BITING THE FEEDING HAND

BY

DR. ALHASAN SISAWO CEESAY, MD

© 2016 by Dr. Alhasan Sisawo Ceesay, MD

All rights reserved. No part from this book may be reproduced in any form without written permission from the publisher, except by a reviewer who may quote passages in a review to be printed in a newspaper or magazine.

FIRST PRINTING

PUBLISH KUNSA.COM

ISBN 978-1-910117-28-6

INSCRIBED TO

My Parents; Wife, Children, Teachers, Friends; Colchester Friends of Manding Charitable Trust UK and Friends of Manding Alpena, Michigan, USA and the downtrodden.

It is criminal to bite the hand that feeds you. And it is very tragic to be ungrateful to those who helped bring relief to your life.

Dr. Alhasan S. Ceesay, MD

PREFACE AND ACKNOWLEDGMENTS

Great is the mystry of commitment and passion. Some sacrificies are never seen until at blooming. Fellow humans demystify and have love and commitment to each other. I write to explore informantion and tease action out of reality. Some have no ability to understanding that others sacrificed for them in a given time of their lowly lives.

At times it looks criminal to expect the ungrateful to understand shallow dignity demonstrated in being ungrateful. The ungrateful lacks restrain and dignity in assuming and using others despite damage their acts may yield. Their minuscule minds sense nothing beyond their noses. They are myopic, insensitive, and fails to appreciate help others enabled them.

A villager once told me thus, "The ungrateful are nothing but scum bats that feed upon victims but careless about the consequences of their acts." This work is about how love and human spirit holds life together despite such heinous bats in human flesh that joined me in Manchester on July 2015. First, I in 2015 relented to pressure from both side of the family isles to let my wife and children in the Gambia to join me in Manchester United Kingdom.

It took a court hearing for their eventual reuniting with me. Hell broke loose when wife met some undesirable characters who told her that "in England life is 50/50 and no man pushes his partner." Wife took this heartless idea literally and rancho, displays that ensued are revealed for posterity and good people to learn from and to avoid repeatition of such madness as happened to me.

The glory in bringing relief to a fellow being surpasses all life's elations. In the mean time allow me express profound gratitude to my wife Mrs. Fatou Ceesay and our children: Famatanding Ceesay, Binta Ceesay and Rohey Yata Ceesay for bearing and persevering patiently through with me in thick and thin during my drive to bring medical aid and service to villagers.

Also I am immensely thankful to illustrious lawyer Ousainu Darboe, Mrs. Lorna Robinson, Eliza Jones, Dr. Laurel Spooner, Dr. Barbra Murray, Dr. Phil Spooner, Dr. Richard Murray, Dr. Malkaight Singh, Cloyd Ramsey, Howard Riggs, Rita Riggs, Dr. Charles Egli, Dr. Cooper Milner, Dr. Nelson Herron, Deidre O'Leary, Margaret Cruise, Bill Cruise, Alison Cruise, Dr. Eunice Kahan, Dr. Betzabi Alison-Prager, Henry Valli, Fr. John Milner, Homer Sheppard, Geraldine Sheppard, Dr. Lamin J. Sise B, Dr. Sulayman S. Nyang, Dr. Aliue Jobateh, Kemo Ceesay, Yankuba Suso, Mustapha Kinteh, Ebrahima Bojang, Bishops Masson & Coleman McGhee of the Episcopal

Diocese of Michigan, Detroit, the Ceesay Committee Diocese of Michigan, Lois R. Leonard, Rev. Walter White, Rev Huge White, Patricia Koblynski, Ishfaue Ahmed, Imran Khurum Ahmed, Khalid Rasheed, Mohamed Nassir (Natz), Saba and Nadia, Ahmed Nizami, Abdinnisir Hassan, Faisal Alim, Abdel Rhaseed Suguelle, Noora Sugulle, Mahmud Adam, Ganem Al Hadied, Abdullah Shahim, Asiya Qadri, Yusuf Ali, and numerous others whose names are not mention but not forgotten.

I write to raise money for the building of a village hospital at Njawara, the Gambia. It is my hope that you would be inspired to join our dream of providing medical aid and service to Gambian villagers and children in the North Bank region.

Purchasing this book or donating in cash or kind would help bring our dream to fruition of Manding Medical Centre for a much needed healthcare delivery and hope to villagers, especially children who frequently die prematurely from childhood diseases because of lack of medical service.

Together we can catch a dream for the villager and children. Log onto: www.publishkunsa.com ; or www.friendsofmandinggambimed.btck.co.uk ; to learn more about our self-help village health project Manding Medical Centre at Njawara. Portions of proceed from sale of this work go to support goals of Manding Medical

Centre. In addition it will in due course offer scholarships to rural candidates wishing to read for a medical or an agricultural degree and return to serve in rural Gambia.

Dr. Alhasan S. Ceesay, MD

Chapter 1

Long lonely lull

He that is low fears no fall but one in solitude craves for companion. Sixteen long years of destitution, joblessness; sleeping rough in safe streets and Manchester City Parks is far from optimum social or progressive admirable life that foreigners come to gain from the developed world. The legend was complicated by immigration foot dragging regarding request change in my visa to enable me pursue my goal for the rural Gambia.

I requested my status to be changed to student visa in 2002 and the sage went on until 2013 before that enigma faded away. I was not, during that time, allowed employment and had to gain income by working underground in shops and restaurants or distributing and dropping flyers for shops to enable me send money to Gambia to feed and educate my daughters.

With help from a few Samaritans I call UK angels who chipped in to buffer a very challenging life event. Some advised that I return home but it was already too late to do so because tyrant at the helm in my country had already labelled, through his Attorney General, that Gambians like me fighting for Human Rights, Justice, Freedom, and development of the masses are nothing but Trojan Horses that should be eliminated upon arrival in the Gambia.

My case became reality after writing my third book: "Country for President, Tribe and Party," which was seen as an affront to the great butcher and self enthrone king of the Gambia.

It took time and hard work by legal luminary like Dr. Angela J. Stull of Lloyds firm Solicitors and backing of Sir Gerald Kaufman MP from Manchester along with good and understanding Immigration officers, such as Charlie Jones and all at the Liverpool branch, that my asylum request was approved after lengthy relentless scrutiny of relevant facts and documentation I presented the officers in December 2012 seeking asylum.

More on this asylum saga can be found in another book of mine titled:" To remove or not to; dilemma of a village Doctor." Let us now digress to the lonely years before arrival of wife and my daughter to the UK in 2015. First, let me make it crystal clear that each second, minute or hour that passes during those years were endless hours of agony and nightmares full of yearning to be with my wife and children.

The need to protect and provide them comfort and education kept whirling endlessly in my head to making me suffer from untold number of pressure headaches.

Yet for love of them and want of providing medical service or proper healthcare delivery to villagers I never contemplated suicide. I kept vigilant on believe that one day and at the Miniminiyang Bolong my folks will raise their hands in gratitude and holy praises to God for keeping me strong to the cause. Let us now dwell deep into period between 2004 through 2013.

This is journey in tapestry of my personal experience on adventure to bring medical aid to villagers and the deleterious dominos it had on my family back in the Gambia. If you had never given help or be charitable this work calls for you to revisit your heart.

Everything in life had a Samaritan's mark to it. The bread you eat or meal over the table is all through hard toil and kindness of others willing to apply themselves for you to get something over to fill the belle.

The teachers, doctors, farmers, solders and mothers all gave their best to let you have chance in life on this earth. Why not do your best to make someone else feel good about this life? This experience is about being a positive contributing member of society no matter where you may find yourself.

It tries to shed reason why we need ignite the spirit and embers of giving not only to illuminate an others' life but to remove dark and despondent moments from those needy hearts. In so doing we let hope and light triumph over darkness and hence allow peace to transcend earth. Hope you be inspired to motivate others do good causes waiting for their mark.

Join in to saying, "We are each other's brother and sister's keeper who we commit ourselves to cater to." Caring comes with passion to do good things and share its rewards with community. The Alice in wonderland or the story of the Wizards of Ooze is more comprehensible than my Manchester days and after mirth dominos.

Chasing a wild goose would have perhaps been more rewarding experience than what you are about to read. It all started in 2001 when I came to Manchester to attend wedding of a friend's and to sit the PLAB exams. I accidentally met Mustapha Kite, a fellow Gambia who was resident in the city.

I knew his family while attending primary school at his home village of Kite Kuna in the lower Caribous, North Bank region. I returned to Colchester in Essex after an hour of reminiscence of the smiling coat and our families. Kite and I kept in touch and it was he who invited me to join him at Manchester while working on the rest of my PLAB exams when life got difficult and job situations were not working out well for me in Colchester.

Naturally, I moved in as quickly as I can into 7 Holton Street to be with Kite where I tried to complete my PLAB requirements. From then on life neither spiralled down wards making me face challenges I never dreamt would be my lot nor foresaw in my acceptance to join Kinte and his wife in Manchester.

His wife Was not comfortable with the arrangement hence I had to relocate to Portland Road at Fustian Fork's, a kind Ghanaian, place where she gave me room free of charge for six months hoping that my situation at the Home Office would have been sorted by then.

Here I tried to reactivate my previous Nursing skills to help me get a job with the NHS until the compulsion of my PLAB exams. This lady treated me like her own family and was generous towards me. However, my joblessness was not encouraging state as my wife and children now lived on the skin of their teeth. I tried my best to concentrate on the exams but their pain in my mind would not allow me leeway to study.

My efforts to rejuvenate my nursing fizzled because of recent rules forbidding NHS from recruiting health personnel from developing countries like mine or so I was lead to understand. My nightmare escalated and I had to move to Mill Hill Road at the end of six months at Port Land Road.

The flat at Mill Hill eventually cost me about three quarters of my weekly income from a part time job I had secured through the help of friends. In the end because of inability to pay my rent in time I was graciously asked to leave because a relative and former occupier was coming back to Manchester.

Hence, I found myself an instant street person for at least three weeks before getting in another flat at 245 Great Western Street. The struggle to get a job became my greatest challenge. The landlord was a very kind man but business does not have a heart and he needs his weekly rent fees met.

Luckily I was able to get a job at Sam Sam's Take Away and was able to pay rent to retain my privacy and carry on my studies. The saying good things hardly last long came to hunt me in this job. One starts from 9:00 Am to 5:00 Pm or from 5:00 Pm to 3:45 Am leaving me with no time to concentrate on my studies. Unfortunately for me business slowed almost to a halt.

We use to get at least 20 to 60 customers daily on weekdays and a guaranteed 300- 500 customers on weekends. All this dropped down to a skeletal drip, drip number of 5 to 10 customers on weekdays and 60 on weekends.

So when the manager decided to retrench the staff, again the saying "last come first to go" became my un-sort luck. The manager called a meeting Friday night and told us whom he was going to sadly let go because his business was no longer able to balance the books and that he had been in the red since the fall of customer levels.

He apologized and told us he did try to maintain us but would not be able to pay his or even us. I left saddened and went without a job for another three months before landing a shoe sale cum security job at a shop at Wilmslow Road, Manchester.

Working conditions were not conducive for studies but I needed the money to send to my family now living on the skin of their teeth and starving. I sold shoes and doubled as security man for the shop under gearing and amid rude attitudes from youngsters and drunken customers.

Here work starts from 9:00 Am to 7:00 pm on weekdays but on weekends we start work from 7:00 Am till 9:30 Pm before wrapping up the day. It gave me no time to study but I persevered for quite a while knowing what had just happened and not wanting my family to suffer.

One day, while I was having mild asthma attack the elder son of the business owner told me to go down the seller and clean everything in them disregarding my asthma. I pleaded with him to wait until my health improves for going into such damp place would exacerbate my asthma. He callously told me that if fail to do as he instruct I should consider myself fired from the job.

After repeating this threat three times I took him seriously and I told him that I refuse to put my life at risk and he can have his slave job, I let him know that God will come to my aid and thanked him while walking away for good. I learnt he got scared and told his father it was my decision to leave the job but a witness later told his dad what transpired between us in his presence. The family still remains my friends and the young man apologized for his tantrums. I still could not understand why he was so callous with me knowing about my precarious health and need to send money to my family.

He later told a friend he met his match who was not going to back down even if it meant going hungry and homeless in Manchester. I left after three years at the shoe shop without being paid the hours I worked for that particular week after the fiasco between us.

I did not wreck the place or cause commotions because I was on a visitor's visa with no work permit issued me by the Home Office. Again I took on board with little pain on my chin and searched for job at other places.

It took another five months before I could land a part time job at the Bell Free House Hotel under the food and beverages manager, Kostas Militias, as a dishwasher and porter, which ended with the summer season activities at the hotel.

With this job gone the noose got tighter and tighter around my neck for I lost lot of time unable to concentrate on my studies and am now in worst condition not able to fend for my family or pay rent. I was served eviction notice after three months up on losing the shoe sales and security job. What a pity and pain for my family.

Five months later Kostas Militias, then manager, called to say he had a job for me in Wales I could not believe my ears and I told him I was ready and parked to move with him immediately.

I parked my belongings horridly amid reminders by the landlord that I need to vacate the flat same day. Some of the 18 boxes were left with a friend while the rest Kostas squeezed in his car and we headed to Wales. After four years 245 Great Western had become my second home and Manchester wet or dry.

Sentimentality set in, as many stories and painful moments passed in that flat, over my misty eyes as I picked the last box out of the room. I now head for an unknown destination in Wales. Kostas came for me on 24/08/09 and we headed for Conway in North West of Wales.

We were there by 1:30 pm. After lengthy discussions with his colleagues I was given part time job as dishwasher and potter at the Abe Conway Park Restaurant and allowed to stay with a Polish couple, Magma and Seamark.

They were very kind folks I am remain grateful to. Kostas was not certain if the caravan owners would allow me stay as long as was expected as he found out from his not so cooperative friends and colleagues at the restaurant.

Yes, there were undercurrent believe that customers might stay away because of the amount of foreigners working for Kostas. It was arranged that I get my meals from the kitchen whenever convenient for the chef and staff on duty at the time. I labelled my container as 'Ceesayconway' food box drawing lots of laughter from the staff and customers. However, it was embarrassing and tears wailed from Kostas's eyes for only he knew how embarrassing begging for food was for me at the time.

The staff never knew I was a medical doctor enduring such mockery and hardship. Kostas was concerned that the kitchen job might trigger my asthma.

He felt my situation to be worse than that of the beggars in the streets of Manchester but he had no warned to stop it right away. We both cried in our hearts and hoped for the best while holding our chins up to hide our emotions. Yes, it was difficult to be begging for food but being unemployed that was the only honest way out for the like of me. I remain incepted to Kostas Shamark and Magda for their kindness, help and friendship shown me while I leaved at the Caravan. I stayed at 11 knights bridge caravan nestled among filthy rich retired Brits. My open personality and simplicity, attitude toward others earned me many friends among the residents.

Abe Conway park caravan lot is surrounded between a horse-shoe shaped mountain on the North and an open sea on the South side and half an hour's walk to maim city Conway itself.

At this cluster of 150 – 200 caravans leaves a handful of youths amid groups of seasoned elderly retired Brits. I can guarantee it's a place not short of British history of empire, wisdom and kindness. The old folks were usually all smiles upon meeting me.

Most of tee time, some would make jokes about Africa and only identified me with countries they visited some forty or fifty years ago in Africa. I stopped reminding them that I was from the West coast of Africa and not Kenya, Uganda, Malawi or Zambia.

We normally discuss current affairs to life in Africa and African leaders. A majority of residents I met warmed up to me and told me that they came to such quite corner of the United Kingdom wanting a peaceful and quite retirement life. They were running away from the noisy and pollution of big city life. Initially, curio city got the better of my neighbours but they eventually became my friends as they noted the polite difference in my approach to their fears. This fear is no new phenomenon regarding newcomers to speculative communities.

Normally people are either concerned, curious or become too friendly to allow no space for the new entrant to the community. All is well that ends well. Things came to a sudden twist when Kostas Miliotis on the 7/8/08 came to No.11 Knights bridge caravan and told me about there being trouble regarding a bomb shell decision taken by the caravan owners.

He, in tears, said there was trouble. Decision had been taken that I neither work for the restaurant nor was I any longer allowed staying in any caravan at Abe Conway Park. It was ordered that l leave as early as the next day being a Saturday.

We were all in tear by the time he was able to finish his sentence. Even though he did his best to keep his pride and emotion controlled the shock of the day welled out. The whole story brewed like a creation of snow on a mountain.

Nothing happens until one day an avalanche devastates whatever was bellow and on its path. Today, Kostas and I stand devastated by the loss of his job for just trying to put food in mouths of my children in the Gambia. The whole affair was due to havoc my unlucky and catastrophic avalanches that buried him. The firm saw his acts of kindness differently.

My being at the Abe Conway Park might have contravened residential rule according to some. Right there and then, Shamark, got on the phone to his friend and asked him give me ride that night to Manchester city. We arrive at 1:30 pm at Knut ford Road in Gorton, Manchester where Ebrahima Gisse let me into the flat he rents. Monday, Kostas called to reassure me of his continued desire to help me out.

He let me know friends of his are trying to both a job a place for me to stay until completion of my exams. They never called and after several attempt to connect with Kostas he could not do much for me any longer.

We still contact each other and he had landed another job though not as lucrative as the former according to him. Mean while Ebrahima Bojang contacted his friend Waseem in my behalf for any assistance he could seek or give to me for my situation was getting desperate.

Waseem arranged a meeting between Ahmed Nizami, a lawyer and editor of one of the Pakistani Magazines in Manchester.

Nizami and I met on 15/08/08 and gelled immediately. We discussed my state and need. I told him that I needed job and money to send my family and pay for my exams. Mr. Ahmed Nizami indicated interest and promised to help in fund raising for the goals of Manding Medical Centre at Njawara village, the Gambia. We even planned to form an extended version of the charity the medical centre in Manchester in due course.

However, he had just moved into Manchester and would like time to settle before embarking on my project.

Wassem called on the 25/08/08 and told me a friend of his in Glasgow, Scotland has agreed to give me temporal help while we look for more permanent jobs.

Five days later we were in Lark Hall, Scotland meeting Malick Illias at his Indian One in all take away food shop. Malik was forthright about the deal. He made it clear that he was just helping temporally but did not need my service as he has more than adequate number of staff to run the business. He would also talk to some of his business friends to seek more jobs for me. He would try me for at least five weeks to see how things fared on for customer level is dwindling.

Three days into my sixth week at his take away, Malik called me to his office. With head held down he told me that he no longer required my service because business was taking down turn with him being over staffed it means getting to the red if he continues with the current role payment.

As a beggar has no choice in most decisions affecting them so did I concur and asked when to vacate the current room I was using. He told me to stay for ten more days while he check or sound other friends to see if there is chance of my getting employed by one of them.

My usual bad luck manifested no opening and I had to leave Scotland the following Friday for Manchester.

I arrived late in the evening and walked straight to 7 Hulton Street, hoping to find Mustapha Kinte, to lodge me temporally until I find my way out of the current situation. He was away and I had to get Yankuba Suso to open the house and let me in for the night.

I informed Kofi Awudoo, a Ghanaian friend and he kindly let me stay at his flat at 55 Eagle Court in Trafford. Later Ahmed Nizami offered to house me at 9 Knowles street in Manchester.

There too the landlord got me out because of Warehouse situation not accepting tenants or lodgers at 9 Knowles. From Knowles I shuttled to 22 Warren Street at Cheetham Hill then back to Hens bury for a short stay before heading to 75 Beresford Street in Manchester and landing in where other than 148 Bedford street South in Liverpool. At this state my life a weathercock or shuttle cock was much more stable than me. I was never certain where I will lay my head next.

Life was just an unceasing whirlwind and like a tornado picks ferocity each time it reaches the next phase of a disastrous vengeful journey. I weathered the seemingly ceaseless storm at Liverpool and prepared for the PLAB exam, which was due on the 21/02/10. Right after the exam I was told to find another place to stay by first week of April 2010.

Yes, life has been endless seesawing saga parked with the most difficult circumstances of my life. A thunderbolt of the saddest kind hit me on the 3/3/10 from an email message from Keith Robinson letting me know that my friend Mrs. Lorna Robinson collapsed and passed away same day.

Her untimely departure shocked me and left me depressed for weeks on end. She was my England and now she left me in solitude and hungry for a true and simple human with a heart for the indigent villagers in Gambia. We have worked acidulously in an effort to providing medical aid to villagers.

Manding Medical Centre has lost a friend, a person who cared and shared what little she had with those less fortunate than her. She was our springboard and the wheel that turns to make things happen for the centre. Lorna was an angel of mercy.

The villagers, my family and I miss her and mourn her premature return to her maker. May she rest in peace? Her departure left me without the England I knew. I moved back to Manchester April 2010.

Life was never the same as Keith Robinson started fazing me out of having anything to do with the Friends of Manding charity his wife started in Colchester, Essex, UK. He called, on the 4/6/10 letting me know for health reasons he no longer can run affairs of the charity and has closed the charity's accounts at the bank. I could not persuade him to hand over the duties to other members of the trust. I plan to speak to the doctors to see if any would help in reinstating the accounts in the earliest possible time. A few weeks after settling in Manchester I wrote appealing letters to the following founding members of the Colchester Friends of Manding Charitable Trust, Dr. Laurel Spooner, Dr. Richard Spooner, Dr. Barbara Murray, Dr. Philip Murray, Dr. Linda Mahon-Daly, and Dr. Peter Wilson. I later found out that most of them were on holidays and I will have to get in touch in a month time. Thank God, Eliza Jones, a Gambian in resident at Colchester agreed to step in and filled void left by Lorna Robinson.

Dr. Alhasan S. Ceesay receiving residency permits from his solicitor, Dr. Angela Stull, Lloyds' Law Firm Stockport Road, Manchester 2013

Chapter 2
Why the United Kingdom?

With the unset of the post independent status in the Gambia, I decided to travel to the United Kingdom for two reasons and only these made me leave blessed Africa once more. They are

(1). Seek to improve my medical skills before returning to serve the rural sector in Gambia.

(2). To further internationalize the village self-help health NGO, Manding Medical Centre, I establish at Njawara village, Lower Badibou District, North Bank Region, The Gambia providing medical aid to villagers since 1993.

We needed to bring awareness of the greater community and developed world about our goals in other to get financial resources to build the hospital before my eventual return to the Gambia.

Interest in the NGO picked up momentum nine weeks after my arrival in Colchester, Essex, UK. Here doctors, nurses and residents joined and formed the Friends of Manding Charitable Trust serving as an arm and liaison for Manding Medical Centre at Njawara village in UK and the European Union. Very soon all the paper work, fees for registration were completed and submitted for approval by the UK Charity Commission.

And sure enough, we got our charitable status for England and Wales by August 2002. We are registered as Friends of Manding Charitable Trust, Colchester, Essex and the charity number is 1088136. While the charity organizers busied itself on fund raising activities on weekends and calling attention to project Manding Medical Centre's goals,

I started on the primary reason of my being in the UK, that is to pursue a course of study leading to the MRCP degree. The devil in the form of a visitor's visa reared its ugly head after the second renewal of it by the Home Office.

The Home Office refused to change my visitor's status to student to allow me work and study in the UK. The decision tantamount either starving to death or returning to the Gambia because of inability to fend for myself.

The Home office failed to realize that going back prematurely will result to conflict at that juncture and would plunge me into disgrace, diminution, and definitely not getting my job back or promotion from lower rank, if one was lucky to be reinstated in the civil service.

I might not get the chance to do private practice and hence my profession would be brought to an abrupt termination. It took me lot of juggling and struggles to get this current visa. The above possibilities made friends in the UK come to my aid to help, even though it would be an uphill battle waiting in a dark tunnel of troubles.

Mean while I authored the legend against all odds and Medicine for the village, with hope of raising money for both the health Ngo and me. Unfortunately my books are not selling well at the moment and those bought still go to paying for publishing them. My financial woes extricated as one will soon find in the next pages.

The direction of my primary goal for coming to this great monarchical Island on the silvery seas did not follow expectation but like a yoyo ricocheted from the sublime to the ridiculous. All efforts to have the Home office reverse its decision of not changing my visitor status stuck with me. Let me reprint what the visa says.

It specifically states: "Leave to remain in the United Kingdom, on condition that the holder maintains and accommodates himself and any dependants without recourse to public funds, does not engage in employment paid or unpaid and does not engage in any business or profession, is hereby given until." My life at this stage veered and became a story of trials that plunged me into a Pell-Mel of a heaving hell on our earth.

The years following the decision left in vagueness, melancholy, chaotic, inept feeling I ever experienced since leaving the Gambia. I knew the villagers relied on my letting them help and this way it might take eons to get help for them.

Mrs. Famatanding Tarawaleh (mother holding baby)

My state brought to mind what floaters at sea who would not or do not think at all, but hope that like cork in the water they will float on the waves of circumstances that in the end things somehow settle down and they will arrive successfully in a hospitable port. Unlike floaters, I refused to let the waves drift along with me.

Hence, I put my heart, head and soul into my goal to catch a dream for the villagers. I went underground in an effort to achieve my medical training but that made it hard. Menial jobs do not pay much hence the little I gather went into paying rent, school fees of my three daughters and food to keep their bone and skin together.

I am left with nothing to pay for review courses for the PLAB exam I did everything the hard way which affected my exams. I faced several evictions that set my life into tatters. It threw me into the streets among the homeless. Being jobless made me sleep rough for a while. I lived on molten bread, semolina, Sardines, when available and at times boiled white rice with salt.

Some sympathizers at food take away businesses do once on a while give me left over meals instead of destroying or binning the food they could not sell the next day. There were those who thought I was stupid to endure such deprivation in one of the world's richest countries. Others suggested that I should take the bull by the horns and marry any cheap girl to get over these inhuman ridiculous visa restrictions.

They just failed to realize how determine I was to achieve my dream without becoming dependent and return to my people in Gambia. Hence the pain was worth the end result in my mind set. I swallowed my pride and called a friend and told him the ugly state my life turned out.

He brought food and offered a day's job at Blackpolls Dog Show. Kostas came to pick me for the job the next day. On this coveted day it was gray, wet and windy. Gales were up to 67 miles per hour but that did not stop 20,000 dogs and their owners attending.

I risked the cold outdoors because of need to feed my family and my dwindling body of bone and skin as well as send a few pounds to my beleaguered family back in the Gambia.

Events picked up at the dog show as well more than 2000 people in attendance despite the stormy weather. They watched dogs being paraded about amongst various officials and judges. Lot of small businesses had displays in McGee's and stalls.

Ours was among the larger emcees able to cater for at least 300 customers with the best food and drinks plus fish and chips, fezzes for juniors. Meals ranged from good old fish in chips to a four-course dinner and drinks of kinds. The atmosphere was festive indeed.

I even started to make friends among the uests/customers, dog owners and officials in the mileage. We were cheerfully serving the best meals of the day. Then all of a sudden hell broke loose. The wind picked more strength and speed with heavy rain on top of it.

Two sudden events followed almost simultaneously. First, our McKee lost one of the pegs holding it causing serious breakage of wine and liquor section. Hundred of if not thousands of pound worth of alcohol went into the ground as bottles crashed and broke at random.

That settled we innocently carried on as usual, cooking, serving amid jokes while rushing to serve customers. To everyone's chagrin the second wave of event happened so fast that all in the Marquee were trapped and shouting get out to safety to ant one nearby or could hear the warning. The destruction was so rapid and devastating that three quarters of the humongous McKee was sent tossing like a kite in the sky and people and animals were running from away from harm from all directions.

Luckily only a few of us were injured. One of our cooks had the most serious first degree burns of the thigh and was rushed by ambulance to hospital and first aid crews were left on the grounds to attend or seek wounded folks out of danger.

I had scald burns running from the right side of my face, forehead up to the middle of my skull. At first the pain was bearable prompting me to refuse being taken to hospital by ambulance.

I knew going to the hospital from this scene would spell trouble for my friend Kostas and it could lead to refusal insurance payment compensation with a possible fine for hiring an over stayed visitor. I did accept paracetamol tablets from the attending nurse, who insisted I should go to hospital for my wounds to be, look at carefully.

I smiled and applied cold compression over my burns and blistering face. Soon there were lots of blisters over my face and my right eye, which closed instantly, blocking my sight immediately. This was followed by the skin literally slough and leaving a pink to red tomatoes surface like on my right face to middle of my skull.

The blisters on my face got bigger and baggy with some busting on their own because of the serum they collected. Kostas became very worried that I am risking my life for him. He became panicky and urged that he take me to the hospital.

I again assured him that my face may look ugly at that time but am able to withstand the pain and assured him that I rather attend Manchester General Hospital, away from the scene than go to this very hospital with media hounding me about when or how and why we were at the dog show despite the stormy weather.

I let him know that it was not worth the repercussion to follow if I have to give evidence to insurance, police and immigration officer who would certainly be involved. I rather save him from any hassles. He was being only kind to my family and me. He had just bought a new home and paying high mortgage on it.

I made it point blank that the help and friendship he showed me meant more to me than few gilders or gold nuggets this accident might yield in the form of compensation and deportation. We both stand to lose in the deal meant to reward us.

Kostas relented and concord for he knew my sincerity for a better outcome was the reality of the situation. Had I reported at the hospital in Blackpoll, I would be declared illegal and that would make the insurance people to likely not compensate his firm.

It was apparent that the business would have received high penalties for engaging the services of a visitor and I would have by now headed for the Gambia as soon as my wounds healed or improved. Yes, sometimes one had to take a few knocks or make such difficult choice life meters if it brings harmony to all concerned.

Hence, I made it clear to Kostas that I will have my wounds managed by burns experts as soon as I made it to Manchester city. He took me to Manchester. It was 11:45 pm and I picked my ID and headed for the A&E at Manchester General Hospital.

My eye was closed completely and blisters were dripping all over me and looked like a watering can. The sight was ugly enough to cause the nurse scream because of the unsightly nature of the wounds. Most of my face had peeled completely making me look ghastly.

The nurse covered it up with acriflavine soaked gaze while prying out how it all came about. Most of the staff told me that the hospital would support evidence of my having been treated by it and the extent of burns for me to be compensated.

They would not buy my story of having incurred the injury by tipping a pan with boiling water onto my head and right face. I did not want the record to reflect that the injury occurred at the dog show to avoid making it worst than it's for my friend Kostas.

I shrugged all questions alluding to it being involved in an accident or from violence or at a job place. The staff felt so sad for me that I am refusing compensation for wounds that may end up defacing me with colloid tissue hanging on my face etc. I understood their empathy but would not burgh or recant my original reason for the injury.

I remembered telling the nurse that doctors are brave lads. She said, "Tell me again!" And we laugh over. She cleaned my wounds thoroughly, dressed it and made an appointment for to be attended at the specialized burns clinic at Wythenshawe Hospital on the same day.

At the burns clinic I met Dr. Chris, a very kind young doctor from Hon Kong, attend me. I was given medication to apply over the wound and to return for follow up and review of my wounds in three weeks.

Dr. Chris feared that I might develop nasty keloid tissue over my face, as it is a prevalent complication common in black people. He wanted to make certain that cosmetic surgery commences at the earliest possibility of such hideous lumps developing on my face. Luckily, I healed completely without any of the foreseen complications. Dr. Chris let a shy of relief when I told him that my face has fully recovered and there were no ugly lumps on it.

I told him all is well and my face was smooth and good-looking again as before the accident. We chuckled about it and he left to see other patients. The nurses at the Wythenshawe burns unit were very kind and professional. I left the burns unit very satisfied.

Most of my wounds healed so fast that it took most by surprise for the skin had recovered fully with only few hairless spots were noticeable by very curious onlookers. However, my right eye continued to be troublesome as I developed temporal mono-ocular diplopia due blister fluid sipping into the obit causing pressure and the ensuing diplopia.

This also settled within a week and I never needed services of an ophthalmologist. My misery escalated on 24/04/08 when the landlord Sharif Azan called me to his office and simply told me he had sold the building and that he and the new owner agreed to review my tenancy by the end of April 2008.

He said they have concluded that I will not be able to secure a job and as a result they want me to leave or vacate the flat and hand over the keys to the office, without delay, by the first of May 2008. I thanked him on my way out. I felt sad and helpless and fearful of what might happen next. My life was once again battered but this instant took me by surprise.

The decision does support dictum that business neither bleeds nor does it have a heart for anyone in my state. It came at my most vulnerable time as my daughters were just bounced out of school because of none payment of fees. The last nail to my coffin was almost put in place when the General Medical Council (GMC) added pepper to my raw wounds with its 16/06/08 decision recanting my PMQ due to wrong Internet entry at the American University at Montserrat, West Indies.

Yes, stars, tears, disbelieve and remorse all crossed my path in this little frame of mine in an instant. Life was turning catastrophically painful. Being in the street and have such bad news all at once is not domain of the weak. The boot became tighter and I had to swim or sink with this miserable state.

Alas! The situation with the GMC did not linger long because my university corrected that mistake. Kostas stepped in and secured a shared rooming at the Caravan in Conway, Northwest Wales.

He arranged some part time potter's job at the Abertconway restaurant kitchen. He would help in this until hopefully things change or are sorted out for me. I kept the rest of my troubles to myself for fear of frightening away the earthly angel and last straw of hope left to me.

On the day to move out of 245 Great Western Street in Moss side, Manchester, I parked my belongings horridly amid reminders by the landlord that I need to vacate the place. Some of the 18 boxes were left with Ebrahima Bojang while Kostas and I squeezed as much as possible of my luggage into his small car and we headed for Conway in Wales the same day.

After four years at 245 Great Western Street, I now have to say farewell to the place I called my Manchester abode. Sentimentally sank in as many stories and painful moments flashed over my mind's eyes and memory.

I still cannot describe how sad I was when I picked up the last piece or box out of that flat. It has been my peaceful Manchester whether rain or dry. I now headed for an unknown destination called Conway in Wales.

We were at the Abertconway Park around 1:45 pm where Kostas then worked. He was not too certain if the firm would allow me stay as long as he had requested from his not so cooperative friends and colleagues at the Restaurant.

Yes, I later found out from him that there was undercurrent believes that customers might stay away because of the number of foreigners working for Kostas. Mean while I stayed with a very kind and helpful Polish couple, Magda and Shamark, also employees of the restaurant.

Mrs. Binta Ceesay, Elder Sister

We jokingly renamed the caravan as Ceesay Miliotis instead of Knightsbridge caravan. It was arranged that I get my meals from the kitchen whenever convenient for the duty chef and staff.

I labelled my container as ceesayconway food box drawing lots of laughter from the staff. On the other hand it was very embarrassing and tears wailed from Kostas's eyes for only he knew how debasing begging for food was for me at that juncture of my life.

Most of the staff never knew that I was a medical doctor enduring such hardship to be able support my goal and family back in the Gambia. Kostas was very concerned and fearful that the kitchen job might trigger my asthma and stop the little chance I had at the place.

He believed my situation was worst than those street beggars but he was unable to wave warn to help me out. We both cried in our hearts and hoped for the best while holding our chins high up to hide our emotions.

Yes, dear reader, it was difficult to be begging for food but that was the only honest source sine I had no job to fend for myself in the UK. I am profoundly indebted to Kostas and numerous Brits and the young Polish couple for kindness help and friendship they gave while I leaved in their caravan at Conway in Wales.

I stayed at 11 knights bridge caravan nestled among filthy rich retired residents. I, the poor of the poorest, am now nestled in ceesay-miliotis caravan among moderate to very rich Brits. My open personality and simple attitude towards others earned me many friends.

Abeconway Park Caravan lot is surrounded between a horseshoe shaped mountain on the North and open sea on the South side and half an hour's walk to the main Conway city itself.

At this rested cluster of 150 – 200 caravans of various sizes and qualities with a handful of youths amid groups of seasoned elderly Brits. I guaranteed it's a place not short of British history of empire, wisdom and kindness. The old folks were usually all smiles upon meeting with me.

Most of the time some would make jokes about Africa and only identify me with places they visited in the continent but hardly about Gambia Britain rule for well over three hundred colonial years.

I stopped reminding them that I was from the west coast of Africa and not from Kenya, Malawi or Uganda where most have serve his majesties colonial power.

The discussions ranged from world affairs to life in Africa. The majority of residents I met warmed up to me and told me to such quite corner of the United Kingdom wanting a peaceful and quite retirement life.

They were running away from the notice of big city traffic life. Initially, curiosity got the better of my neighbours but eventually everyone became my friend as they noted the polite difference in my approach to their fears.

This is not a new phenomenon regarding newcomers to speculative communities. Normally people are either concerned, curious or become too friendly to allow no space for the new entrant to the community. Things came to an abrupt twist when Kostas Milliotis on 7/08/08 came to the caravan and told me about a bombshell decision taken by the caravan owners.

He, in tears, said, "There is trouble. Decision had been taken that you neither work for the restaurant nor were from today allowed to stay in any caravan at Aberconway Park." He said they want me move away as early as the next day, being on a Saturday.

We were all in tears before he finished his sentences, even though he did his best to keep his pride and emotion controlled. The whole story brewed like an accretion of snow on a mountain.

Nothing happens until one day an avalanche devastates whatever was bellow and on its path. Today Kostas and I stand devastated by the loss of his job on account of helping me and from havoc caused by my unlucky and catastrophic avalanches in trying in his trying to help me support my family in Gambia.

He was just helping and now became casualty of being kind to other people from faraway lands. It is believed that my being in the Abe Conway Park Caravan might have contravened residential rule to put it mildly.

No reasons were given why the sudden dismissal of my friend to this very day nor was I ever paid the fifty-two hour I had already worked for the restaurant firm. Right there and then, Samark got his friend to drive me back to Manchester city over night.

We arrived at Knut ford Road in Gorton, Manchester at 1:30 Am and Ebrihama Gisse, a Gambian at the flat, let me in. Monday, Kostas called to reassure me of his continued desire to help and that his friends promised to seek job and look for place for me to stay.

He was very concerned about my family in the Gambia and where to get money to pay for my exams which he was certain am going to have to postpone till the next seating.

Mean while Mr. Ebrahima Bojang contacted his friend Waseem for assistance who eventually arranged that I meet with Mr. Ahmed Nizami, a lawyer and editor of one of the Pakistani magazines operating in Manchester.

Nizami and became blood brothers from then to now and he supported me in various ways. He helped pay my exam fees and asked a friend of his lodge me until when I can sort myself out. He became interested in project Manding medical Centre and even suggested we set up an annex of the charity here in Manchester.

His travels to Pakistan slowed that moment but the plan is still afoot pending approval of the Colchester branch of the charitable trust. Luckily Ahamed Waseem called on the 15/08/08 and told me that friend in Glasgow will give me a temporal job at his take away in Lark Hall, Scotland. We left together three days later and arrived at Lark Hall by 5:54 pm where I met with Malick Illias, owner of Indian All in One Take Away.

Malick is youngish and a nice fellow who showed me round while introducing me to his staff. He was very frank, a quality I liked in a human, and he told me that he was over staffed but will give a chance to help raise school fees for my children.

He made sure I know that my engagement not permanent even though he would be talking to friends in the business to see who can give additional helps. As the saying goes good things never last long hence after five weeks Malick had to terminate my service. The customer level had fallen from well more a hundred in the evenings to less than thirty at most.

So he had to offload me to avoid being in the red during the cold season. One week later I boarded the National Express Bus and headed for Manchester my home away from home. This time I spent three months of the winter at 55 eagles Court in Strafford, Manchester before moving to 9 Knowles street as guest of Ahamed Nizami.

It was during this hectic period that my second book, Medicine for the villager, was publishing by Publish America, Frederic, Maryland, USA. I did all sorts of petty jobs like delivering adverts door –to- door for Union Cars taxi-company, even tutoring biology for three days and cleaning.

I mean washing very dirty freezers and refrigerators for a use refrigerator repair company. These only help to defray food money and school fees for my children in the Gambia. I moved from Knowles Street to Warren Street at Cheethamhill and ended up five months later at Hens bury Street in Moss side before moving to Ganem Hadied's flat at Beresford Street in Manchester where I met Mahmud Adam.

Ganem and Mahmud had been exceptionally kind to me and did made the arrangement for me to temporally stay at Mahmud's flat at 148 Bedford street south in Liverpool till February 2010. Being jobless I concentrated on my review for the PLAB and completion of some of the manuscripts I started but had to stop writing for lack of time.

The duo solicited monetary help for me from both mosques in Manchester and Liverpool most of donations I sent to my family to keep food on table for them. One of the completed manuscripts, titled: "When hearts melt in love" has already been accepted for publishing by Publish America, Frederic, Maryland, in the USA.

And unlike my other books I hope it net me large costumer numbers to cause a change in my downtrodden life and help me build the Manding Medical Centre to provide a much-needed medical service to villagers. I now have a permanent Liverpool memorabilia, a Central library membership card.

It and the heavy snowfall pictures I took will one day be worth reflecting on as these are trying moments for my family and me. I stayed at the above flat until the 10/02/10 before heading for London to take the PLAB exam February 2010.

The sudden loss of Lorna Robinson did not make life easier. She was the wheel that turns and makes things happen for both the Colchester Friends of Manding Charitable Trust and I. Lorna Robinson stood firmly by me in thick and thin moments of my stay in the UK. Her collapse and sudden departure left a devastating blow if not a bitter pill to swallow.

Life after this benevolent angel of mercy will never be the same again for none showed as much zeal and interest in the running, promoting and organizing activity to get money for the building of the children and maternity units of Manding Medical Centre at Njawara, the Gambia West Africa. Much more can be read about her from another book of mine titled

The Measure of Wisdom. My life followed a downward spiralling after Lorna. I moved from Beresford and had to spend few nights in the open cold Alexandra Park before Mohamed Salam let me used his vacant flat at 81 old hall Lane waiting for tenants to move in three weeks.

My aberrant visitor's visa and GMC problems lead to an untold suffering of my family back in the Gambia. It turned me into a destitute begging for food and money to send my beleaguered family in the Gambia.

A month before leaving Liverpool my elder daughter, Famatanding Ceeesay, sent me the following heart wrenching text. "Good morning dad, yesterday Social Security came here and they brought along notice which says that it is the final demand for arrears and if we do not make any attempt to for it within 14 days it will they will take legal proceedings against us and it could result in our being evicted from the house making us homeless."

I contacted Sulayman Cham, one of the officers handling the case and pleaded for more time as the precarious nature of my visa along with my wife delving into extension instead of paying the mortgage caused the arrears.

Being unemployed the inevitable were almost lurking at the door. I tried every friend I thought might help to get the money Social security requested in other to quell the legal proceedings against Brusubi plot E605 in the Gambia.

Social Security finally entered correction regarding allocation of the plot by inserting my name in it and let it be known that it will also so read in the final deed when all monies due the company is being settled.

However to my disappointment and surprise not long after the adjustment. None other than Sulayman Cham sent the following text. It read, "Hi Mr. Ceesay. It is being a while, any way once your request was met and your promise is not fulfilled.

Well then we will go back to where we started and forward the matter to our solicitor for repossession. Thanks." My life has seesawed between difficult life threatening poles as above and the GMC saga did not dampen my pain nor did it help for people now doubted my medical education than previously implied.

It is now battle for survival and regaining of my professional status besmeared by the GMC's June 17th 2008 recanting its recognition of primary medical education but eventually recognizing it after it found their previous information erroneous and misleading.

Luck has it that after introducing me to the next-door neighbour, Abdullah Shahim and Wife Asiya Qadri, a Bangladesh cum Pakistani couple, they decided to put me up into their flat at Sway field Street in Long Side Manchester.

This kind and generous couple gave me clothing and food plus one hundred and ten pounds sterling to pay for the IELTS exam. They adopted me wholeheartedly.

Nonetheless, I was more than aware that this caviar was not lasting and that time will come when these lovely couple would reach the end of their tether.

Not surprising by the end of December and having contacted Abdul Shahim he made it clear that he was no longer able to help because other obligations and financial difficulties he was then enduring. In the mean time I text a thank you note to Abdullah Shahim and his lovely wife Asiya Qadri.

It read: "You have been very kind and generous to me. Thanks a million. May Allah reward your efforts. I need a job to care for my life. Please keep in touch." In the same vein I contacted Mohamed (Nazt) Tufail and told him the eminent and desperate state my situation turned.

After series of text message between us Nazt showed up at my door around 1.30 Am with thirty pounds sterling in an envelope for me to pay the landlord.

Dr. Ceesay with Mr. Sisawo Ceesay (father)

Mean my life continued staring into the abyss as destituteness plummeted me into unbearable experiences. The drama got so bad that I had to spend a few nights at the Alexandra Park in Manchester while I gather my sanity.

My mood was down cast and hardly brilliant. Thanks to intervention of Abdul Shahim, Asiya Qadri, Asfaq Ahamed and wife my life escaped catastrophic ends. Asfaq would bring food every other day to keep my skin on bones alive.

On the other hand Shahim and wife made certain that they help me have shelter and roof over my head during the winter months. These young couple rented a flat for me at 12 Hanna Street for five months before I was again forced to move to Ganem Haidied at Beresford Street, Manchester.

Ebrahima Bojang, alias Alkali Bojang continued visiting and at times donating food money. Late entrance or Salvatore was Yankuba Gassama and wife Rugie Liegh both of who are Gambians.

These constant dislocations, unemployment and inability to send money to my wife and children placed an added burden on my being able to get through my exams. My wife had at this time given up on me. She started being belligerent towards me despite being told the true state I found myself in the UK.

Chapter 3
FROM THE DAYS OF YORE

Father once counselled to always do my best at what I planned at the time. I will have bumper harvest later. He specifically warned that the first approach to getting what one wants out of life was to decide what goal one intend to pursue and follow or stick to it to the end. Well dear reader, you are about to ply through pages of forty-one years of relentlessness full of surprises of catastrophic proportions.

My legacy would be better than my experience sounds and it would be a sharing one with the needy. Hence, let us start where it all started, Njawara village on the 14th of February 1942. I started Primary school in 1953, against the wishes of my father; at Kinte Kunda village a stone throw from Njawara.

After four years of walking on bare feet seven miles daily I passed the secondary school entrance examination and was assigned to Armitage School, the only boarding secondary school located at George Town some 175 miles from my village.

It was difficult boarders' life but I made the necessary adjustment and completed five years of secondary schooling and then enrolled at the Gambia Nursing School at the Royal Victoria hospital Nursing School in Banjul in 1960.

I received the State Registered Nursing certificate in 1963 and served at the Royal Victoria Hospital before proceeding to Alpena Community College to start my premed courses for medicine in 1967. These phases are well documented in my first book, the legend against all odds, published by Publish America, Frederic, Maryland, USA in 2002.

I had the Associates of Arts degree in Biology from Alpena Community College in 1969 then proceeded to Olivet College September'69 where I completed the BA degree in Biological Sciences in 1971.

The trail took me further to Michigan Technological University in Houghton, Michigan. Here I earned the Master of Science degree in biological Sciences in 1973. I thank God that the snow avalanches never buried me by the time the M. Sc. Degree was conferred on me.

I applied to a dozen and more Medical Schools but residency and funding became accessible or un-crossable bridges for me. Some gave interviews and insisted that the Gambia foot the bills for my training before I could start my medical education, while others asked that I present them a USA resident status permit before proceeding to the next phase of enrolling into their universities.

The Gambia not only delayed replying until six month after the deadline that the universities gave. Things seesawed to a discouraging point that friends advised that I do a PhD program while sorting things out hoping for better responses from medical colleges. Thus, I decided to enrol at Hayward University in Washington, District of Columbia to do a PhD program in entomology in 1975.

It was there that I learnt bitter news that such candidates were seen as either buccaneers in search of the green card or already qualified enough to carry on well in life from recent PhD graduates wanting to enrol in medical college.

Hence, I had to make a quick detour to trying to get into one before it became late. I stopped attending Howard and got admitted at the A. M. Dogliotti School of Medicine in Monrovia, Liberia, West Africa. January 1979. Here things initially took a brighter sing and there it seems the prospects my becoming a doctor was finally afoot.

How wrong it turned out to be for in 1980 sergeant Samuel K. Doe along with 17 others decided that AK47 should rule and violently overthrew the government of President William Tolbert under guise that the government was corrupt and does not care for indigenous Liberians.

This excuse for removing democratically elected African governments installing them with executive AK47 trigger happy nuts became a frequent reverberation over our young Africa continent leaving a cancerous trial of destruction, carnage, and retro ration.

The little infra structure or educational institutions, bequeathed by colonial rulers went to the dust and awaiting repair whiles the majority of Africans starve for want of food or means of producing it.

Things got unbearable and unsafe for me in Liberia that, Mr. Clyod Ramsey, an American friend spirited me out of Monrovia back to the USA in 1982. A limited visa status of six months ended fast before was able to plan the next step.

My experience at Liberia made me made me write supporting letters for Latif T. Sanyang, a friend landed me into hot waters causing my request for a temporal asylum in the USA. This took its course of lawyers and INS officers battling which culminated in an initial approval of my asylum request pending the recommendation being accepted by the state department.

To everyone's utter surprise, then vice president George W. Bush, Senior, denied the offer on the bases that Gambia was a friendly nation and one of Africa's democratic countries.

Simply put a crony of the west but not the interest of its citizen's plight. I had to opt for the applet courts routing. This took a foot dragging silence or inactiveness until 1986 when my defense was asked to plead our case before an INS judge.

Four years has lapsed and my case was in hands of someone nick named hanging judge of Atlanta by those who passed through his dockets. All Africans brought to his chambers were sent matching home with a stroke of the pen.

Deliberations of hearings on my case started from noon and ended after 6 Pm. The verdict came six months later with lengthy legal mambo jumbo about how democratic the Gambia was and that the minuscule impact of my protest letters were insufficient reason to grant asylum.

The judge blindfolded himself to the nature of African executive's sensitivity to being criticized. These were the days of Communism versus democratic ideologies.

The West was concern about which way Africa follows. Students like me telling the truth about behavior and corrupt practices of our fledgling pseudo democrats in seat of government were given deaf ears and the West smothered democracy in Africa by being complacent about these banana republic.

I spent all these years unemployed at the behest of Bishop Coleman McGhee and the Episcopal Dioceses of Michigan, in Detroit. Dr. Harvey Sloan, Mayor of Louisville, Kentucky and Miss Joyce R. Racer, Director of Health Affairs were able to get a $45,000 school fee from the University of Kentucky Medical School upon my presentation of a resident permit and my willing to pay back the money by working at the Appalachian region for two to three years as contribution.

Appeal after appeal to the state department and other branches of government failed because they believed Gambia as special friend to American hegemony.

Yes, she was special because city tsars and vying forces continue corrupting the state leading the president to make warning statements about it and the introduction of declaration of Assets Act, which never saw daylight. The big boys muscled through and had it thrown out of the window by forcing the firing of the Attorney General who spearheaded it.

In summary, all the other difficulties farmers encountered at the hands of pseudo city politicians went unchallenged nor were adequate resources of state given to aid empty bellied villagers. Hence, like Liberia, a few solders miraculously brought to close of democratically elected government of the Gambia with world watching gleefully with folded hands.

The first question that came to mind was where are all those who purportedly claim Gambia democratic and a friendly nation to refuse asylum to citizens from her territory? Again we see AK47 becoming executive in peace smiling coast of the Gambia.

Knowing that the system was incapable of challenging vice president George W. Bush, Sr., I left America reluctantly to start medical school all over at the American University of the Caribbean in Montserrat, West Indies in 1987.

I graduated from Medical school in 1992 and returned to the Gambia. There I met more opposition from none other than my medical colleagues. Hence after setting up my village self-help health NGO I left them and I am now on study leave fighting to do the MRCP degree in UK.

It is not easy access to grants because new rules state that priority must be given to United Kingdom and European community citizens in most of the training programs.

With the upset of the post independence status co, I decided to go to the United Kingdom and two things: improve my medical skills to the MRCP/FRCS level where possible and second, to internationalize the Self-help village Health NGO, Manding Medical Centre, I established at Njawara village in the Badibous in the North Bank region to get resources to build the center before my final return to the Gambia. The second aspect of my trip regarding the NGO picked up momentum just nine weeks to my arrival in Colchester, Essex, UK. Here doctors, nurses and resident of Colchester joined and formed the Friends of Manding Charitable Trust serving as an arm of Manding Medical Centre at Njawara village in the Up and the EU.

Very soon all the paper work, fees for registration were completed and submitted for approval by the UK Charity Commission. And sure enough we got our charitable status for England and Wales in August 2002. Our Charity number is registered as 10836.

While the organization busied itself on fund raising activities on weekends and calling public attention to Manding Medical Centre's goals, I started on the primary reason of my being in Uk, i.e. to pursue a course leading to the MRCP degree.

The devil in the form of visitor's visa reared its ugly head after the second renewal at the Home Office. HMO was not willing to change my status to student status nor allow me engaged or seek job in the UK.

This tantamount to either starving to death or returning to one' place of origin... disregarding the conflicts that returning prematurely entails. It meant going back to face disgrace, diminution, and definitely no promotion if one was lucky to be reinstated in the civil service.

The possibility caused certain friends to come to my aid to help even though it would be an uphill battle waiting in a dark tunnel of trouble. This saga relating to my pursuit of the MRCP is detailed in 'Doctor in Tattered Rags' with the GMC's senseless verdict in my case.

With the forming of Friends of Manding some Colchester doctors went to visit Njawara village in the Gambia to check out the districts interest and confirmation or commitment of the villagers to Manding Medical Centre.

They found an overwhelming enthusiasm beyond their wildest dreams. A second visit to the region in 2003 gave a different verdict and picture for it reported conflict of interest among Njawara residents regarding attempts to drum up false lies that I had purportedly had agreed upon their dubious conditions.

I set up and established the Manding Medical center in 1993 and the only agreement was an understanding between the local authority, Toro village and I was never to use the allotted plots of land for personal use, except hospital and health related facilities.

Hence, I reassured members of the Colchester Friends of Manding that I would sort things out with Njawara and local authority to stem opportunist from derailing the center. The effect report of the second visit to Njawara still revive rates because of the phenomenon of Africa fatigue, meaning people being tired of passing hard earned cash into well meaning and needed projects only to find that money used wrongly and not delivered to the intended recipients or goals. The Africa fatigue also gave the unwilling excuses for not participating no matter how much good said project would yield to indigenous villagers.

The organization mended as much of the damage as possible and villagers are still actively interested in the goals of the center. Momentum had been recently dampened by the current world wide global economic recession and massive unemployment of people who would normally give to organization like Friends of Manding.

In my drive to internationalize NGO Manding Medical Centre, I decided to invite the leadership class at Alpena Community College, a college I attended from 1967 to 1969 before transferring to Olivet College in 1971, to visit Njawara and help at the schools.

This rejuvenated more interest on locals and Njawara and the surrounding villages. These chipped in to make the visit a successful one. The twelve students' contingent and their instructor, Mr. Tom Ray, were very pleased and expressed desire to return to the region if the opportunity arises.

Right after the visit, I nudged with Carol Shafto and Penny Boldery, Alpena city Council to enter into a sister-city relationship with Njawara and Kinte Kunda villages in the North Bank Region of the Gambia. In the same vein I urged Colchester City Council to consider twining with Toro Bahen village.

Alpena acted instantly after hearing from the students and friendship they made at Njawara. As for Colchester, it took the Brits way of doing business.

It was not until 2007 that I finally heard from Mayor of Colchester Borough that at the time Colchester had twined with three European Union towns and could not add another at that moment of contact about Toro Bahen.

With the enacting of the Alpena- Njawara and Kinte Kunda proclaimed, Dr. Avery Aten got interested in the Manding Medical Centre and together we started work on idea of generating awareness of the Manding Medical Centre in the state of Michigan.

This lead to the formation of the Alpena Friends of Manding Charitable Trust and later Dr. Richard Bates and his colleagues joined and offered their service to the center.

Also I authored the legend against all odds, Medicine for the villager, Measure of Wisdom, Dare stand for Justice, Three Princesses of Badibou Manding, when hearts melt in love and Doctor in tattered rags.

Portion of proceed from sale of the above go to support the running of Manding Medical Centre at Njawara village, the Gambia. In addition I set up the Badibou Cultural dance troupe to tour Michigan in a fund raising drive for the Centre.

The visas and fares were still sticky points but we hope it will be resolved in 2009 according to Dr. Avery Aten, co-coordinator of the Michigan Tour. Many universities and colleges had offered venues for the dancers' tour once it got into gear.

My life at present had been a story of trials and the current economic meltdown, call it monetary crash if you may stands as man's doing as he plunges the rest of us little ones into a Pell Mel of a heaving hell.

The last years left me with vagueness, melancholy, chaotic inept feeling I ever experienced since leaving the Gambia 1967.

My state brought to mind what Floaters at sea who would not or do not think at all, but hope that like corks in water they will float on the waves of circumstances that in the end things somehow settle down and they will arrive successfully in a hospitable point.

Hence putting my heart and soul into my goal I too could wriggle out and lift myself to work again with head held high without stigma for the Gambia.

Mr. Faruq: PIA and Dr. Alhasan Ceesay, Manchester UK 2007

Miss Binta Ceesay Bundung, Gambia 2001

Chapter 4

NAIL THAT ALMOST.....

One of life lessons in parenthood was untraveled to me on the 27/9/2013 when my Famatanding Ceesay divulged a serious mistake she had just made. I was at first shocked because I was not prepared for such a disappointing revelation from the jewel of my heart. Famatanding Ceesay was one I wanted her sibling sister to emolliate and her confessing of an irrevocable mistake led me to ask what I did wrong as a father.

I loved my daughters more than anything and I stand confused as to reason why Famatanding did such backward act and how Famatanding's mistake came about.

Yes, to err is human and to forgive divine. The question for me was that was I wrong in staying away in search of a golden chance and solid education for my progeny? I stayed only to hopefully bring or afford my daughters good university education and fighting chance that would enable them compete in this turbulent doggy doggy world of their generation.

Was Famatanding aware of how much I pleaded for her admission to the Pre-med courses at Alpena Community College, Alpena, Michigan, USA?

Back in April 2010 Dr. Avery Aten offered Famatanding a place to stay once in Alpena, Michigan. He wrote:

To: alhasanceesay@hotmail.com
From: maten@chartermi.net
Subject: lodging
Date: Thu, 22 Apr 2010 00:19:01 -0400

Dear Dr Ceesay,

With great delight, we offer lodging, meals, transportation, and any other assistance that may be required for Famatanding Ceesay while she attends coursework at Alpena Community College.

Please see the attached letter to Michael Kollien, Admissions Representative at ACC concerning our offer.

Best Regards,

Dr Avery J Aten MD.

Again when things got delayed I contacted Dr. Aten thus:

On Dec 23, 2013, at 8:50 AM, Alhasan Ceesay wrote:
Dear Dr. & Mrs. Aten,
Please accept sincere apology for my not having written earlier. Bellow event was overly stressful and took most of my time. Merry Christmas and a happy new year in advance.

The reason for this long silence was that Famatanding Ceesay ran into difficulty while at a visit to distant relatives in Guinea Conakry.

The past years were hell for the family but to cut a long sad story I am happy to report that we got her back in one healthy piece. We thank you for your patients. Let me know current standing of her enrolment offer.
Regards
Dr. Alhasan Ceesay

Even under such bleak circumstances my friend wrote back saying:

<u>AVERY ATEN</u>

Re: AN UPDATE... AND WISHING YOU

AVERY ATEN
12/29/13

To: Alhasan Ceesay

Dr Ceesay, Merry Christmas, and a hopeful New Year, in which dreams may come true. Our previous offer remains in effect. I am retiring from medicine in Feb 2014, with the exception of volunteer or mission projects. If you can raise the cost of her tuition and international travel, she has a place to stay with us. Dr Aten.

Was this opportunist worth it better for her than sacrifice we put in to educate her and to give her chance to become a doctor serving more needy people than one most likely not only to throw her away on the wayside when things get rough or upon meeting a pretier and richer girl?

Was this act of Famatanding that weak-minded folks meant about my having nothing but girls? I still say girls are special jewel and my daughters are my heart's joy. However the pain of the curse almost became the nail that almost sealed my coffin.

Life turned upside-down as I saw most of thirty five years effort go down the drain of hopelessness with no real future for her. I had spent most of the energetic years of my life not only fighting against the odds but preparing this girl for the best there is in life and I got for it was advent of very serious irrevocable mistake.

Wife's reaction added peppers to a raw wound for me. It left my heart laden with sadness for having lost a daughter to a dishonest fellow. Et tu Brutus! I cried. Luckily after a week of soul searching I called my Famatanding and assured that I not only forgive her but will unflinchingly stand by her through her new encounter.

Selfless folks like me never balk in the face of a trial but I am against opportunists. The disjunction between perception and reality is due to belief that feelings last. The lopsidedness in infatuation with some proofs me right.

Understandably the victim always belief in his/her perception and follow their hearts instead of brains. It was painful but the right thing and stance as she will always be my genes whether she had a perfect or not so perfect life.

She is mine and I am duty bond to love and support her from my heart and core. I still wake up late at night hoping that it was all a dream or a prank my daughter pulling on me. However, in reality it was real and I only pray that such mistake never happen to her remaining sisters who took her as their role model. It at one time made me look back into my trail in UK and the USA to find reason for her behaviour.

Making both ends meet was not easy for me as my visa classification prohibits from engaging in gainful and even voluntary employment. Life in the UK was not an easy experience for the jobless. We all agree job is the only rewarding avenue to a balance formal or functional life. As stipulated my visa disapproved my getting a job even if it were offered.

Then the economic downturn made it more unbearable as those would like to offer a few pennies now those pennies for family and self. I was let stranded and sleeping in parks or open safe streets most of the time. This made it difficult to show how much I adore my girls and wanted them better prepared for life than their generation.

Never in my wildest dream did the thought that teenage life was more difficult for girls than boys. Why did God/nature made it so hard for women in this life? Famatanding Ceesay and I continue to see eye to eye and I begged her younger sisters to learn from the mistake and not cause dad go through such pain in his aging days.

Famatanding text: "I admit this is my mistake. I know that I have let you down!" To add insult to injury her purported Knight on a white horse text: "Be assured that I am willing to take good care of your daughter and I will always stand by her. All we want is your continuous love and support. Once again, I am sorry for the shame and embarrassment. I am sorry."

I straight away went into damage control and preventive mode and decided to follow plan B so as not to lose the other girls to a similar opportunist. I called Binta, my next eldest daughter, and told her that was going to try and reactivate her admission for the BSc degree in business and management at the University of the Gambia.

Roheyata Ceesay will complete her high school hopeful by that time the horizon would be much brighter for the family than it is at the moment. Binta still held onto desire to join me in England but as much as I would love the family to join me there isn't the monetary means with me at present.

I spoke to Aminata Njie, Director, Admissions and Finance Aid at the Finance section about letting my daughter start her courses. I made it clear that I will transfer the whole year's fees as soon as the request is answered.

My Famatanding Ceesay; Daughter, Gambia 2004

I never claim to be a supper parent but have burnt both ends of the candle for want of giving my daughters the best possible start and fighting chance in this life. Famatanding said of me thus: "My hero, my best friend! My daddy! He is sweet n loving!

Always respect and understands me, He has never hurt me! He always tries to put a smile on my face even when his days are not good!"And I am not ashamed to say that I have never loved any man as much as I love my dad!"

Additionally Famatanding Ceesay sent the following moving birthday greeting on my 72nd year which ran thus: "Feeling excited with Alhasan Ceesay. Happy birthday to an awesome #DAD.

Despite all that we do, you still love us unconditionally and we're so grateful to have you as a Dad. You're more than just a father to me-You're my hero, my guru, my inspiration. Happy birthday #DAD. Thank you for been caring and loving through the years! Happy Birthday to you #ALHASAN CEESAY"

Growing up without a dad to show the path to take is the worst thing that could ever happen to a little girl! It has been 14 years since I last saw my best friend n dad.....How unfortunate! In conclusion, my darling daughter, never take things for granted but always is humble while doing positive things with your life.

Always have faith, be honest, truthful and trust worthy and above all just and none judgmental. Learn from your mistakes and love un-adultratingly. In assertion let faith be your guiding pillar as you ply through life's trials and tribulations. Never give up trying to better yourself and others. Enjoy life to the fullest but work to earn a decent living.

Furthermore keep in mind that all that glitters is not gold. In short, earthling parents like beggars, would gallop to heaven had wishes been horses. Rest assured of unflinching support as long as I live.

Dudou Ceesay, elder brother in green, with family

Chapter 5

PRISONER OF MY AMBITION FOR THE VILLAGER

The burning embers of a wish and hope for my people became a prison wall that kept caving onto me any time I relaxed my effort. Ambition to bring the Golden Medical Flees, in the form of medical aid, to the villager constantly hunts me and reminds me of my covenant for the Gambia.

There were no doubts in my mind that I was rightfully engaged in bringing much needed medical service to the region served by Manding Medical Centre in the Gambia. I literally became the fugue of the family as I pushed to bring my desire to provide proper medical aid into fruition for the villager in the North Bank of the Gambia.

This quest for a better medical service to neglected villagers led to my disappearing from the family horizon to America as early as 1967. There I started the challenge of my life in a drive to become a doctor of medicine serving the Gambia.

The path of this adventure is well documented in my first book, "The legend against all odds" published by Publish America, Baltimore, Maryland, USA in August 2002. The strength of my conviction along with a mindset to do something concrete for my people made me give up today's pleasures for a better tomorrow for the Gambia.

An Armchair psychologist, Dr. Kube Lonna (nick named Dr. Hamham), once told me; "Dreamers are a pain in the neck." I asked why? And he replied, "They wake up with one of the most ridiculous ideas and try not only to live in that nonsense but implement them for the rest of their lives.

Us pragmatics and wise become sceptical and weary of the dreamer and brand him either a total loony or living in a planet by himself or herself." I replied quoting Lawrence of Arabia. Who said "All men dream: but not equally.

Those who dream by the night in the dusty recesses of their minds wake in the day to find that it was vanity; but the dreamers of the day are dangerous men, for they act their dream with open eyes to make it possible."

I further made it clear that none the less many dreamers have converts. I asked what converts the sage to the dreamer' path? To this he gave the most amazing reply in favour of the dreamers and people with strong convictions like mine.

My armchair psychologist told me, "We only become flabbergasted as the dream unfolds to bits of reality opening up wide realms unknown to us before that day." He continued by illustrating what he meant. "Take for example the case of the Rights brothers and their attempt to fly.

Boy oh boy! Some critics who strongly believed that only birds, goblins, and angels had the privilege of flight ridiculed the Rights brothers as witches. Today you and I know better for we now use the Rights brother's dream to fly round the world at ease and by it we have catapulted to the moon and beyond."

I hope this has cleared the air for the reader as to why some of us are considered as whacks and a challenge to my friend the sage armchair psychologist Dr. Kube Lonna. Very early in my high school days friends labeled me as a reclusive person not knowing that my whole psyche was based on going aboard and becoming one of the future doctors of the Gambia.

I am fully aware of all work and no play not only turns us into monsters but also indeed a very dull one at that. I just moderated my life and made certain that I never lost track of my direction in life and my ambition for the Gambian villager.

After ten years in America my family considered me being lost in zealous desire to gain book knowledge or Western education. I learnt that my father, while on his deathbed urged that prayers be offered so that I, the family fugue would return home.

Like Mac polo or Sinbad's adventures mine had seen me fly on several times to America, Liberia, the West Indies and the United Kingdom seeking more skills with which to serve my people.

It is said that life is lonely at the top but I found it even lonelier when struggling from ground zero with no hope of financial assistance at sight. Every hour of my life had to be organized in a way to minimize loss of income and to maintain progress in my academic pursuits.

Hence I worked on three jobs during the summer breaks and at school libraries to raise funds for my education or repayment of loans which enable me continue schooling. To me every ounce of energy and sent spent on my aspiration to become a doctor in the Gambia was as exhilarating as becoming an overnight multimillionaire.

It is a joy I wish I could share with you. Graduating from medical school and my first patient in the Gambia are indelible blessed moments I hold dear to my heart. The rewards will forever be for my people and humanity.

Fatou Koma-Ceesay and daughter Rohey Ceesay, 2015

Chapter 6

DISTIGUISHED 2005 GRADUATE

AWARD TO DR. Alhasan CEESAY

I attended Alpena Community College (ACC) in Michigan, USA, from September 1967 to December 1979. My contact with friends at Alpena never waned. Hence the wheels of profound recognition by the institute started rolling when Mathew Dunckel called me to let me know he read my book, "The Legend against All Odds."

He was very impressed and intrigued by my experience and fortitude since my leaving Alpena Community College in 1979. I met Mathew when he was twelve years old. His father Dr. Elbridge Dunckle was my academic advisor while I was at Alpena community College.

I will without any reservation still recommend Dr. Dunckel for academic advisor to any foreign student attending the college.

It was during one of our telephone conversation (02/01/05) that Mathew told me of the possibility of ACC recommending me for the Distinguished 2005 Graduate award offered annually by Alpena Community College to its outstanding Alumni.

Alpena Community College foundation recognizes its graduates annually for their academic and their career accomplishment for their communities. It simply recognizes the aspirations of Alumni for their people.

The Pandora's Box was opened by innocuous telephone conversation in recognizing my aspiration and goal for providing medical aid to Gambian villagers. Mathew asked me to fax him any and all possible documentation about me and work I do in the Gambia.

He would then speak to the relevant authorities regarding my being nominated for the Distinguished 2005 graduate of Alpena Community College coming May 5th 2005 spring/summer commencement. Mathew did just as promised. In a nutshell, here is the letter from Mrs. Penny Boldrey, Executive Director Alpena Community College Foundation. It read:-

Alpena Community College

666 Johnson Street

Alpena, MI 49707

January 6, 2005

Alhasan S. Ceesay, MD

245 Great Western Street

Manchester M14 4LQ

Dear Dr. Ceesay,

Mathew Dunckel shared the information that you recently provided to him regarding your professional achievements since your early years at Alpena Community College.

I'm extremely pleased to share with you that your many outstanding accomplishments have earned you the distinction of Distinguished Graduate of Alpena Community College (ACC) for 2005.

We commend you for your humanitarian efforts in founding and developing the Manding Medical Centre in Gambia, West Africa. I'm anxious to read your book. "The legend against all odds" once Matt has finished with it. Without a doubt, you serve as an example of how a solid educational foundation from Alpena Community College can launch a lifetime of achievements.

You will be honored at our spring commencement exercises on Thursday, May 5, which begins at 7 pm, in the Park Arena at ACC. We invite you to join us on that evening. However, we certainly understand that making a trip to the United States, on so short a notice, may not be feasible. During the commencement program, I will share a synopsis of your extraordinary career that has earned you the honour of Distinguished Graduate. If you are able to join us, you will be invited to join me at the podium to receive your award and to address the audience if you wish.

Would you be willing to provide us with the following: 1) a copy of your professional resume; 2) a paragraph on your memories of ACC and how your experience helped you achieve your goals; 3) a professional photo for use in our alumni newsletter as well as in an ad that will appear in AlpenaNews.

Please feel free to call me or e-mail me with any additional questions you may have. Again, congratulations! We look forward to hearing from you in the future.

Sincerely

Penny Boldrey

Executive Director

My response to this honour and invitation to my second home America was swift and obvious as penned bellow. I e-mailed Penny forth with as my heart was overwhelmed by joy for being recognised by my Alma Mata ACC. It simply stated:-

13/01/05,

Manchester, UK.

Dear Penny Boldrey,

I am overwhelmed and do not know where to begin this note of thanks to Alpena Community College. In my mind it's the American people who deserve such honour and distinction for I am only recipient of the goodness of the Americans.

I am humbled and further rejuvenated by the thought and recognition of my goals and work for the Gambia. I remember in the 60s when people used to tell me, "You will end up just like all foreign students who came to America.

They end up getting trapped by the greener pasture syndrome of America." To such challenges my response had always been; I for one will disappoint a lot of you for I will never rest until I bring to my people the American know how and willingness to share with others.

This stance has never changed and will not ever change because the only way I can, in a small measure compared to what you did for us poor ones, pay back is to be able to show what the USA is all about and her stand for the little guy anywhere on this planet.

I will look into my schedule to see if I can afford to be in Alpena May 2005. I will let you know by the end of February 2005. Mean while I'm faxing a resume and will try to send my photos by e-mail.

Where it is not possible for me to attend in May, would it be okay for my first Alpena family friend, Mrs. Rita Riggs to represent me at the ACC' spring Commencement Ceremony. She was the first people in Alpena that opened their homes to me. She and her family will certainly appreciate recognition of their help to this simple Gambian.

None the less rest assured that I have not yet slammed the door to my seeing Alpena once more. Timing and visa problems might make it unattainable. Again, please accept profound gratitude to all of you and to Alpena Community College. God blesses you and rain peace on earth in 2005. Cheers and regards.

Sincerely

Dr. Alhasan S. Ceesay, MD

My lovely daughter: Binta Ceesay

Mrs. Boldrey replied thus:

ACC, Michigan 49707

13/01/05

Hi Dr. Ceesay,

Yes, I did receive your curriculum vitae and thank you for forwarding that to me! We are extremely proud of you and your accomplishments! Once I get my hand on your book, I will pay special notice to the ACC chapter.

The best part of my job is the opportunity to meet former alumni and learn of the impact ACC had in their lives. Please believe me that we understand if you are unable to join us at commencement on May 5.

Indeed we would be pleased to have Rita Riggs accept this honour on your behalf. Rita is remarkable and kind woman. My husband speaks fondly of her and has stayed in close contact with her.

I look forward to getting to know you better through our correspondence! And meet you in person someday. Regards

Its

Mrs. Penny Boldrey

Executive Director

At the end it was not possible for me to attend the ceremony in person. So Rita Riggs and her family stepped in for me. Her elder son Robert Riggs was designated to receive the award in my behalf as representative of Rita who was in her 80s at the time.

I emailed the follow short remarks to be read by Robert Riggs at the time the award is given. It is titled:-

A FUTURE FOR ALL

Mr. President, staff, Graduates, Ladies and Gentlemen; I am deeply moved and humbled being chosen Alpena Community College's Distinguished Alumni for 2005.This recognition belongs to America.

Without the good will and foresight of the staff, students and the community of Alpena in 1967, I might never have had the chance to earn education with which to help my people move forward in life.

Hence, allow me reiterate profound gratitude to Alpena Community College, my fellow students, people of Alpena and America at large. My life after Alpena has been full of trials and tribulations detailed in my first book, "The legend against all odds".

One relief in it is the robust blessing and peace of mind I have knowing that I am right in what I am doing for my people. There are those who claim Heaven in being rich but for me it is reaching out to help others that matters in life. Upon graduating from medical school, I returned to the Gambia and setup a self-help village Health organization (Manding Medical Centre) at Njawara village in an effort to provide a much needed medical service to the rural sector. I am happy to report that membership has grown beyond twenty thousand villagers.

Please join me to catch a dream for my villagers. Manding medical centre will help portray the America we all dream of and yearn to be part. We are on the verge of building the children's unit and do need monetary, equipment and medicines assistance in our drive to provide this unique service to villagers.

To the graduates, I would like to remind you that, the great tide of history flows and as it flows it carries to the shores of reality what binds us as one human race. Be aware of the extent, depth and gravity of the challenges ahead as you set out to transform, reconstruct and integrate America into a global icon.

Sincere congratulations for your march towards success and fulfilment. Alpena Community College has given you the first footprints. Walk your way with head held high and determination to succeed in the world. Confucius said, "Our greatest glory is never failing, but in rising every time we fail." Stockpiles of atomic bombs or weapons of mass destruction and dictators do not measure greatness.

I believe strongly and sincerely that with deep-rooted wisdom and dignity, innate respect for human right and lives, the intense humanity will make us more cherished and better leaders. This will make us able to contribute towards the future and progress of mankind. I am happy for you and hope that you will fly the American flag for it is the great American constitution.

Finally, I would like to pay tribute to pass and present staff, students of ACC and Alpena community for having given me the opportunity to forge for my people. Allow me make special mention and express thanks to the remarkable and noble friends I met in Alpena.

Sincere thanks from my family, villagers and I to Howard & Rita Rigg, Judge Philip & Viola S. Glennie, Mr. Henry V. Valli, Dr. Elbridge Dunckel, Dr. Strom, Bill & Magritte Cruise, Dr. Charles T. Egli and the Alpena medical association, Mr. Cloyd Ramsey & the Medical Arts Clinic and all who helped make my sojourn to Alpena a remarkable success.

If I have a million friends, I would like many more to be like you. I hope you will believe in, as well as join me, in my dream of providing modern medical aid to the Gambian villagers. Thanks a million and God bless America!

BY: DR. ALHASAN SISAWO CEESAY, MD

Mrs. Penny Boldrey called to let me know she confirmed the details with Robert Rigg, who was selected by the family to deliver the speech.

She assured me that Bob was all set with my remarks and had been practicing many times. Rita and Donna will also be attending with other friends. To make it official she sent this note to Robert Rigg (Bob).

April 21, 2005

Robert Rigg

312 Liberty Street

Alpena, MI 49707

Dear Bob,

Dr. Alhasan Ceesay has informed that you will be representing him at our commencement ceremony and accepting the Distinguished Graduate Award on his behalf.

Our spring commencement exercises will be held on Thursday, May 5, at 7 pm. There will be VIP seating near the front left section of the Park Arena for and your family. During the commencement program, I will share a brief synopsis of Dr. Ceesay's career.

I will invite you to join me at the podium to receive Dr. Ceesay's Distinguished Graduate Award. Following the presentation, you will have the opportunity to share Dr. Ceesay's remarks.

I shared with Dr. Ceesay that his comments must be kept brief (2-3 minutes) because our program consist of many individuals who will also be addressing the graduating class.

After the ceremony we would like to take some photographs, so if you could remain near your seats, I will come to you.

A reception at the Jeese Besser Museum follows commencement and you are also invited to join. Enclosed you will find a copy of Dr. Ceesay's remarks. I look forward to hearing from you. Please call me to confirm your participation.

Sincerely

Penny Boldrey

Executive Director

Two weeks prior to the ceremony I received an e-mail letting me know that Karen Eller, administrative assistant in the president's (ACC) office of Public information will be writing about me in the Lumberjack Link spring and summer alumni newsletter publication.

Penny also told me that Kerrie Miller (also alumni) and news writer for The Alpena News would like to feature me in the local paper. I immediate e-mailed the following to Kerrie Miller at the Alpena News.

Hi Kerrie, I just received Penny's email with the good news that you want to feature me in the Alpena News. For me this would be a dream come true. Yes! By all means go ahead and feel free to contact me should you want more information about me or the work I'm doing in the Gambia.

I am a simple person that loves to help others get on with life the best way they can during their short sojourn on mother earth. I strongly believe that those of us who had the privilege to learn from America have responsibility to share American goodwill with our people.

That is the only way they, our people, can experience the real America that stands for the down trodden and the innovative. I still feel very happy when come across an American.

If your paper is able to help me get Manding Medical Centre at Njawara out of its current limbo, then you would have participated in the most noble and worthy course that will outlive us and will be a spring board of hope and medical service for generations we can ever dream of.

It is my Binta Ceesay

We are still on fund raising stage to build the first phase, the children's unit, which according to estimates will cost around £250,000 or about $500,000 dollars. I committed all proceeds of my book, "The legend against all odds", to the centre but it is not selling enough to get things in fast gear.

I need help to bring relief to my villagers. Well, this is enough introductions until I hear from you. God bless you and thanks a million for being kind towards us.

Sincerely

Dr. Alhasan S. Ceesay

Kerrie Miller replied and asked that I send her a synopsis of how I found out Alpena in the 60s. So I sent her the following summary. "I came to be in Alpena by simply going to the then American Consulate in Banjul, the Gambia and asked for a catalogue with information on American colleges.

As a beggar normally has no choice, I started from the top alphabets. Well, Alpena Community college was there and was the first that accepted my application among the schools that replied to my desire to pursue further education in America. T

his part is well expanded in chapter in my book "The legend against all odds" highlighting my experience at ACC from 1967 -1969.

I was born and bread in abject poverty and I'm only fighting for my villagers to have a chance to proper medical care etc, etc nothing more and nothing -less.I hope you will help get your readers interested in Manding Medical Centre and its objective for the villagers.

Thank you for taking upon the task of writing about me and my work in the Gambia. Manding Medical Centre is in limbo and we year for a boost or a short in the arm to get things moving faster. Please visit our website: www.Friends of manding gambimed.com

It's

Dr. A. Ceesay

I will later reproduce both articles written by Karen Eller for the Lumberjack Link and Kerrie Miller's in the Alpena News respectively. For now let us head to the spring commencement podium and listen to what Mrs. Penny Boldrey has in mind about this simple village doctor.

Bob and his family attended in time and it was now time for Penny's remarks about my achievements from the days of Alpena Community College to now.

It is simple and movingly started thus:-

"Good evening and congratulations graduates!

The Alpena Community College Foundation created the Distinguished Graduate award not only to recognize, but to honour our graduates who have gone on to contribute to society through successful careers. Our recipient tonight serves as an example of how a solid education foundation from ACC can launch a lifetime of achievements.

I'm pleased to share with you that our 2005 Distinguished Graduate is Dr. Alhasan Ceesay from the Gambia, West Africa. Dr Ceesay received his Associates of Arts Degree in 1969, exactly two years after leaving the Gambia. He credits many individuals, and the generosity of others, as the driving force behind his success.

Following his graduation from ACC, Dr. Ceesay transferred to Olivet College, on a full-tuition scholarship provided to him by the Besser Foundation. In 1971, he earned a Bachelor of Arts Degree in Biology from Olivet, and in 1973 completed his Master of Science degree from Michigan Technological University at Houghton Michigan, USA.

Dr. Ceesay taught biology for several years in the Gambia before entering into medical school in 1992; he was awarded his Doctor of Medicine Degree from the American University of the Caribbean. Dr. Ceesay again returned to the Gambia, and provided free medical assistance to the villagers for an entire year before he took a position as House Officer at the Royal Victoria Hospital, Banjul, the Gambia, and was eventually promoted to the post of Medical Officer in 1999. He is the proud founder of the Manding Medical Centre, a self-help village Health organisation located in the Gambia, which has provided much needed medical care to over 8000 villagers.

In his autobiography, "The legend Against All Odds", Dr. Ceesay shares his struggle to survive in his quest for an education. All the proceeds from his book go to supporting the Manding Medical Centre. Dr. Ceesay and his wife have three daughters, ages 14, 11 and 7. In my correspondence with Dr. Ceesay over the past few months, he shared his profound gratitude for his American education.

He said, "In my mind, it is the American who deserved such honour and distinction, for I'm the recipient of the goodness of the Americans." Due to travel difficulties, Dr. Ceesay is unable to be here tonight to accept this award. However he has asked his first American family, the Howard Rigg family to represent him.

At this time I'll ask Bob Rigg to join me at the podium to accept the award for Dr. Ceesay. Indeed, it is truly an honour to recognize Dr. Ceesay for his many accomplishments and humanitarian efforts.

We congratulate him on earning the Distinction of Distinguished Graduate of Alpena Community College. – Penny Boldrey-

Robert Rigg eloquently delivered my remarks aimed at the graduates and residents of Alpena city. It was welcomed as I was later told by those who were able to e-mail me. Alpena city and ACC were very happy. This Distinguished Graduate award came thirty 36 odd years since I last visited Alpena, Michigan.

Mathew Dunckel sent me the following comments about the evening of the award. "Alhasan, your address was given at commencement. It was the portion of the evening that was enjoyed by most.

Partly because it was delivered well and partly because of my father was mentioned. I think what you said was inspirational for our students and brought home the need for them to think internationally.

Tom Ray is making final preparation to depart for Gambia early next week. What a great adventure for the students. I am looking forward to hearing about it on their return. Thank you for helping make it happen.

Your friend

Matt.

I sent Penny Boldrey the following; "I received both the award and enclosures. Accept my deepest appreciation for the kind words spoken about me in your presentation speech during the spring graduation ceremony. Thank you very much for your kindness."

I suggested we pursue the possibility of twining Alpena with two villages in the Gambia. Dear reader, I hope your patience is not running out as you eagerly look forward to the publication for alumni and friends of Alpena Community College.

Karen Eller wrote to let me know that she was assigned to write a news article for the local paper announcing my receiving the Distinguished Graduate award. She read my book, "The legend against all odds," to garner more information about me to help her on the matter at hand. She continued by letting me know that she found my story very interesting and she intend to do a good job at the article.

Here without further ado is Karen Eller's article about me. This idea unfolded to reality in the chapter on sister city proclamation.

THE LUMBERJACK LINK: ALPENA MICHIGAN

DR. CEESAY NAMED DISTINGUISHED GRADUATE

Dr. Alhasan Sisawo Ceesay of the Gambia, West Africa, was recognized with the Distinguished Graduate award at the ACC spring commencement ceremony in May 5th, 2005. On hand to receive the award for Dr. Ceesay was members of the Howard Rigg family, his first host family when he came to Alpena in 1967.

According to Dr. Ceesay, "The Riggs were the ideal American, an average working class who readily shared the little bit God gave them with others less fortunate."

Dr. Ceesay earned his Associate of Arts degree from ACC in 1969 and went on to Olivet College to earn his Bachelor's degree in biology with the help of a full-tuition scholarship from the Besser Foundation.

He earned his Master's degree in biological sciences from Michigan Technological University in 1973.

In 1979, Dr. Ceesay returned to Africa and entered the University of Liberia Medical School in Monrovia. Because of political unrest in the Gambia in 1981, Dr. Ceesay escaped to the United States in hopes of completing his lifelong dream; "to provide medical relief to the villager who is forced to walk miles on end to seek medical aid for his already dying child, wife or friend."

During the time he was seeking political asylum in the United States, Dr. Ceesay never gave up his quest for education, and he continued to take classes at Michigan State University and Wayne State University.

He was finally accepted at the American University of the Caribbean in the West Indies, and he began the final segment of his journey to becoming a doctor. In 1992, after 25 years of educational struggles, Dr. Ceesay was awarded his Doctor of Medicine degree from the American University of the Caribbean.

He returned to the Gambia where he provided free medical assistance to the villagers for an entire year before taking a position at the Royal Victoria Hospital, Banjul, The Gambia.Dr. Ceesay founded Manding Medical Centre in 1993. This is a self-help village health organisation which provides much needed medical aid to the villagers of the Gambia, West Africa. His autobiography, "The legend against all odds," chronicles his struggle to survive in his quest for Western education.

Proceeds of his book go to support Manding Medical Centre at Njawara village and provide scholarships in medicine and agriculture for indigent rural candidates in the Gambia. To learn more about Dr. Ceesay's ambitions, you can e-mail him at alhasanceesay@hotmail.com.

Dr. Ceesay was honoured to receive this distinction from ACC and would like to "express thanks to the remarkable and noble friends" he met in Alpena. He credits the goodwill and foresight of the staff and students at ACC for giving him the chance to earn an education and help move his people forward in life.

-Karen Eller-

I thank Karen Eller for this revealing commendable article. Here now is that featured by the Alpena News written by news staff Kerrie L. Miller. This is Miller's version about me and my goals.

ALPENA NEWS, MICHIGAN, USA 2005

A LONG ROAD FROM GAMBIA TO ALPENA

When he was about 14, Dr. Alhasan S. Ceesay saw a family tragedy unfold that would change his life forever. As he was walking to school, he saw a woman, pregnancy full-term, who was obviously ill.

Her husband was carrying their young son who was nearly comatose from illness. Ceesay later found out the pregnant woman's baby died in uterus and she died from the toxins built up in her body as a result. The young boy also died three quarters of a mile before his family was able to reach the health centre at Kerewan village.

"That day I said, "If God will help me, no one will ever have to go through that again. That picture is what made up my mind for me," Ceesay said. Ceesay, a native of Njawara, Gambia, is a graduate of Alpena Community College, class of 1969. He earned his Associate's of Arts degree from ACC before attending Olivet College, Michigan Tech and Howard University, earning his doctor of medicine degree from the America University of the

Caribbean in 1992. But how does a young man from a village in Gambia get to Alpena to attend its community college? In an e-mail message, he stated that after reaching the American Consulate, and asking for a listing of American colleges, Alpena Community College was at the top of the alphabetical list.

And Acc was the first to respond to his application. Once here, life was not without challenges. In a telephone conversation, he said it was the first time he had left his country, and when he got here no one spoke his language. "But I don't give up," he said.

Another goal Ceesay never gave up on was making it possible for village families, such as those like the one who affected him as deeply as a young man, to have access to health care services. With the creation of the Manding Medical Centre, which has helped over 8000 patients free of charge, he is doing that.

Though progress has been very slow in coming to the centre; Ceesay said officially he is employed by the central government and is only on the weekends is he able to man the centre, along with three or four other doctors who volunteer their time. Ceeesay say the centre sees no fewer than 500 patients and as many as 1,500 patients in a weekend.

He said currently the centre is in limbo and is a little more than a shed. He has been working on fund-raising to get the first phase, a children's unit, built. It is expected to cost approximately $500,000. Members of the ACC Leadership Class are currently conducting fund-raising to go to Gambia and help with the children and volunteering at the centre.

The trip will last two weeks. Ceesay is the author of a book chronicling his life's experiences called "The legend against all odds" (available at Amazon .com) and he has committed all proceeds of its sale to the centre. He said he's never regretted the decision he made to become a doctor. "Sometimes I feel like I have oil on my feet and I'm climbing a very steep hill." Ceesay said.

"I have always believed I'll reach my goal... you have to be crazy like me and you have to ignore lots of things that take you away from your goals." A typical day in Ceesay's life begins at 5 am with prayer, before boarding public transportation to the hospital where he works, 7 miles from his home.

From 7 – 11 am he does morning rounds, followed by clinics, then evening rounds. Days can last up to 10 or 11 pm before he heads back home. "In between, I try to please my wife and children. It's a very simple life really," he said. He and his wife have three daughters, the oldest of which has dreams of attending Alpena High School and

ACC before going onto medical school like her father. Ceesay's long-term goals revolve around the medical centre, which he hopes will continue to grow for generations, helping thousands more patients. "I plan to stay at the centre until the day they bury me. That and have my children educated. That's it," he said.

-Kerrie Miller-

Kerrie sent me a copy of the Alpena news. And I sent the following in appreciation of the good work in the article. Kerrie, I just received a copy of the Alpena news featuring me. It was a job well done.

I hope it help move my dream of providing medical aid to villagers a notch higher for Manding Medical centre and the Gambian villagers. The Gambia and I are most grateful for enlightening your readers about us and our need for a medical facility.

Extend our thanks and deep appreciation to the staff and Alpena-news. We shall definitely be in Gambia in due course. We look forward to your crew attending the ground breaking ceremonies in Gambia soon. I have started a collection of documentations about me to be placed in Dr. Alhasan S. Ceesay's achieves.

Kerrie Miller replied saying that they missed me for the ceremony but she look forward to attending the grand opening of the centre. Penny Boldrey simply said, "I will certainly make sure you receive a copy of our alumni newsletter once it's completed. Indeed, we are very proud of your accomplishments and humanitarian efforts."

Alh Kebba Sanneh, Japine, Gambia 1867: Friend That lifted my feet when my wings forgot how to Fly.

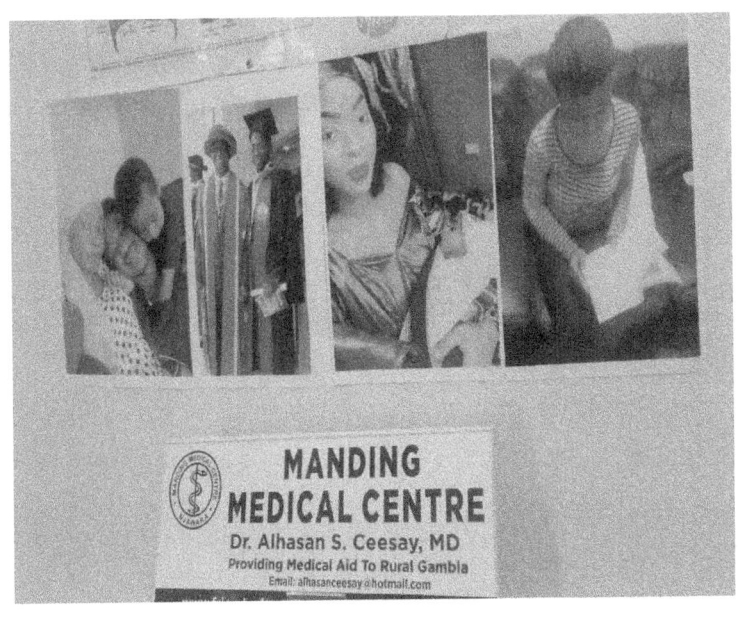

Chapter 7

AMERICAN GUESTS VISIT MANDING MEDICAL CENTR, NJAWARA, THE GAMBIA, IN MAY 2005.

The telephone call on 5/01/05 from Mr. Mathew Dunckel as well as that from Mr. Thomas Ray (TOM) four days later opened the Pandora's Box and became harbingers to a remarkable trip to Manding Medical Centre, Njawara village, Gambia by the Alpena Community College's Leadership class headed by none other than their instructor Mr. Thomas P. Ray.

I contacted Mr. Thomas Ray as soon as it was brought to my attention that some ACC students were contemplating visiting my centre at Njawara in May 2005. My message on the 6/01/05 to Mr. Ray ran thus:-

"An old friend, Mr. Mathew, staff of ACC, had a long chat with me last night and he brought to my attention of a possibility that a class wanting to travel to the Gambia as guest of Manding Medical Centre at Njaswara. I am more that willing and happy to pave the way for those that would venture the trip.

I do need an e-mail or fax from you indicating desire to go to the Gambia on a mission for Manding Medical Centre. I will speak to both the schools and the district authority about your most welcomed trip to the Gambia.

Manding Medical Centre is a self-help village health organisation I setup in upon returning to the Gambia in1992. We provide medical service to villagers and land has been donated for the location of the centre and its ancillaries.

We only have a corrugated shed as clinic. We are now on the verge of building the first phase, being the children's unit of the centre and need monetary assistance. I am delighted to know of your intentions. Please contact me as soon as you speak with the class."

Thomas Ray replied on 7/01/05, "I was thrilled when Mathew discussed the possibility of a trip to Gambia for our leadership students. I will meet with the whole class next week to discuss the possibility.

As I am sure you are aware the cost of airfares from Alpena to Gambia is high, so I will need to be certain the students are committed to raising the money needed before we begin making plans. I have travelled to many locations, but never to Africa, so I am also very excited about the prospects for myself.

After I meet with the students on Tuesday of next week, I will e-mail you with further information. I wish to also commend you for your personal achievements; I plan to purchase a copy of your recent book to share with my students and for my personal reading. Thank you for your help and enthusiasm."

I emailed Tom advising that to bargain for insured group tickets. Tom further contacted me on 12/01/05 stating that he has spoken to the students and they have agreed to take on a service trip as part of the course.

He told me that they would only be able to travel in a group for 10 – 14 days in May 2005. Tom wanted to know if there was an existing program at Njawara that would be able to accommodate the students.

He assured me that the students would be comfortable in a dormitory housing or make shift dormitories. In addition I let him know on the 14/01/05 that I have spoken to the commissioner, North Bank Division and the local authority in Lower Badibou district regarding their pending trip to Njawara as guest of Manding Medical Centre and the region.

I assured him that these authorities would be more than happy to have his class visit with them. I requested an e-mail from him stating that they are visiting in behalf of Manding Medical Centre at Njawara and specify what they would want to do while in the Gambia.

I suggested that they can help teach in some of the schools. I assured them that even though business and some residents have moved out there is still some activity at the village. Tom in reply sent the following on the 15/01/05. "Thank you for the great news.

I am very excited about the prospect and have begun searching for group airfares with special student rates. I will inform the students on Tuesday and contact you immediately afterward via email. I have a few questions. What costs do we need to expect in Gambia and in your village?

How will we travel from Banjul to the village? We need to be certain we have a clear idea what expenses we will have to help us set specific fundraising goals both for ourselves and for the foundation from which we hope to receive grants.

When I write the other e-mail, are there tasks other than tutoring that I should include? Are there other ways we can help while we are there? I am more excited about the prospect of this service trip everyday and the students are quite enthused."

In another e-mail dated 15/02/05, Tom wrote, "The students in the leadership class are so committed to this project that they voted to contribute their own money toward the travel if they cannot raise enough. This means that the number of students who actually travel will likely be fewer, but that we will be able to travel to Njawara in May.

I have begun drafting the letter to the commissioner many times, but I have some questions. Am I asking the commissioner to help organise local housing for us? Do I want his permission to visit Njawara? Should I tell him what we would like to do there? What subject might they tutor? Are there any construction projects for the centre or the village with which we could help?

I would also like to know if there are any material supplies we could bring with us to donate to the centre or the village. One possible way for us to save money would be to fly into Dakar, Senegal and travel from there overland to Njawara.

All the above concerns and questions were answered but a small hiccup in fundraising occurred leaving a distinct possibility that the students will not be able to raise enough to make the trip.

The reason being the major source of funding for the trip fell through. This left all of us jittery but Tom and his students were in no mood to change their plans to travel to the Gambia in May 2005.

On the same day 15/02/05 I received the following from Mr. Jay Walterriet, Director of Public information for Alpena Community College. It stated that he was asked to contact me for more photos of myself and the clinic at Njawara.

He wanted more information regarding the Leadership planned trip to Gambia. I was told that the local television station would like to do a segment on the

Leadership class and their trip. As part of the segment photos were needed. I sent all photos that were relevant to enable the reporter to do his TV-segment on the planned Leadership trip to Njaswara, Gambia.

Mr. Jay on the 17/02/05 emailed thanking me for providing the requested photos and assured me that ACC has received good deal of interest from the local media regarding the Leadership class trip and both he and Penny Boldrey were trying to provide all of the information they could.

My e-mail was given to reporters who might want to contact me for more information. The entire twenty students could not enlist for the final take off to Africa. So Thomas Ray and 11 students took on the venture of their life time to the Gambia as guest of Manding Medical Centre at Njawara village.

On 17 February 2005 Tom sent me a copy of the final letter he sent to the commissioner and the local authority at the Lower Badibou district spelling out their intentions and wish while guests of the Manding Medical Centre for a two weeks duration. Here it is.

Thamos P. Ray

Alpena Community College

666 Johnson Street

Alpena, Michigan 49707

17 February 2005

Dear Commissioner Batala Juwara,

I am pleased to inform you of our plans to visit Njawara on behalf of the Manding Medical Centre. I am the advisor and instructor for a group of college students from Alpena Community College in Michigan in the USA. We plan to visit Njawara in May and hope you will help us find lodging with local families during our stay. Our plan as of now is to fly out of the US on May 6th to Banjul via London and to return on May 19th 2005.

During our stay in Gambia, our hope is to provide any assistance we can to the community on behalf of the Manding Medical Centre. We would like to visit the school in Njawara and tutor the children and share stories and activities with them.

I also hope that we will have the opportunity to visit the important centres of the community and learn as much as we can in our short stay about the people and life in Njawara and Gambia.

I have communicated our plans with Dr. Alhasan Ceesay, who has kindly extended the invitation to us on behalf of the Manding Medical Centre.

Sincerely

Thomas P. Ray

English Instructor

This letter was acknowledged by the commissioner and the district authority in the Gambia. Now that I was certain of the trip I set to inform my board members in like manner. The certainty of the trip was concretized by the following sent by Tom on 10 March 2005.

It simply updated me on the progress made regarding the trip; that the students have raised half the money needed to travel to Gambia. He affirms the fact that everyone concerned is working hard on the remaining sum. The arranged inoculations and are preparing to apply for visas to Gambia.

He said they were all enthused and has used my address in Gambia for the visa information requirement. Again, I was delighted for things are now heading the right direction for the historic and unique trip to Njawara.

I am now certain that more doors to boost ours and the centre's goals for the Gambia will be open by this simple friendly act of ACC. Here finally is my despatch the board members of Manding Medical Centre at Njawara village.

MANDING MEDICAL CENTRE/NJAWARA

UNITED KINGDOM CONTACT

245 GREAT WESTERN STREET

MANCHESTER, M14 4LQ

ENGLAND

E-MAI:alhasanceesay@hotmail.com

Tel/Fax: 44+161-342-0854

Date: 25/03/05

DEAR BOARD MEMBER,

I am pleased to bring to your attention about American guests to Manding Medical Centre at Njawara. Mr. Thomas Ray along with 11 Alpena Community college students will be visiting the Gambia as our guest in May 2005. They will be leaving the USA for the Gambia on May 6th, 2005 and depart for United States on the 19th, of May.

I would be most grateful if you give some of your time to meet them and make their visit memorable. There are many benefits to be accrued for the centre and the

Gambia. I am at present arranging in the form of scholarships or placements in various fields of study at my previous college in Alpena Michigan.

I have been in constant contact with Commissioner Batala Juwara at Kerewan and I would like all of you to brain storm and make this an ongoing link between us and Alpena Community College and other Michigan cities I am now in negotiation with. Alpena city has developed interest in our project.

I am also happy to report that my former college, Alpena Community College has awarded me, "Distinguished 2005 Graduate." Find enclosed correspondence from Mr. Thomas Ray, in behalf of the Leadership class of Alpena Community College, to Commissioner Juwara and Sefo Fafanding Kinte.

I look forward to your understanding and participation to help open up the Pandoa's Box of goodwill for the Gambia. This is a onetime opportunity for the Gambia that would make our two people linked for good goals and noble courses for generations of Gambians.

My regards and keep in touch.

Yours truly,

Dr. Alhasan S. Ceesay, MD

Founder/co-coordinator

Cc: Mr. Ousainu Darboe

Mr. Fafa E. Mbai

Dr. Dawda Ceesay

Dr. Ayo Palmer

Mr. Saim Kinte

Mr. Sambou Kinte

Mr. Mustapha Njie

Mr. Maja Sonk

Mr. Dodou Ceesay

Mr. Sisawo Ceesay

Mrs. Mbee Sonko

On April 7th 2005, Tom updated me stating that the visa applications were going well and that most of the students have received their visas. In addition let me privilege you the reader with some of the reactions emailed to me about the pending trip and what it would mean to them.

Alison Jane Smolinski said: "Hello Dr. Ceesay. I am one of the students in the Leadership class at Alpena Community College. I am really excited about the service trip, only a couple more weeks. Right now we are trying to prepare for the trip, just getting the basic necessities and what we should be packing.

I just read about how you are building a bakery at Njawara. Even though our resources are limited, is there something we could do to help out? I thought we could help in some way.

I also just wanted to say thank you for the wonderful experience you giving to us. I realize it will be truly an eye opener. I feel as if I could never be able to repay you for these two weeks that you about to give us. Thank you Dr. Ceesay!"Another email from Brittany Postumus simply stated; "I am one of the students from Alpena Community College that will be coming this May to help.

After learning all the things that you have done I must say you are an inspiration and the world can use more people who care as much as you do. I can't wait to come to Njawara. I am very excited to be able to help and thank you for the invitation."

Lastly, Ms. Grace Schimitz sent in the following before leaving for the Gambia. "I am a member of the Alpena Community College class that will be assisting you this May at Njawara. I am greatly looking forward to my visit to the Gambia.

Thank you so much for the invitation! The Friends of Manding, a charitable Trust at Colchester had the following in its web site about the trip to Njawara, the Gambia. It read as "News flash 12 American visiting: A class of 11 students and their instructor Mr. Thomas Ray from Alpena Community College, Alpena Michigan, will be visiting the Gambia as guest of Manding Medical Centre from the 6th to 19th May 2005. They will be visiting communities and tutor at local schools.

Alpena has developed interest in project Manding Medical Centre at Njawara. We are negotiating to have this exchange as an ongoing affair between Alpena and Njawara." As time drew near to the flight to the Gambia Tom contacted the Commissioner on several occasions to clear last possible huddles that may surface.

None the less preparations went smoothly and Thomas Ray and his ACC Leadership class left America on May 10th 2005 via Madrid and then Dakar, Senegal before embanking at Banjul, the Gambia.

As fate would have the team instead hired a bus from Dakar to Hamdali village in the North Bank which was nearer to Njawara. I learnt they were given a VIP escort from Hamdali via Kerewan to Njawara village.

As expected, I called the Mayor of Njawara, Mrs. Hadi Panneh enquiring about the American visitors. She told me they were fine and housed at the village centre, a semi motel used for foreign guest to Njawara. Tom and I spoke at length along with Sefo Fafanding Kinte.

Sefo Fafanding reassured me that everything possible will be done to help make "our guest comfortable and likewise a memorable visit in due course. I spoke briefly to the commissioner the next day to get a feedback from him. The two week flew fast for the students most of who did want to leave at the time for kindness rendered by the villagers.

It is said that good things never last long and this is the experience of the student who went to Njawara in May 2005.Here is the reaction of Americans after the trip to the Gambia. The ACC students started sending their report and experience as guest of Manding Medical Centre, Njawara, The Gambia. Starting with Alison Jane Smolinski reported as bellow.

"Hello Dr. Ceesay: The trip to Njawara was incredible! I did not want to leave. It was an experience of a lifetime that I will never forget. Everyone in the village was very kind and helpful. I have never met such kind people in my entire life.

I found the villagers doing everything possible to make their lives better. I realized that many people work together to get a job done or finished. This is absolutely wonderful. Everyone was so helpful in the village.

The people of Njawara gave us such wonderful hospitality. The food and shelter was more than we deserved. Also your wife, Mrs Fatou Koma-Ceesay, was all too good to us.

We had a remarkable time with her at Bundung,

Serekunda. Her cooking was excellent. And the gifts she gave all of us, we did not deserve. Your family is wonderful and was too kind to us.I would like to thank you for the incredible experience you have given me. I could not have asked for anything more.

I immensely enjoyed my self. I want to go back one day. I also want you to know that I will do my best to help in whatever way I can. I realize that action are louder than words and hope I can prove that to everyone.

Thank you Dr. Ceesay." Another reaction came from Grace Schiminitz. "I really enjoyed my time in Njawara. The people treated us very well and it was a pleasure to spend two weeks with them.

Your wife is a wonderful person and was very hospitable to us. I will always be grateful for her kind treatment.I hope to make another visit to Njawara in the future. It is a wonderful place. It was an eye-opening experience. The people were absolutely marvellous.

They treated us as their own family and welcomed us with open hands. I had no idea that they would be that hospitable. I really miss walking to the river and spending time with the children. It was my first experience in Gambia and hopefully it will not be my last. I hope I can return their kindness.

I would love to see how the kids have grown up." The last but not the least came from Mr. Thomas P. Ray, English instructor at ACC. It read; "I want to thank you for the opportunity you provided my students on this trip. The entire experience was enjoyable and valuable as a means of teaching my students something about the responsibility that comes with the privileges they enjoy here. Everyone was kind to us on the trip and the students came away with many great souvenirs and memories. I have many digital photos and am working on producing a CD of them to send out.

I also plan to type up a version of my journal for posting on the internet and I will send parts of that to you. I plan to call the village this weekend to extend my appreciation to everyone. Do you know anything about the proposed potential sister city relationship between Alpena and Njawara?

I would like to start making some local contacts here to help that process. I am also hopeful that future trips will be possible for my students.

-Mr. Thomas P. Ray-

As you know very well man proposes but God dispose things. Tom took over the running of the department and with that came a hand full challenging responsibilities. He was not able to provide the CD until 11th of October 2005 after several reminders from me and those visiting my

Website (www.Friendsofmandinggambimed.btck.co.uk). Finally, Tom contacted me on 4/11/05 to let me know he had the college mailing office send the CD of photos and other material registered delivery to me.

Then he made donation of $1000(one thousand us dollars) in the name of Friends of Manding, a Charitable Trust at Colchester Essex organising fund raising activities for Manding Medical Centre at Njawara the Gambia, West Africa. This cheque was duly received and forward registered mail to the Secretary of the Friends of Manding for depositing into our account at LLyod's Bank in Colchester Essex County.

Tom asked about the state of the proposed sister-city program between Alpena and Njawara. Yes, this was one of my goals for inviting the Americans to my village in the Gambia.

I just believe that unveiling the false masks and stigma others have about Africa will create harmony in its unique way. People need to accept differences in the cultures.I transmitted all reactions presented by our American visitor to the Commissioner, the chief, and the village heads especially Hadi Panneh of Njawara village.

ALPENA: THANKS FOR TWINING WITH US/SISTER-CITY PROCLAMATION.

Having now been recognised as Distinguished 2005 Graduate by Alpena Community College I made a proposal for a twining relationship or sister-city status between Alpena and select villages in the Gambia. I, you guessed right, contacted Mathew Dunckel as a sound board or trial balloon for the above idea.

He replied that it was a sound idea and suggested my contacting the Alpena City Council members on the subject. He gave their web site thus:

http://www.alpena.mi.us/council/members. In addition he gave the names of Councilman Dave Karschnik and Councilwoman Carol Shafto for me to initiate direct contact with the Alpena City Council. He told me that the mayor was John Gilmet and the City manager was Mr. Alan Bakalarski.

Armed with all this information and more I made my first push through Mrs. Penny Boldrey, Executive Director at Alpena Community College. I had no doubt if I get her interest in this unique wish she would do all within her power to not only contact the right people to make it eventually happen but would open up more doors for my villagers and our health project at Njawara.

Penny Boldrey upon hearing from me linked with Councilwoman Shafto on the June 14th, 2005 thus; "Hi Carol, from one Distinguished Grad to another….. I received the enclosed message from our 2005

Distinguished Graduate, Dr. Alhasan Ceesay. I'm wondering if perhaps you can help me with his inquiry regarding the possibility of twining between Alpena City and two villages in the Gambia, West Africa."

Penny in turn informed me that she had contacted a good friend, Carol Shafto, who is a member of Alpena's City Council and also an Alpena Community College Distinguished 2003 Graduate, regarding my request for twining between the above communities.

She enclosed Councilwoman Shafto's response to the idea. My reaction was swift and my message to Councilwoman Carol Shafto ran thus:-"Hello Councilwoman Carol. Mrs Penny Boldrey sent me correspondence she had with you regarding a proposal I made to the city of Alpena.

My initial e-mail kick starting a twining proposal between the city of Alpena; Njawara and Kinte Kunda villages in the Gambia West Africa was sent to Mayor John F. Gilmet, Dave R. Karsctunick, Mike Polluch, Sam Eller and Carol Shafto.

It read, "I'm pleased to write and inform you that I am deputized by village heads of Njawara and Kinte Kunda to contact you and initiate a twining/sister city status proposal between Alpena and the above two villages. Njawara is my home village and Kinte Kunda is where I attended primary school in the early fifties.

Tom Ray and the Leadership students visited both places during their two weeks stay in the Gambia. They met the chief of the district, Sefo Fafanding Kinte, at Kinte Kunda. Kinte Kunda has been the seat of many chiefs of the region and Fafanding is the most recent of several from this village.

Njawara is historically a trading centre connecting Gambia and the Northern part of Senegal. Today she has become a tourist destination. One can easily log onto information about Njawara village on the internet. It boasts of lots of female education oriented projects.

In addition it has an agricultural training centre."The contact was made in behalf of the village heads of the above and the local authority at the North Bank division of the Gambia.

This twining would be a very rewarding interaction and educational for both yours and the villagers. The people are eager to make worthwhile friendship with America. The chiefs and village heads have urged me to initiate their wish for the twining between them and Alpena or any city willing to go into such relationship with the villages.

You can link up with Mr. Thomas Ray and his students for feed back on their experience as guests of Manding Medical Centre at Njawara village, the Gambia. The villagers and I would be most grateful if given the chance to link up with Alpena City. Carol Shafto sent in this hiccup. "Dr. Ceeasy, I cannot proceed with any more discussions with the City Council of the City of Alpena until I am much clearer about what a Twining proposal entails. Could you please describe to me what you have in mind?

Although we may be supportive of your work at Njawara and Kinte Kunda in the Gambia; we cannot really act on your request until we know what we are agreeing to. Could you send me a brief outline of what you are seeking from the City of Alpena?

I will be happy to act as a liaison between you and the City, but cannot do so until I have a clear idea of what I am advocating for. Thank you most sincerely."

Carol Shafto

On July 13, 2005 I sent the required clarification to Councilwoman Carol Shafto as follows. Hello Carol, I am glad to hear from you. To be simplistically clear, twining means a sisterhood relationship between two cities for the mutual rewards of those involved.

Hence it is a friendship like affair where people from Alpena can be part of and likewise the villages involved but at no cost to either party. For example Councilwoman Shafto can choose to spend two weeks in Gambia helping reorganize or create a more functional administrative system or even learn from the villagers. In brief it is a two way international relationship. Or cultural dance - troupes from the Gambia villages can be coming to entertain Alpena, possibly more cities, during the summers.

This will help raise funds for the city, the villages, like wise for our health project at Njawara. It will provide much awareness and understanding of the two people merged in friendship.

It is like adopting each other and opening up rewarding human adventures at no cost involved. In a nut-shell, it means ratified friendship between Alpena and the two villages. I hope this makes it palatable for Alpena to want to be part of such endearing relationship.

I thank you in behalf of the Kerewan local authority, the villagers and Commissioner for North Bank Division, the Gambia. God blesses all of you."

Yours Sincerely

Dr. Alhasan Ceesay

Needless to say Councilwoman Carol Shafto was very pleased with the above clarification and appealed to Alpena City Council to consider the idea of twining in behalf of the Gambian villages.

Hence, Carol on the 13/7/05 sent me this e-mail following the receipt of the above message to the councilwoman. It simply states that, "I have forwarded this information to the mayor and city manager and offered to be the liaison if the City should consent to comply with this request.

I will keep you posted with any development." I updated the Commissioner and all concern at the Lower Badibou district regarding progress of my initiative with Alpena City few weeks after hearing from Councilwoman Carol Shafto.

The Commissioner and the local authority sent me the bellow covering letter in support of my push for a twining relationship with Alpena City Michigan, USA.

Njawara/Kinte Kunda

Lower Badibou District

North Bank Division

The Gambia, W. Africa

E-mail:njawaranato@yahoo.co.uk

November 5th, 2005

To: Dr. Alhasan Ceesay

Manchester, England

Subject: Twining of Njawara, Kinte Kunda & Alpena Michigan

Dear Dr. Ceesay,

Your first letter dated September 23rd, 2005 has been received and the content of which is understood, both the Commissioner, the Chief and the Alkalos (village heads) of Njawara and Kinte Kunda are very much interested in having Njawara, Kinte Kunda and Alpena City twined.

The Communities of both villages met and discussed the issue and they are very much happy about the lofty ideas. Njawara and Kinte Kunda are located in the Northern part of the Gambia.

They are just about 60 kilometres away from the capital City Banjul, the Gambia. Kinte Kunda is just 2 kilometres away from our administrative headquarters Kerewan where both the Commissioner and Area Council stay. Where as Njawara is located 9 kilometres away from Kerewan. Regards

Sincerely

Aja Hadi Panneh (Alkalo)

Alh Fafanding Kinte (Chief Lower Badibou)

Cc: Mr. Batala Juwara (Commisioner NBD)

I replied to the above support with this note despatched immediately to the village Akalos, the Chief and Commissioner North Bank Division at Kerewan village.

245 Great Western Street

Manchester M14 4LQ

England

16/11/05

A BIG THANK YOU TO ALL

Dear Commissioner,

I'm profoundly grateful to you, Sefo Fafanding, the local authority (area Council and chiefs) and especially Alkalo Arfang Bah and people of Toro. Lastly but not the least a big thank you goes to the people of Badibou, Njawara and my sister Hadi Panneh Alkalo of Njawara village. I am very happy for support and understanding given to Manding Medical Centre.

I'm pleased to inform you that I have initiated a twining process between Alpena and the villages of Njawara and Kinte Kunda. I have forwarded your note of 5/11/05 to the Alpena City Council. Copies were also sent to Mr. Thom Ray and the college.

Again, thank you for making our American friends happy and welcomed to our beloved country. God bless all of you. I will continue working for our development.

Sincerely

Dr. Alhasan S. Ceesay, MD

Director/Founder

Manding Medical Centre.

I then sent Carol Shafto the letter from the district authority plus this note urging action from her end.

245 Great Western Street

Manchester M14 4LQ

England

8/11/05

Mrs. Carol Shafto

Councilwoman

Alpena City Council

208 North First Avenue

Alpena, MI 49707

Dear Mrs. Carol Shafto,

The enclosed is reply to your last e-mail dated 25/9/05 regarding the twining proposal made to the Alpena City Council earlier on by me in behalf of Njawara village and Kinte Kunda, the Gambia, respectively.

The enthusiasm about having this relationship with Alpena is immeasurable. The villagers are looking forward to a warm and fruitful relationship between the two people. They all pray that you would be as eager to consummate it as they have already done in their wishes and hearts.

Finally, may friendship and human kindness be an everlasting link between all humans. God bless you and we look forward for a positive reply soon.

My personal regards and thanks to the City Council and all of Alpena.

Yours Sincerely

Dr. Alhasan S. Ceesay, MD

It was not until September 21, 2005 that I sent Councilwoman Shafto the following reminder and follow up note. "Hi Carol, I hope you had an enjoyable summer. This is a follow up of that lofty idea of twining Alpena City with Njawara and Kinte Kunda villages in the Gambia.

Has there been any movement forward at the Mayor's Office about the proposal made to the city? Is there anything I or the district authority in Gambia need do to bring this to fruition?

I have not heard anything about it since your last email of 14/7/05. Again, regards and thanks. I bank on your continued interest. God Bless."

Yours Sincerely

Dr. Alhasan Ceesay

The next day God smiled onto our dream to befriend America. Councilwoman Mrs. Carol Shafto sent me the following reply to the inquiry about the status of my dream for America and the Gambia.

It rang in the most melodious and cherished message I ever had for a long, long time after my being admitted into medical school and upon treating my first patient in the villages.

Here is Carol's email to me. "Good morning Dr. Ceesay: I appreciate your persistence in accomplishing this goal. Without that it surely would have failed. I do apologize for this delay.

I have just returned this week from a wonderful month long tour of the UK and Ireland. My last communication, before I left, with the City Manager was that this was a good idea, will be good for public relations, and that we should go forward with the proposal. The Mayor is also in favour. So there is absolutely nothing standing in the way of this happening.

I am willing to do the work of it, but I honestly have no idea what to do. Do you know procedures or paper work or any such thing from your end? Is it as simple as a proclamation?

I would like to have more information about your village, your people, and why you are interested in twining with Alpena – what connection there is.

I would then put together a presentation for the City Council and ask them to decide that we are sister-cities (the term used here, although I know the UK and Europe use "twining) with the villages of Njawara and Kinte Kunda.

We could erect a sign at the City entrance, etc. If you have any idea or directions for me, please let me know. Also any information you can provide on your village would be helpful. I will continue to work with you on this until it is accomplished.

Your friend in Alpena

Mrs. Carol Shafto

This was followed by my forwarding the bellow addendum to whatever had reached the Councilwoman's desk. Being the architect of this union much was expected from me.

And so I never relented supplying as much information as many times as I can afford. My phone bill sprouted to a Warping £600 etc. Most important was this addendum bellow.

SYNAPSIES OF NJAWARA/KINTE KUNDA VILLAGES

Njawara is a 350 years old market village situated on the bank of the Miniminiyang bolong, a creek of the River Gambia, in the Lower Badibou District of the North Bank Division of the Gambia.

Njawara has a population of a thousand residents and is 95 kilometres from Banjul, Gambia's capital City.
The village lies close to the Senegalese border and has been the trade links between Gambia and Senegal during the colonial days.

Njawara was established and founded by the Panneh family of the Wolof tribe and initially called "Panneh village". The elderly still fondly refer to her as Mpanneh.

Among the residents of now Njawara are Mandingkas, Fulas, Sereres, Jolas, Konyanginkas, and Mabara tribes. All of whom are farmers, with few serving as petty traders, growing Peanuts, Rice, Coos, and a variety of vegetables. The nearest government administrative post is 9 kilometres away at Kerewan village. Njawara lacked modern luxuries of electricity, proper telephones, sewer system, pave roads but water is now pumped from a nearby borehole.

The village has a thriving school and a dynamic citizenry working hard to improve their lot and the future of the younger generation.

KINTE KUNDA village has been the political base of Lower Badibou District for decades. It has provided us with several chiefs in the past and Sefo Fafanding Kinte is the most recent contribution. Kinte Kunda village comprises of mostly Mandinka tribes men and women.

It is the home of venerable late Sefo Njako Kinte who, in the 30s ruled the district with an iron fist. It was he who imposed one of his brothers, Almami Kinte, to take over the administration or village headship of then Njawara (Mpanneh). None the less he was a respected chief.

Kinte Kunda was the first village that had a school in the entire Lower Badibou district and I am told that he chief insisted that the school be built in his home village leaving a row that lasted through his rein.

The village is now a smaller population than Njawara and the current appointed chief of the district, Sefo Fafanding Kinte resides there. Residents of Kinte Kunda are all farmers eager to improve their lives and those of their children. They are friendly, peaceful, charming, descent hard working people who contributed a lot to growth of the Lower Badibou District in the North Bank.

These two villages along with the entire Lower Badibou District yearn for this twining/sister-city status to come to realty. Hence, I enclose relevant messages regarding the proposed twining from the district authority as per fax from the Gambia.

The villagers and I are interested in twining with Alpena Michigan n an effort to open up the Pandora's box of friendship, goodwill and more understanding of the people and cultures that would allow us relate in this shrinking globe we all share.

There is a lot we can do for each other once the ugly veil of ignorance, misunderstanding and fear is removed. And this can be done only learning and interacting with one another. I am sure the students, who went to the villages, can tell how much warmth and friendship they received from the villagers they met.

Exchange visits and whole host of beneficial programs to both parties can be organized within the framework of this twining. Once again, I personally appeal to the Mayor and City Council of Alpena to give this desire of the villagers a chance of fruition for Alpena City and the above villages in the Gambia.

BY: DR. ALHASAN SISAWO CEESAY, MD

In short while, I received the following reply from Councilwoman Carol Shafto of Alpena City Council letting me know of the final details, date of the be proclamation for the sister-city relationship between our villages and Alpena Michigan. Without further ado I present the message as sent on the 17th of November 2005.

"Good Morning Dr. Ceesay

After many months of communication with you, I can finally announce a DATE for our Twining/Sister City Resolution! The Alpena City Council will adopt a resolution to establish a Sister City Program with Njawara/ Kinte Kinda on December 5th, 2005.

I am going to be personally preparing the resolution. Since it will be a part of permanent records for both the villages and the City of Alpena, I would like be sure all of the information is accurate.

Penny Boldrey suggested that I email the text to you after I complete it. If you are willing, you could read it for any factual errors or omissions before I send it on to the City. If you are willing, I will send that via email when it is ready, sometime next week.

Meanwhile I am meeting with Tom Ray from the college who led the Leadership Class expedition to the villages. He is VERY enthusiastic about this proposal and is going to give me information and even share some pictures. We will be meeting next week. Finally, I have invited several people to come to the City Council meeting to provide testimony and support for this proposal. Both Penny Boldrey and Tom Ray will be there.

Also they are inviting some of the students who went to the villages to also be present and speak to the issue. So it would be a very nice presentation and will be more than just a formality.

Also, if you would like, I can arrange to have a tape of the meeting sent to you. Our meetings are videotaped and played for the public on the public access television channel several times a week, between meetings. I can make a copy of the tape of the meeting and have it send you or to the village officials or both if you would like.

Also, the resolution will have an official seal of the City of Alpena and the signature of the Mayor. I will have as many copies as you need made and will laminate them so they will be preserved.

I will send those to you and/ or whomever you designate. I will get several if necessary. I am so pleased to finally be able to bring this to completion. I know it must have been frustrating to you to have this take so long and to have us seen to be so unresponsive.

I hope this totally enthusiastic ending makes up for all of that!

Your friend in Alpena:

-Carol Shafto

On the day of ratification or passing of the resolution for sister city relationship between Alpena and the two above villages several speakers were heard. These included, among many, Penny Bodrey, Mr. Tom Ray, two student representatives who visited Gambia in May 2005 and Dr. Avery Aten.

This was buffered by loop of fifty photos of the villages taken by the student while in the Gambia. At the end of the presentation Mayor John F. gimlet read into the record the above proclamation and vote was tabled to pass it.

This Sister City proclamation between Alpena with Njawara/Kinte Kunda, Lower Badibou District, the Gambia was moved by Councilwoman Carol Shafto, seconded by Councilman Karschnick, that the proclamation to establish a sister city program with the villages of Njwara and Kinte Kunda be approved. The move was carried by unanimous vote.

A copy of the sister City Resolution passed by Alpena City Council on December 5th 2005 is reproduced for your pleasure to read.

Dr. Alhasan S. Ceesay holding favourite photo

Chapter 8

PROCLAMATION TO ESTABLISH A "SISTER CITY" PROGRAM WITH NJAWARA AND KINTE KUNDA, LWER BADIBOU DISTRICT, GAMBIA, WEST AFRICA

WHEREAS, the City of Alpena recognises and supports the concept of global cooperation and community; and

WHERAS, the villagers of Njawara and Kinte Kunda, through their local leaders and Dr. Alhasan S. Ceesay, have reached out their hand in friendship and goodwill, and

WHEREAS, relationships were established by students and faculty of Alpena Community College when they were warmly welcomed to the villages for a service project earlier this year, and

WHEREAS, mutual understanding of our diversities as well as our similarities and the cultural exchanges that will result, will be beneficial to the citizens of both areas, and

WHEREAS, true global community is often established one person at a time, and one city and village at a time, leading to beneficial relations and programs for all;

NOW, THEREFORE, I, John F. Gilmet, by virtue of the authority vested in me as Mayor, DO HEREBY PROCLAIM, a "Sister City" Program with the villages of

NJAWARA/KINTE KUNDA

LOWER BADIBOU DISTRICT

GAMBIA

And urge all area citizens to extend the hand of fellowship and an embrace of genuine fraternity to their friends in NJAWARA/KINTE KINTE KUNDA and pledge support and loyalty as these communities of two great nations join together as "Sister Cities"

Signed at Alpena Michigan, United States of America, on this 5th day of December, 2005. Councilwoman Carol Shafto read the following reply from me to Council and residents of Alpena City.

ALPENA, THANKS FOR TWINING WITH US

Honourable Mayor John F. Gilmet, Alpena City Council and residents of Alpena; please allow me convey heartfelt thanks as well as greetings from the Commissioner, NBD, Kerewan Area Council, the Chief of Lower Badibou, the Alkalos (village heads) of Njawara and Kinte Kunda. I am today full of joy and gratitude for twining resolution ratified by the Alpena City Council.

I am speechless as one of my dreams for the villager and America has now materialized in this twining resolution passed by Alpena. We are two good people now merged in good will for humanity and friendship.

This coming together will archive a lot for both of us. There is a lot for us to gain as well as learn from each other and generations to come will thank us for having taken the first footsteps of bringing people of diverse cultures and understanding together.

Enclosed is message from the Gambia in response to the most welcomed news in your last email. This is the top of the iceberg for there is lot more benefit in this act. In addition, as long as I am alive Alpena and Gambia will not only benefit from this unique venture but will smile yearly for having dreamt along with me.

Let me, in passing, mention with thanks the first harbingers of this day. They are Mr. Thomas P. Ray and his Leadership team of students from Alpena Community College who visited Njawara village in May 2005. Thomas Ray and the students laid the marvellous foundation we today concretize.

Mrs. Penny Boldrey and Mathew Dunckel deserve our appreciation for remaining interested and in constant contact with me. The Gambia, the district authority of Lower Badibou and villagers remain eternally grateful for giving us the chance of twining with you.

A Huge thanks Alpena City, the Mayor of Alpena and Alpena City Council for work well done. Councilwoman Mrs. Carol Shafto who relentlessly steered the twining proposal to completion also deserves our profound gratitude. The villagers and I are eternally indebted to all at Alpena. In addition, we look forward to working hand in hand for the reward of all parties. Finally, I would again like to pay tribute to past and present friends at Alpena who helped me reach this pedestal.

All of you helped make my sojourn to America a remarkable success. I would like many more of my friends to be like you at Alpena. I hope you will believe, as well as join me, in my dream of providing modern medical aid to the Gambian villagers. Thanks a million and God bless America!

Signed: DR. ALHASAN SISAWO CEESAY, MD

FOUNDER/COORDINATOR

MANDING MEDICAL CENTRE

NJAWARA, THE GAMBIA

Two weeks later I received three copies of the "sister City Proclamation" along with a video tape of the Alpena City Council Meeting of December 5, 2005. Also enclosed were the Alpena news and copy of Alpena Public Notices showing minutes of the City Council meeting which carried ratification of the sister city proclamation by a unanimous vote.

I must confess exhilaration in my heart for Alpena City Council having done so much for my villages without reservation and accomplished with great speed. I sent the following communiqué to the current representative to the Gambia, Ambassador Joseph D. Stafford in preparing them for the arrival the package from the Alpena City Council for forwarding to the Commissioner of the North Bank Division, the Gambia.

MANDING MEDICAL CENTRE

245 Great Western Street

Manchester M14 4LQ

Email:alhasanceesay@hotmail.com

Date: 10/12/05

Ambassador Joseph D. Stafford

Embassy of the United States of America

Kairaba Avenue

P. M. Box 19

Banjul, the Gambia,

West Africa

RE: Manding Medical Centre/Alpena USA Twining

Dear Ambassador Stafford,

I am Dr. Alhasan S. Ceesay from Njawara village and currently on studies in the UK. This is to introduce the above self-help health organization at Njawara as well as kindly request favour of your good office's service in behalf Alpena Michigan and the villages of Njawara and Kinte Kunda, the Gambia.

I pioneered the above centre, after graduating as a doctor and upon returning to the Gambia in 1992. It became an NGO in 1994 after being fully registered by the Justice Department and recognized by the Ministry of Health in 1993.

In addition, we are now a registered Charitable Trust, as Friends of Manding, in England and Wales by the Charity Commission of the UK. Our website is: friendsofmanding gambimed.btck.co.uk. It will show our home page as "Friends of Manding."

Alternatively, one can used a short cut by typing in "Manding Medical Centre, Njawara" and click search. The same home page plus lot more will appear. I have also written two books and a hefty portion of proceed from the sale of both books is earmarked to help support Manding Medical Centre at Njawara and our goal of providing medical aid to the villager, especially children.

More information about my work and commitment to providing much needed medical service to the region in conjunction with the Gambia Ministry of Health can be seen in our website as above. Finally, I am more than delighted to report that Alpena City, Michigan, USA has just ratified a sister city program with my home village

Njawara and Kinte Kunda village in the Lower Badibou District, North Bank Division, the Gambia. Hence, I have asked the Alpena City Mayor's Office to send five copies of the final proclamation declaring the sister city status between Alpena and the above two named villages in Badibou to you for your office to kindly deliver the documents to the Commissioner North Bank Division at Kerewan.

Thank you for taking time to assist us in the above matter. Please feel free to contact me any time convenient to you. Best wishes for good health and achievement in the coming year. Regard to your family.

Yours Sincerely

Dr. Alhasan S. Ceesay, MD

Founder/Coordinator

Manding Medical Centre

Njawara, The Gambia, West Africa.

This letter was followed with two telephone calls to the Embassy of the United States in the Gambia to verify receipt of the package sent from Alpena to Joseph D. Stafford.

The Secretary to Mr. Stafford, in the last phone call let me know it usually take a month or more before none official mail arrives at their desk.

He assured me that the office will do as request whenever the package reaches the Embassy. I called Sefo Fafanding Kinte and Alkalo Hadi Panneh and told them to check with either Ambassador Joseph Stafford directly or one of the officers in the know at the office for their copies of the sister city proclamation of which the villagers are unsung heroes for having received the ACC students who visited Njawara in May 2005 with open hearts, hospitality, generosity and warmth.

It was not until Thursday, February 16th, 2006 that Ambassador Joseph D. Stafford and team where able to deliver, in person amid tumultuous reception and celebration, the sister-city proclamation between Alpena City, Michigan USA, with Njawara and Kinte Kunda villages in the North Bank of the Gambia.

I made it clear that the brief ceremony at Njawara on the 16/2/06 marked the end of phase one of the sister city relationship between us and Alpena Michigan. I suggested the following four areas for food for thought by all concern. They are:-

1. Education

This already started in earnest as some in Alpena have expressed desire to sponsor worthy candidates at the primary level for an experimental period of one year. Higher levels, such as college education and nursing training and or other relevant skill areas will in due course be included.

2. Health

A lot is planned for health oriented programs and Manding Medical Centre will be enhanced to a much functional status. There will be training programs for health personnel etc.

3. Tourism: I am studying ways of creating tourist attraction with facilities erected in due course to the region.

4. Cultural: Exchanges entailing having cultural dance troop(s) from the Lower Badibou District travel to Alpena Michigan, and other cities in the USA during the summers to display our fabric of entertainment, history and arts.

These are few ideas in the pipeline. Feel free to add yours to enrich the program. This is by no means binding or final but seeking more suggestions on how to benefit both parties in this unique twining program just approved by Alpena City. Let me make it crystal clear that there is no financial commitment from Alpena.

However, the cultural show can raise lot of money upon performing in America. I thanked the Commissioner North Bank, Sefo of Lower Badibou, District Authority and Kerewan Area Council for having worked so hard with me to provide this excellent opportunity to our people. I promised that more is on the way. Three weeks earlier I received this e-mail from Councilwoman Mrs. Carol Shafto announcing the good news of her efforts. "Dr. Ceesay, we have sent five copies of the proclamation to the America Embassy- which you provided the address for.

I also have three copies of the proclamation for you as well as a copy of the tape of the meeting; a copy of the newspaper where the action appeared; and a copy of the newspaper with the official minutes. I will get these out to you today. It was a most wonderful evening as you will see on the tape. Five people, your friends old and new, spoke in favour of the proclamation.

This included Dr. Avery Aten who I have now spoken with and who is very enthusiastic about working on the medical aspect of things with you. He will be in touch with you by phone he said. But you will be able to see him and hear what he had to say during City Council meeting of December 5, 2005.

Also speaking where two students who have visited the Gambia; Tom Ray and Penny Boldrey. (And me, of course). I read your wonderful letter for the record. We also had a loop of over fifty slides showing on the screen during the presentation. It was the nicest sister-city ceremony we have ever had-by far! Usually we just read the proclamation and that is it.

I think this ends my part in all of this-except for one thing. My sons and I were going to "adopt" a family through Save the Children. This involves sending a letter each month and with an amount of money. We would be happy to adopt some children from your village instead if there is an easy way to do this. We would need a name and address and what form we could make our donation in (money order?).

We are not really wealthy- but could send $20 -$25 a month for at least a year to a deserving child. Of course; we would hope that they might send a note now and then... but this all up to you. I hope you are pleased with all that has happened.

I remained your friend.

Carol Shafto.

In reply I sent my friend Carol Shafto the following.

Hello Carol; Now I am able to response to your email. First, please accept our eternal ineptness' for having worked so hard to bring the twining into reality. Only God can reward your efforts.

Please kindly extend our heartfelt gratitude to the Mayor and your fellow Councillors at Alpena. Send me the Mayor's telephone. I need to convey our appreciation to him. I had a long chat with the village and they were in cloud nine about the approval of the sister city program.

I will be forwarding the names of deserving school children you might want to sponsor/adopt. I will cal you, before forwarding the names, about it when I get the list that the parents and headmaster promised to send me. Thanks a million and God blesses you and yours. Best wishes for good health and successful 2006. I look forward to our travelling to the Gambia soon. Regard.

Sincerely

Dr. Alhasan S. Ceesay, MD

In the mean time Mrs. Penny Boldrey was also busy doing a story for the ACC Alumni News. In addition Carol was able to have a feature about the just approved sister city program done by the local news paper. She was very happy about it as the email bellow from Carol shows.

"Good Morning Alhasan, "our story" is headline, above the fold, in the Alpena News today! It is wonderful publication for your project.

I will send you copies but you can read it on-line today only at www.thealpenanews.com. It reads "Alpena's sister-city- ACC graduate initiates partnership with Gambia villages." And there is a wonderful colour picture of one of the ACC students with village children.

I hope you enjoyed the story and are pleased with my efforts for publicity.

The news reporter, Sue Lutuszek, will do a follow-up story about people "adopting Children for education purposes", like I am doing with my son(s).

It is a good day for celebration. Check the website.

Your friend

Carol

Here is one of several features about the twining between Alpena City with Njwara and Kinte Kunda villages in the North Bank Division, the Gambia.

ALPENA NEWS MICHIGAN, USA

SISTER CITY PROGRAM HAS TIES TO

ACC STUDENT OF 1960s

A link dating back to the 1960s has helped Alpena establish a sister city program with Njawara and Kinte Kunda, Lower Badibou District, the Gambia.

The program was initiated by Alhasan Ceesay, MD, an Alpena Community College of the 1960s and the 2005 Distinguished Graduate who lives in the Wes African country. He was assisted by ACC staff and Councilwoman Carol Shafto.

"He feels this is his American home and villages in Gambia are his African home and wanted to link the tow together." Carol Shafto said.

When Penny Boldrey of the ACC Foundation first put Ceesay in touch with Shafto for assistance in the venture, Shafto was leery of his intentions. "I did not get it," she said.

"I wanted to know what we are going to gain?" the whole idea is simply to put out information on the situation in those villages in the public eye, Shafto said Ceesay's dream is to build a medical centre to serve the villages, since care is many miles away and roads in and out of villages aren't passable by ambulance.

Currently patients are transported out of villages without ambulances for distances to health centres from their homes. Avery Aten, MD, of Alpena also has become involved with the project. "The medical aspects of this relationship can be long-term," he told city council members.

He said so medical statistics regarding the area, such as the average life expectancy is 53 years old and 85 out of 1000 children die during birth.

According to Shafto, some of Aten's hopes include sending medical equipment which is no longer used here to the villages and even possibly having nursing students experiencing practicing there. "I just see all kinds of goodwill things happening," Shafto said. "For us to have the opportunity to lead about a totally different culture is good for us."

"One aspect Shafto highlighted is the opportunity for elementary classroom in Alpena to communicate with the village school. Although she assisted in having the proclamation made, Shafto gives credit for making it happen to individuals at ACC.

"My part is minor compared to what ACC has done," she said. They are the ones who really got this started."

During the trip the students met with various village leaders who showed them what projects they were working on and where the greatest need was. In addition, the students taught some short classes on the United States.

One day the group helped with the construction of a mosque. They also visited the agricultural centre and health centre. Ray said the trip "contributed greatly" in making the sister city proclamation a reality "because it gave people in Alpena a connection to the village.

"The Gambia District Authority of Lower Badibou and villagers remain eternally grateful for giving us chance of twining with you.

Huge thanks to the City of Alpena, Mayor of Alpena and Alpena City Council," Alhasan wrote. "The villagers and I are eternally indebted to all at Alpena. In addition, we look forward to working hand in hand for reward of all parties."

-Sue Latuszek: The Alpena News 2005-

The first hatchling of this merging of diverse hearts is as follows:-

Njawara Basic School

Lower Badibu District

North Bank Division

The Gambia, W. Africa

19/01/06

Dear Sir/Madam

RE: To whom it may concern.

These students are promising students whose parents are not able to fully support their educational needs. As a result, we would be very grateful if a concern person(s) can assist the students and their parents in taking care of some of the financial difficulties they are encountering to earn education.

These include school fees, uniforms, book bills and other school needs. Thank you and in anticipation, I remain,

Yours Faithfully

Lamin K. Juwara/Principal

These where the initial list of needy student to benefit from what was going to be the Manding Medical Centre/USA scholarship grants.

NAME ADDRESS	AGE	CLASS	PARENT	
1. Ismaila Ceesay Njawara	14yrs	8B	Dodu Ceesay	
2. Edrisa Barry Njawara	14yrs	8B	Adoulie Barry	
3. Alieu Dem Njawara	12yrs	7B	Modou Dem	
4. Mamud Panneh Njawara	12yrs	7A	Ousainu Panneh	
5. Adama Jallow Ardo	12yrs	7B	Assan Jallow	Ker
6. Kally Bah Ardo	13yrs	8B	Saikou Bah	Ker
7. Njammeh Bah Bah	12yrs	7B	Musa Bah	Toro
8. Hammed Dem Bah	12yrs	7B	Musa I. Bah	Toro
9. Ebrima Kanteh Bah	15yrs	7B	Baboucar Kaneh	Toro

10. Mustapha Jawo   15yrs   8A   Omar Jawo   Toro Bah

11. Modou Touray   11yrs   6A Sohna Jaw   Panneh Bah

12. Nuha Krubally 10yrs   5A   Modo Krubally   Samba Musu

13. Matarr Panneh   10yrs   4B   Bora Panneh   Njawara

14. Modou Loum   14yrs   7B   Bintou Jammeh   Ker Jebal

The above list and letter were faxed to Councilwoman Carol Shafto on the 23/02/06. The fax simply read:-

Hi Carol,

I hope you are okay and back at work. I hereby forward a list of school children from Njawara school needing sponsorship. Feel free to contact those you think would like to participate in this educational project. The first three candidates in the list are earmarked for you and your son(s). See names 1 – 3 in the list.

Send all monies via Western Union in the name of Aja Hadi Panneh, (Alkalo of Njawara village) to any Gambian Bank that Western Union deals with in Gambia. Then email me stating amounts, date sent and for who.

I will follow up by contacting the Principal of Njawara School, the parents and the chief of the district to ascertain prompt and proper distribution. In addition, I will have Aja Hadi Panneh (Alkalo), the parents, Headmaster and were possible the recipient students to write acknowledging the amounts received.

Please feel free to contact me if you have any questions or ideas to promote the above noble educational commitment. Once again, thanks and we remain grateful for your stand.

Your Friend

Dr. Alhasan S. Ceesay, MD

Lovely smiling Alasan Mballow Jr, 2015

Chapter 9

CHASING TIME TO CATCH A DREAM

It is said that time and tides waits for no man. For me I have been chasing elusive time from time immemorial. The chase started at birth when I stopped breathing in the first hour of my life. In those precious minutes and hours to follow time left me behind and I was declared none existent and was to be buried first thing in the morning.

I woke up before dawn and have been chasing time since February 14th, 1942 to the present time. My peers in other villages started schooling at the age of 5 years and I started primary school at the raw age of 12 years old. And I enrolled at college at the age of 22 years. I graduated from medical school at age 50. There has always been this huge gap between time and when things happen for me.

I wish there was a way I can reverse or stop time so that all delays in my life would level up with elapsed time. All my peers have grown grey or have complete white hairs or totally bald but I look like some 28 year old lad and as fit as a 16 years old athletic kid, even though I never ceased chasing after time.

Time for that precious priceless record of history has not arrived for me. William Shakespeare said of time thus: "Come what comes May. Time and the hour runs through the roughest day." For me it kept flying and irreversibly so. Friends console me by telling me; "Your time will come." In desperation I ask when?

Time cares less for it will stick with or without us. Hence, it is my duty to catch up and do well to live footprints worth following when my time comes. Navigating through the valleys and gorges strewn at us on life's path is a nightmare.

I came to England just to do the PLAB and MRCP degree in medicine and return to my home land in the shortest possible time. This time would not allow as I unknowingly fell into the deepest gorge of visa and job problems. I arrived as a visitor and hence more of tourist than student status.

The Home Office's refusal to change my status to student left me in limbo and a destitute. This made it difficult to pass the PLAB because of being torn between hunger and struggling to find help to send money to feed my equally beleaguered wife and three daughters.

I became catechetic and weak that even the arch angels of death and hell would feel sad and sorry upon meeting me. Again time and tide refused to wait for Dr. Ceesay.

All my compatriots got through the PLAB because they had monetary help enabling them to pay for PLAB review courses. For me I had to feed from the surface of my teeth while I chased time to take my exams under very difficult circumstances that would drown most people.

Time was far ahead and I needed to catch up before it becomes too late for me and my dream for the Gambia. Let me reiterate that the greatest of all faults is to be conscious of none.

Hence, time would have not slipped from my fingers had I taken a moment or two to seek for student visa while at the British Embassy in the Gambia. Anyhow hind sight is always too wise as I later learnt from bitter experience. Despite this long and hash experience, I never gave up and things happen at a surprising and lightening speed for the arrival of a new dawn in my life and goal for the Gambia.

Chapter 10

THE PARADOXICAL SCHISMS

Back in Africa life is simply or mostly of an agricultural or rural type. It usually starts with education and guidance from parents, initiation, which connotes the day one, is circumcised or inducted into manhood/womanhood, and finally the individual's return to our maker and reunion with our ancestors in the world beyond.

For sojourners like me, it's the beginning of endless challenges and changes we have to adapt to quickly for our survival. Life becomes an endless long hours, 16 or more hours a day, of work with the earning paid to schools, universities, landlords and sending whatever is left to family back in Africa for their sustainers.

It is full of surprises and unfamiliar behaviours, customs, and outcomes. First the weather one encounters unravels in four seasons; spring and summer being the most tolerable but autumn and bone chilling winters are for Eskimos not warm blooded Africans.

Winter curdles my blood and frizzes every bit of me no matter the number of thermal layers I manage to put on. Thanks to technology and kindness of the people over in these frigid places I survived my wintry days in Europe and America.

Paradoxically, the expression of freedom and degree to which it is adhered to far exceeded my imagination and expectations. One of the most surprising paradoxes or schism was being castigated when I attempted to settle a simple dispute between husband and wife friends of mine.

In Africa and most places one can give genuine counsel to warring factors for them to resort to reconciliation instead of being at each other's throat over trivial matters mostly emanating from misunderstanding or failing to listen to the other's point of view.

Let me reiterate what St. Francis of the Franciscan order in Assisi, Rome, eloquently admonished us regarding incidence as above. He said, "Where there is discord, May we bring harmony; where is error, may we bring truth, where there is doubt may we bring faith. And where there is despair, may we bring hope."

A dear friend made matters worse for me, by repeatedly asking that I consider moving out of his premises. The demands made on December 5th, 2000, May 30th, 2001, and again on August 11th, 2001were painful experiences. However the July 13th, 2001 order to relocate from his place was the last straw that made me move. Can you imagine how difficult it was for me to hear that from a friend?

I quote, "You have to move any where you can relocate." This brought endless tears of remorse running down my chicks. It came a year after my wife returned to Gambia living me in solitude and un-employed.

There was still no sign of a financial relief by means of acquiring a temporal job until after my being registered with the GMC. Joblessness cum intolerable circumstances catapulted me to Manchester City in the North West region of the UK. Life did not turn out all roses for me in Manchester. It was a struggle against failures! No pass, No job and no money or peace of mind.

My plan to serve as a nurse in UK, until the time I could get my GMC registration, was set a terrible blow when the Overseas Nurses Association stopped processing my request for assistance because the NHS has ceased accepting nurses from regions like mine.

NHS feared draining the health personnel of developing countries by accepting nurse and doctors from underdeveloped countries.

What a farce! In the same vein the very people can go to our countries and shamelessly pick up our gold, diamonds and other mineral wealth without a second thought to poverty their pilfering was doing to the so called developing country.

To make matters worse, if not very grim for me, the Home Secretary announced in April 2006 that from that time hence forth the NHS will only give training priority to UK and EU doctors.

Such pronouncements left self-sponsors like me in limbo as we have to fight harder in other to get training placement in teaching hospitals. This tantamount to a stab from the back from an institute we relied upon.

This announcement ignored efforts people like me have been putting in to help improve our medical skills we wish to serve our people back in our countries. The current state of affairs along with my age nudged me into devoting the rest of my life building Manding Medical Centre to a fully functional health unit serving the Gambia.

Alasan Mballow, Son-Inlaw posing forthe cameras, 2013

Chapter 11

MANNA NEVER CAME FROM HEAVEN

I am among few doctors whose life retrograded to the level of living on exactly £5 (five pounds) a week on a nine hours seven days shoe selling job. The hundred and five pounds weekly earning this slave life brought was split £50 for rent, the other £50 goes towards paying loans I took to pay for my exams, my children's school fees and sustenance of my family back in the Gambia.

Oh! I had a paradoxical raise in salary of £1a day which propped up my income to £16/day. It was disheartening time for me. It was a nightmare neither member of the family will ever forget.

Most painful for me were the times when my daughters ask for shoes or other things their peers have and I had to come out clean and explain that daddy was, even though I would like them have their requests, at no monetary position to provide such items at that time.

I would promise to do my best to get it for them as soon as feasible.

I can hear them cry before putting the telephone down or simply passing it to their mother to talk to me. I do not wish my worst enemy to have to go through such experience or be embedded in hell on earth as my life was. I love my family and missed being with them. Mean while for those who know me, my state was pitiful. Most would ask "Doctor, what on earth are you doing in a shoe shop and not by the patient's bedside?" I simply reply this is what fate has for me at the moment and I have to feed my family back home.

The next day one or two would return to the shop with offering of £2, £5, or £10 for me to send to my children. Yes, I was literally turned out into a silent street beggar and my pride was trampled to the lowest earthly level.

At the end of the day I return to my flat with a heavy heart knowing that I had nothing to eat but two slices of bread with sardine sandwiched in-between. After this kingly meal I try to study for as long as my wondering mind would let me. The ringing of the telephone brings palpitation and anxiety to me.

I fear whether our landlord, back in Gambia, has not gotten impatient with my family or if food has ran out because of uncontrolled daily high prices of food commodities in the Gambia. My wife and I use to pray, over the phone, for relief and yet we both know and agreed that life could be worst if I failed my villagers and Manding Medical Centre.

So we bit the bullet and continue trying to get more awareness on the good cause Manding medical Centre would bring to the children and villagers. There are those who think that my enduring such painful experience was predicated on sheer stupidity on my part. For family, especially my wife and I, it was a worthy self-sacrifice for humanity. Life, as ordained, did change for the better and my daughters' education was never set back by the above financial limbo I endured while in the UK.

This is further propounded upon in the following chapter titled, Failure conquered amid roadblocks. Tears do not solve difficult moments like these dark days. Only faith and hard work solves small economic pains as I encountered.

Two year old Alasan Mballow Jr, 2015

UNCLASSIFIED

Given the discrepancies noted above I cannot be satisfied that you are the wife of your sponsor as claimed.

- You have submitted a solicitor's letter from Rochdale Law Centre dated 14.02.2014 stating that since your sponsor's arrival in the UK, he has "been in constant contact with his wife and children". There is no documentation to demonstrate any contact between you and your sponsor to support this.

In light of the above, I am not satisfied that prior to your sponsor's departure, you were part of your sponsor's family unit at the time he left The Gambia, which was his country of habitual residence, to seek leave to remain in the UK. You therefore fail to meet the requirements of Paragraph 352A (iv) of the UK Immigration Rules.

Taking into account your circumstances, based on the information you have provided and considering your application as a whole, I am not satisfied, on the balance of probabilities, that you are genuinely seeking entry for the purpose of settlement as the spouse/ civil partner of a recognised refugee in the UK.

I have therefore refused your application because I am not satisfied, on the balance of probabilities, that you meet all of the requirements of the relevant Paragraph of the United Kingdom Immigration Rules.

Your right of appeal

You are entitled to appeal against this decision under section 82(1) of the Nationality, Immigration and Asylum Act 2002. If you wish to appeal you must complete the attached IAFT-2 Notice of Appeal form. An information sheet has also been provided. Should you require further advice or assistance please visit www.justice.gov.uk

If you decide to appeal against the refusal of this application, the decision will be reviewed with your grounds of appeal and the supporting documents you provide. You are strongly advised to complete all sections of the form and submit all relevant documents with your Notice of Appeal, as it may be possible to resolve the points at issue without an appeal hearing.

The completed Notice of Appeal form must arrive no later than **28 days** after the date you received this notice and you must make sure that it is signed and dated.

Entry Clearance Officer: TAA
Date of refusal: 07.04.2014
Date sent to applicant:
How sent: Via Visa Application Centre
If notice personally handed to you by an Entry Clearance Officer, please sign below:
Applicant's signature:
Date

UNCLASSIFIED

UNCLASSIFIED

GV51 (FRA)
Rev 10/11

UK Visas
& Immigration

NOTICE OF IMMIGRATION DECISION

In compliance with the Immigration (Notices) Regulations 2003 made under section 105 of the Nationality, Immigration and Asylum Act 2002

REFUSAL OF ENTRY CLEARANCE

Post reference: ACCRA \ 819667

To: ROHEY CEESAY

Date of Birth: 28/02/1997   Nationality: GAMBIA

Your Application

You have applied for entry clearance to the United Kingdom to join Alhasan Ceesay who is a recognised refugee in the UK. I have considered your application under paragraph 352D of the United Kingdom Immigration Rules. You can read these rules at:
www.ukba.homeoffice.gov.uk/policyandlaw/immigrationlaw/immigrationrules/

I have used all the information provided by you to determine if the Immigration Rules have been met. In reaching my decision, which has been made on the balance of probabilities, I note the following points:

The Decision

- In assessing your application I have referred to Home Office records in the United Kingdom concerning your sponsor's application to remain in the United Kingdom in a permanent capacity. I note that your sponsor arrived in the United Kingdom 2000 and was granted limited leave to remain on 18.12.2012. Your sponsor was granted a visa to visit the UK on 09 June 2000. Home Office records show that your sponsor was interviewed on 03 December 2012. During this interview your sponsor stated he was married and declared a child by the name Roheyata Ceesay born 28.02.1997. You have stated your name as Rohey Ceesay and submitted a birth certificate bearing this name. Given there is no further documentation given other names, I am unable to establish you are one and the same person.

- During your father's interview on 03.12.2012, he stated he last saw you and your siblings on 31.12.1999. Your father states he entered the UK on 06.01.2000, however local records show he was issued a visit visa in June 2000. I am therefore not satisfied you have demonstrated you were part of your sponsor's household at the time he left The Gambia for the UK.

UNCLASSIFIED

> UNCLASSIFIED
>
> • You have submitted a solicitor's letter from Rochdale Law Centre dated 14.02.2014 stating that since your sponsor's arrival in the UK, he has "been in constant contact with his wife and children". There is no documentation to demonstrate any contact between you and your sponsor to support this.
>
> In light of the above, I am not satisfied that prior to your sponsor's departure, you were part of your sponsor's family unit at the time he left The Gambia, which was his country of habitual residence, to seek leave to remain in the UK. You therefore fail to meet the requirements of Paragraph 352D (iv) of the UK Immigration Rules.
>
> Taking into account your circumstances, based on the information you have provided and considering your application as a whole, I am not satisfied, on the balance of probabilities, that you are genuinely seeking entry for the purpose of settlement as the child of a recognised refugee in the UK.
>
> I have therefore refused your application because I am not satisfied, on the balance of probabilities, that you meet all of the requirements of the relevant Paragraph of the United Kingdom Immigration Rules.
>
> **Your right of appeal**
>
> You are entitled to appeal against this decision under section 82(1) of the Nationality, Immigration and Asylum Act 2002. If you wish to appeal you must complete the attached IAFT-2 Notice of Appeal form. An information sheet has also been provided. Should you require further advice or assistance please visit www.justice.gov.uk
>
> If you decide to appeal against the refusal of this application, the decision will be reviewed with your grounds of appeal and the supporting documents you provide. You are strongly advised to complete all sections of the form and submit all relevant documents with your Notice of Appeal, as it may be possible to resolve the points at issue without an appeal hearing.
>
> The completed Notice of Appeal form must arrive no later than **28 days** after the date you received this notice and you must make sure that it is signed and dated.
>
> | | |
> |---|---|
> | Entry Clearance Officer: TAA | |
> | Date of refusal: 07.04.2014 | |
> | Date sent to applicant: | |
> | How sent: Via Visa Application Centre | |
> | If notice personally handed to you by an Entry Clearance Officer, please sign below: | |
> | Applicant's signature: | |
> | Date: | |
>
> UNCLASSIFIED

I transmitted the above to both Lauren Butler and Joan hooper of the Redcross for an appeal to be lodge before the 28/4/14. Joan called few days later to affirm that an appeal would lodge as soon as Lauren returns from her holidays on 22/4/14.

After several exchanges Lauren Bulter and I agreed that we need submit witness statements from friends and relatives.

Witness statement, evidence to be adduced for appeal

Lauren Butler
13/05/2014
To: Alhasan Ceesay
Cc: Joanne Hooper

Dear Dr. Ceesay,

Thank you for your email. To answer your queries and concerns:
Yes, it would be fine if your friends/relatives would like to email statements directly to me. Of course I believe you about the marriage certificate; however our objective is to adduce evidence to support the fact that you're married and lived together.
We cannot assume that the judge will know anything about Gambian society. There is need for suggestions of alternate sources. Are there any other documents available which would confirm your relationship and your shared family life?
I note that you mention Justice Department records. Do you mean Gambian Justice Department records? I'm afraid that I haven't seen Justice Records confirming your family relationships so I would be glad if you could let me know how I might obtain these.

Kind regards,

Lauren Butler
Senior Immigration Caseworker
Rochdale Law Centre
15 Drake Street
Rochdale OL16 1RE

From: Alhasan Ceesay
[mailto:alhasanceesay@hotmail.co.uk]
Sent: 12 May 2014 14:31
To: Lauren Butler
Subject: RE: witness statement, evidence to be adduced for appeal

Dear Lauren,
Is it possible for friends or relatives who wish to make statements send them by email directly to you? My current political muddy waters are of concern to would be contributors.
Second: less than 0.001% of Gambians have marriage certificates.
It is not our culture and I am the first in all my linage. My marriage happened 27 years ago and we do not have wedding pictures like is done in the UK.
One has to accept that the Justice Depart records are valid and that Fatou Koma-Ceesay is my wife and Rohey Ceesay, Binta Ceesay and Famatanding Ceesay being our daughters. Thanks
Dr. Alhasan Ceesay

Subject: witness statement, evidence to be adduced for appeal
Date: Fri, 9 May 2014 17:28:15 +0100

From: lauren@rochdalelawcentre.org.uk
To: alhasanceesay@hotmail.co.uk;
alhasanceesay@hotmail.com
CC: JHooper@redcross.org.uk

Dear Dr. Ceesay,
Witness statement, evidence to be adduced for appeal

Lauren Butler

09/05/2014

To: Alhasan Ceesay, Alhasan Ceesay

Cc: Joanne Hooper

Dear Dr. Ceesay,

Thank you for your telephone call earlier today and for the statement which you have submitted. I write to provide some advice around your statements, and to advice around the evidence that would strengthen our upcoming appeal.

Witness statements:

I note that you have provided a notarized witness statement for your wife, stamped by notary public in the Gambia. You have also included a statement from yourself, unsigned, with the text "sworn at Banjul", the date of 30 April 2014 and including the stamp of a Banjul-based notary public.

You have instructed that you received these documents from your associate in Banjul who is a notary public. Whilst your wife's witness statement is a useful explanation of your daughter's nickname, I must advise you that it is not necessary to have witness statement notarized.

Furthermore, I recommend that you do not sign the unsigned notarized statement which you sent to me as it specifies that you were in fact present before the notary public in Banjul on 30 April 2014.

You have instructed that you did not go to Banjul but only received this by post.

A signed document confirming your presence before the notary public in Banjul would cause you to be at risk of having your refugee status revoked, as the conditions of your leave are dependent upon not returning to your country of origin.

Grounds of appeal and further evidence:

Your witness statement and our submissions are our opportunity to rebut the findings of the Entry Clearance Officer. I will below outline the grounds we are rebutting and the evidence that would support our appeal.

1. Rohey

A. **Grounds of Refusal**

For Rohey, the visa was refused on the following grounds

    1.   Name inconsistency (320(3))

    2.   Failure to establish that you and she shared family life before you fled the Gambia (352D (iv))

    3.   No evidence of contact—although this is not a requirement for the visa, it would be helpful if you would provide evidence of ongoing parental contact

B. Evidence that would be helpful

You have already provided a statement from your wife explaining Rohey's nickname. It would be helpful if you would obtain additional evidence of shared family life before you had to flee the Gambia. This could be in the form of family photographs, statements from friends/family/neighbours verifying that Rohey and you shared family life before you fled the Gambia.

These statements do not have to be notarized, but they should include the name and address of the person making the statement, and they should be signed and dated. For ongoing evidence of contact, I recommend that you endeavor to obtain telephone records.

2.   **Fatou**

A.   **Grounds for Refusal**

For Fatou, the visa was refused on the following grounds:

1. The marriage certificate was signed by yourself in 2001, whilst you were outside of the Gambia, and therefore is not considered to be valid evidence (352A (i) and (ii))

2. There is not sufficient evidence of shared family life before you had to flee the Gambia (352A (i) and (ii))

3. There is not sufficient evidence of ongoing contact (352A (iv))

B. Evidence would be helpful

It would be helpful to obtain evidence of your marriage in 1987, your shared family life before you had to flee the Gambia, and evidence of ongoing contact. Evidence of your marriage could be statements from persons who attended, or persons who knew you to be husband and wife.

Evidence of shared family life could take the form of witness statements, property records, employment records listing your marital status, etc. Evidence of ongoing contact could be telephone records or other evidence showing your ongoing correspondence. I would be grateful if you would review the evidence you and your wife might be able to adduce.

I would be very happy to meet with you to discuss how I can assist in collating this evidence. Please do not hesitate to contact me for another appointment if you would like to discuss the evidence in more detail.

Kind regards,

Lauren Butler

Senior Immigration Caseworker

Rochdale Law Centre

15 Drake Street

Rochdale OL16 1RE

Lauren Butler

16/05/2014

To: Alhasan Ceesay

Cc: Joanne Hooper

Dear Dr. Ceesay,
Thank you for these notes.
I can confirm that I received a statement from a lady called Eliza Jones; however she has only known you since you have been in the UK and so her witness statement would not address the issues raised.
I note your mentioning last time that you believe you made an error in your initial instructions around Rohey's date of birth. I would be grateful if you would confirm her date of birth, so that I can include the revised info in our bundle of evidence. I wonder if it would be more

productive to meet in person to discuss the evidence, including your witness statement. Would you have time on the afternoon of 20th May to come to the law centre?
Kind regards,
Lauren Butler
Senior Immigration Caseworker

Rochdale Law Centre
15 Drake Street
Rochdale OL16 1RE

Statement of Alhasan Ceesay (draft)

I, Dr. Alhasan Ceesay, make the present statement in support of the appeal against the Entry Clearance Officer's decision to refuse the refugee family reunion visas for my wife and my youngest daughter. I confirm that I was born in February 1946 in the Gambia. I worked as a medical doctor in the Gambia before I had to flee to the UK in 2000. I have been recognised as a refugee in the UK.

I was married to my wife Fatou Koma Ceesay in December 1987. We were married in a small traditional ceremony in Latrikunda. As is often the case in our culture, we did not register our marriage with the government. We did not consider that there was a need to do so, as the marriage was valid in the eyes of our community.

We got on with our family life. Much later, in 2001, when it was clear that I would not be able to return to the Gambia, my wife registered our marriage with the authorities.

We corresponded by post so that I would be able to sign the appropriate forms. We did this because we knew that it would be important to have documentation of our marriage in order to facilitate our eventual reunion.
My wife and I have three daughters,

Famantanding Ceesay born in September 1991, Binta Ceesay born in March 1994, and our youngest Rohey Ceesay born in February 1997. We all lived together as a family before I had to flee the Gambia.

In separate matters, my two elder daughters are also applying for family reunion visas under paragraph 319V of the immigration rules. We are anxious to be reunited after our long separation. Since fleeing the Gambia I have done everything possible to be involved in family life.

I communicate constantly with my daughters and my wife via mobile telephone. We refrain from sending post or using landlines as I fear drawing the adverse attention of the authorities to my wife and daughters.

I have as far as possible been involved in the upbringing of my daughters, encouraging them to stay in school and sending money for school fees whenever I was able. I note that the Entry Clearance Officer has pointed out that during an asylum interview in 2012 I referred to my youngest daughter as "Roheyata". I wish to explain that the suffix "ata" means "beautiful."

Therefore, the addition of "ata" to a girl's name is an expression of affection. I concede that it is possible that I referred to Rohey by this affection nickname during my interview. I am afraid I did not anticipate that this would cause confusion around her identity.

My wife has submitted a statement that Rohey is sometimes known as "Roheyata" among her close friends and loved ones. I also wish to clarify a point around my wife's travel to Guinea Conakry. Her family is from Guinea Conakry and for the past several years she has travelled regularly to Guinea Conakry in order to look after her elderly mother. She would sometimes stay there for a period of several months.

I confirm that my relationship with my wife and my youngest daughter is genuine and subsisting. I am anxious to be reunited with them so that I may better support them, and so that we can resume our family life after a long separation. I confirm that this statement is true and complete.

Signed: Alhasan S. Ceesay

A cousin Mrs. Rohey Sey Corr sent the following in support.

Fagi kunda, Adjecent

Fagi Kunda

Health Center

TO WHOM IT MAY CONCERN

I Rohey Sey Corr the undersigned hereby confirmed that Fatou Koma-Ceesay is the wife of my cousin Dr. Alhasan Ceesay and were living together until his travels to the UK in 2000.

For further information please do not hesitate to contact me on yahoo.co.uk

Signed: Rohey Sey Corr

20th May 2014

Scan AttestationDoc

Lauren Butler

21/05/2014

To: ceesay mendy

Cc: Alhasan Ceesay

Dear Dr. Ceesay and Mendy Ceesay,
In order to rebut the Home Office's findings, we must provide evidence confirming that the marriage is genuine and that the couple shared family life. The statement from Rohey Sey Corr will not be strong evidence for the court as it stands.

The witness statement is not meant to "confirm" facts but is a chance for the witness to give evidence around what he or she saw/observed/experienced relating to this couple's marriage and shared family life. The witness statement should answer questions such as:

1. How did you first meet the couple?
2. Did you attend the wedding? If not, when/how did you hear that they were married?
3. How do you know that they lived together? You lived near them and saw this? You visited the house? You worked with them?
4. What other things did you see/hear/observe/experience which causes you to believe that the couple shared family

life? You will also note that the validity of the marriage certificate was called into question. The whole purpose of witnesses to a marriage is to provide evidence at times like this, to confirm the validity of the marriage. For that reason I have asked for a statement from Dembo Kujabi, who served as a witness to the marriage in 1987 and signed the registration in 2001.

(Sadly, the other witness, Mr. Sey, has passed away.) However the witness statement you provided yesterday from Mr. Kujabi shows a completely different signature from the one on the marriage certificate and spells his name differently as well.

Submitting this evidence to the court will likely be construed as further evidence that the marriage certificate is in fact invalid. I look forward to receiving further evidence as I have advised above and as I have outlined in previous correspondence.

Yours sincerely,

Lauren Butler
Senior Immigration Caseworker
Rochdale Law Centre
15 Drake Street
Rochdale OL16 1RE

In response I got the following statement sent to Lauren for consideration etc.
Bundung Mauritanie
Kanifin Municipality
The Gambia
20/5/2014
ATESTATION
I Dembo Kujabie of Bundung mauritanie at Kanifing Municipalty witnessed the marriage between Dr. Alhasan

Ceesay and Fatou Koma-Ceesay in the year 1987 at Bundung mosque.
Singed by thumb-print
I da Corr

22/05/2014

To: Alhasan Ceesay

This is what I sent her
I Mariama Sey cousin of Dr. Alhasan Ceesay would like to confirm that I was at the marriage ceremony between Him and his wife Fatou Koma-Ceesay in 1987. I can tell you that they lived together with their later three daughters until Dr. Alhasan Ceesay's travel to the UK in 2000.

Our house wasn't that far apart so we saw each other on regular basis. I also know he's been sending them money for food and school fees. In brief, I have known Dr. Alhasan Ceesay all my life; he is my cousin & my father Sherif Sey who passed away was his uncle.

Sent from my iPhone: Ms Eliza Jones also sent the following "I live in Colchester (6 Albrighton Croft, CO4 9RB), Essex.

I got to know Dr Ceesay around 2001, through my GP, Dr Laurel Spooner, who was a member of the charity. Dr Ceesay set up to provide medical care in The Gambia and had visited the Gambia to support the centre. Dr Ceesay and I found out that we had a number of Gambian friends in common and he became a family friend.

He got to know my parents, who lived in The Gambia but spent the summer months in UK, and when they returned my mother met up with his wife. Dr Ceesay has told me about his family circumstances (his wife and 3 daughters) and I was able to confirm this personally when I met them during one of my visits to The Gambia. Mutual friends have also confirmed this to me

I attest to this fact.

Eliza Jones

13/5/2014"

I received the greatest surprise of the day in my struggle despite all the above effort and statements from those in the know. The letter from Lauren read:

Rochdale Law Centre

15 Drake Street

Rochdale, OL16 0RE

23 May 2014

Dear Dr. Ceesay:

Re: Conflict of Interest

I note with thanks your instruction to submit the enclosed statement from a Mr. Dembo Kujabie/Kujabi to the Immigration and Asylum Chamber First-Tier Tribunal in support of the pending appeal against the refusal of refugee family reunion visas for your wife and daughter.

I note that when we met on 20th May 2014 we discussed our submissions for the upcoming hearing. We noted the fact that the Entry Clearance did not accept the validity of your marriage certificate, dated 2001.

I advised you on other evidence that we could rely upon to challenge the Entry Clearance Officer's findings and to support our argument that you and your wife were married and sharing a family life before you had to flee the Gambia. We discussed witness statements, photographs of family life, and other documents.

We reviewed the 2001 marriage certificate together and I suggested that the witnesses to your marriage might provide a statement confirming your marriage.
You told me that one of the witnesses, your uncle Mr. Sey, has passed away. You said that the other witness, Mr. Dembo Kujabi, could not provide a statement because he was illiterate.

I pointed out that Mr. Kujabi had evidently been capable of reading the marriage certificate and providing a legible signature. You then said that it was perhaps a different person who had signed the marriage certificate; and that you would look into the matter.

Later that day I received an email from a Mendy Ceesay with an attached statement dated 20 May 2014 from Dembo Kujabie of Bundung, in which he states that he witnessed your marriage. In place of a signature there is a thumb-print.

When I asked about the difference in the name speling and the difference in the signature, you instructed that Mr. Kujabi/kujabie suffered a stroke in 2001 and that the statement had been dictated to his son. You have instructed me to submit the statement as it is to the court. Rochdale Law Centre and I are governed by the Solicitor's Regulation Authority Code of Conduct. Whilst I have a duty to act in your best interest and to comply with your instructions, at the same time I also have a duty not to mislead the court.

My duty to the court outweighs my duty to a client. If I submit the 20th May 2014 statement from Mr. Kujabie to the court I would not be able to mislead the court about how this had been obtained or the fact that you had previously given conflicting information about Mr. Kujabi/kujabie.

The judge would most likely make negative credibility findings against you and Mr. Kujabi/kujabie and this would confirm the Entry Clearane Officer's suspicions about the genuineness of the arriage certificate. Additionally, if I submitted this evidence to the court and our files were later audited to reveal your instructions around the statement, this would cause professional embarrassment to me and to our firm.

Unfortunately, after discussing the matter with my supervisor and our senior solicitor, I have to inform you that due to the conflict of interest arising in this matter I must cease acting on your behalf. You are of course free to instruct new solicitors or act on your own behalf in the court. A copy of your file will be sent to you by recorded delivery in due course.

I am enclosing the relevant extracts from the Solicitor Regulation Code of Conduct explaining our position further.Please note that I will write to the First-Tier

TribunalCourt and to the Home office and inform them that we are no longer acting on your behalf.

Yours Sincerely

Lauren Butler

Senior Immigration Caseworker

For Rochdale Law Centre

CC: Joane Hooper, British Red Cross Refugee Services

My reaction was swift and I sent Lauren Butler the following reply to further clarify point she raised as well as correct assumptions she had about the whole transactions.

Need to know sooner...

Alhasan Ceesay

29/05/2014

To: lauren@rochdalelawcentre.org.uk

Cc: jhooper@redcross.org.uk

Dear Lauren,

I called but was told that you are with a client. I read your letter of 23/5/14 and found out that some conclusion you arrived were based on not understanding what I said. Hence:

1. Mr. Sherif Sey, signatory to the marriage certificate passed away ten years ago. Yes, it is fact that Dembo Kujabi is second signatory to my marriage certificate and that he suffered from stroke a few years ago. Therefore

someone had to write his statement and reason why Kujabi thumb- printed it adding a telephone contact. Latrikunda is a ward of Kanifing Municipality which is same as Manchester is to Lancashire.The Mosque is commonly referred to as Bundung or Latrikunda mosque. Both names imply same worshiping play.

2. "Mendy Ceesay" is an Internet Centre where those who contacted you from the Gambia go to email you. 99.7% of Gambians have no computers or Internet facilities.

 They travel to centres like MENDY CEESAY to have their messages sent.

3. When it comes to spelling of names in Gambia many forms for same exist i.e. Ceesay can be written as Cise, Sisay, and sisse. So Kujabie and Kujabi stand for the same sure-name.

4. In my entire linage I am the only person with a marriage certificate. Our people and culture does not request marriage certificates as it is not within norms of acceptability.

5. I selected to have one on coming to UK as safe guard for my daughters and wife in event of a sudden death.I sincerely think this slight misunderstanding lead to your interpretation of the statements.

 I reiterate gratitude for your help and urge you to know we need your help were possible. I need to know your final stand today because time is not on my side especially if you slipping away. Ms. Joan Hooper's email and telephone with me are not working because I tried to reach her but none worked. Again, thanks a million but there is no fraud in me or in my people's dealings.

My reference to illiteracy was just implying on how simple they take thinks as they assumed rightly that a thumb-print and telephone number were sufficient. I am anxiously awaiting your reply in the soonest possible time. Regard

Dr. Alhasan S. Ceesay, MD

FW: Need to know sooner...--from Dr. Ceesay

Shabana Ahmad (shabana@rochdalelawcentre.org.uk)

29/05/2014

To: alhasanceesay@hotmail.co.uk

Cc: Lauren Butler

Dear Dr Ceesay,

I have been asked to reply to you by my colleague Lauren Butler.

As Supervisor to Lauren, I have overseen her work on your file in this matter. I am therefore familiar with the facts of your case and the reasons why Lauren had to withdraw representation for your wife and daughter.

Whilst I am sympathetic to your plight and the difficult situation you have found yourself in, unfortunately, due to very limited resources available and an excessive demand for the free services provided under the Family Reunion project, the Rochdale Law Centre has to justify use of the funds that we have been allocated.

Lauren had previously requetsed clarification and information from you which had not been forthcoming. It is not a good use of public money to constantly chase up clients for information when client's clearly understand what is being requested of them.

I am therefore very sorry, but the Rochdale Law Centre will not be able resume representation in this matter on behalf of your wife and daughter.

Once again, I apologise for any incovenience this may cause and wish you and yoru family all the best with this matter. Kind regards,

Shabana Ahmad

Solicitor

For Rochdale Law Centre

Rochdale Law Centre

15 Drake Street

Rochdale

OL16 1RE

Need to know sooner...--from Dr. Ceesay

Alhasan Ceesay

29/05/2014

To: Shabana Ahmad

Dear Shabana Ahmed,

Thank you for writing. I do not agree that clarifications were not submitted or that statements were conflicting. I believe there is difference in cultural perception. For instant we, in Gambia neither have marriage photos nor marriage certificates. I just did it as explained to Lauren because of need to safeguard my wife and daughters in the event of sudden death.

Second point in contention deals with Mr. Dembo Kujabi the second signatory of my marriage Certiificate. Mr. Dembo Kujabi is very old and had a stroke making it difficult to write. He speaks and has some ability to walk etc. Hence he had asked one of his sons or a helper to write the statement and he thumb-printed and attached his telephone to it.

Anyhow read the attached to further clarify things to you. Other contributors are cousins and friends who knew me and my family through these twenty seven years.
Finally I am deeply grateful to Lauren and the Rochdale law Center, even though all is well that ends well. I refute vehemently any implied fraudulence by me or my people. The marriage took place some twenty seven years ago. God bless all of you with good health. Bellow is the last clarification submitted.

Dr. Alhasan S. Ceesay, MD

A series of exchanges between Luaren and I pointed to downward spiral than match towards the court room.

I was no surprised when I received the bellow letter from her and later her boss Mr. Shabana Ahmed and Joan Hooper at the British Redcross

Alasan Mballow Jr.& Rohey Ceesay

Need to know sooner...--from Dr. Ceesay
Alhasan Ceesay

29/05/2014

To: jhooper@redcross.org.uk

Hi Joan,

I got the bellow email from Shabana Ahmed of Rocdale Law Centre, this afternoon and I am sending you copy of my reply to Shabana Ahemed and Lauren Butler. I reiterate deep gratitude for help give thus far. Regards

Dr. Alhasan S. Ceesay, MD

Mrs. Famatanding Ceesay-Mballow

From: alhasanceesay@hotmail.co.uk
To: shabana@rochdalelawcentre.org.uk
Subject: RE: Need to know sooner...--from Dr. Ceesay
Date: Thu, 29 May 2014 16:05:27 +0100

Dear Shabana Ahmed,
Thank you for writing. I do not agree that clarifications were not submitted or that statements were conflicting. I believe there is difference in cultural perception. For instant we, in Gambia neither have marriage photos nor

marriage certificates. I just did it as explained to Lauren because of need to safeguard my wife and daughters in the event of sudden death. Second point in contention deals with Mr. Dembo Kujabi the second signatory of my marriage Certiificate.

Mr. Dembo Kujabi is very old and had a stroke making it difficult to write. He speaks and has some ability to walk etc. Hence he had asked one of his sons or a helper to write the statement and he thumb-printed and attached his telephone to it.

Anyhow read the attached to further clarify things to you. Other contributors are cousins and friends who knew me and my family through these twenty seven years. Finally I am deeply grateful to Lauren and the Rochdale law Center, even though all is well that ends well.

I refute vehemently any implied fraudulence by me or my people. The marriage took place some twenty seven years ago. God bless all of you with good health. Bellow is the last clarification submitted.

Dr. Alhasan S. Ceesay, MD

Need to know sooner...

Alhasan Ceesay

To: lauren@rochdalelawcentre.org.uk

Cc: jhooper@redcross.org.uk

Dear Lauren,

I called but was told that you are with a client. I read your letter of 23/5/14 and found out that some conclusion you arrived were based on not understanding what I said. Hence, Mr. Sherif Sey, signatory to the marriage certificate passed away ten years ago.

Yes, it is fact that Dembo Kujabi is second signatory to my marriage certificate and that he suffered from stroke a few years ago. Therefore someone had to write his statement and reason why Dembo Kujabi thumb- printed it adding a telephone contact.

Latrikunda is a ward of Kanifing Municipality which is same as Manchester is to Lancashire. The Mosque is commonly referred to as Bundung or Latrikunda mosque. Both names imply same worshiping place.

2. "Mendy Ceesay" is an Internet Centre where those who contacted you from the Gambia go to email you. 99.7% of Gambians have no computers or Internet facilities. They travel to centres like MENDY CEESAY to have their messages sent.

3. When it comes to spelling of names in Gambia many forms for same exist i.e. Ceesay can be written as Cise, Sisay, and sisse. So Kujabie and Kujabi stand for the same sure-name.

4. In my entire linage I am the only person with a marriage certificate. Our people and culture does not request marriage certificates as it is not within norms of acceptability. Gertificates are Western culture and formality.

5. I selected to have one on coming to UK as safe guard for my daughters and wife in event of a sudden death. I

sincerely think this slight misunderstanding lead to your interpretation of the statements.

I reiterate gratitude for your help and urge you to know we need your help were possible. I need to know your final stand today because time is not on my side especially if you slipping away.

Ms. Joan Hooper's email and telephone with me are not working because I tried to reach her but none worked. Again, thanks a million but there is no fraud in me or in my people's dealings.

My reference to illiteracy was just implying on how simple they take thinks as they assumed rightly that a thumb-print and telephone number were sufficient. I am anxiously awaiting your reply in the soonest possible time. Regard

Dr. Alhasan S. Ceesay, MD

Need to know sooner...--from Dr. Ceesay

Joanne Hooper (JHooper@redcross.org.uk)

May 2014

To: Alhasan Ceesay

Dear Dr Ceesay,

I have just spoke with Lauren and the decision at the Law Centre is definitely to close your case due to the reasons in the letter sent to you. I am regretful that we were unable to help and I hope that you are able to find another solicitor soon. If you require advice about other solicitors nearby, please let me know. Revive and GMIAU might be able to assit you.

With kind regards,
Jo Hooper
Family Reunion Support Project Caseworker,

British Red Cross,
10 Brindley Road,
City Park, Cornbrook,
Manchester
M16 9HQ

I thanked Joane and the Bitish Red Cross for coming to my aid even though their lawyer bowed out before we reach the court room to present the case for a judicious action.

Back tow: Binta Ceesay, Rohey Ceesay, Famatanding Ceesay

And Alasan Mballow

Dr. Ceesay and Kula Samba, Olivet College

Chapter 12
First –Tier Tribuanal:All is well that ends well

If experience maketh the man then mine is a plethoric complexion here in black and white print. I had at this stage reached my theter and patients for it looks like that other cultures'finger prints can not be accepted as real or valid. Time being agains me I made the required £280 court fee payment and seeked a replacement solicitotor immediately.

Luckily Dr. Angela Stull at the Llyods Law firm on 580a Stockport Road, Manchester agreed to step in and help my cause in the courts. We had our first meeting and set out a stretgy to undo damage the visa refusal implied about the appeal on Tuesday 3rd June 2014. After which I sent her the email bellow.

Dear Angela,
The above attachment is reason for refusal sent by the British High Commission in Gambia. Am I right in believing that all I need is the paternal and maternal DNA results plus an authentic note from the Imam?
I just spoke to wife and the JPs will charge £40 for each statement. Is it necessary to have witness statements? Kindly let me know when you hear from DNA legal world wide.
Again my family and I remain indebted to you for being so kind to us. Regards
Dr. Alhasan Ceesay
Then I followed this with a clearification request to Mr. Russ Cowley of DNA legal world wide thus:

Quote for: AC/Ref Maternity Test Legal

Alhasan Ceesay

To: Russ Cowley

Dear Russ,

Thank you for the quote. Now my name is Mr. Alhasan Ceesay and not ms Alhasan Ceesay. I am one requesting both a maternity and paternity tests for immigration purpose. Ones to be tested are:

1. Myself: Mr. Alhasan Ceesay, Flat 1 96 Birch Lane, Manchester, M13 0WN, UK (Tel.:0.........)

2. Mrs. Fatou Koma-Ceesay (wife), Phase 2 EXT, Brusubi, Banjul, The Gambia (Tel.00220..........)

3. Rohey Ceesay (daughter), Phase 2 EXT, Brusubi, Banjul, the Gambia

My lawyer Dr. Angela Stull had already contacted you about it. Your reply to my lawyer was not very specific on how to pay. It just said BACS or by credit card or debit card.

Do you have an account with sort code and A/C number to pay into? Which bank do I go to make debit card payment for your service? Awaiting your reply. What is the total cost? Regards

Alhasan Ceesay

DNA Testing

Russ Cowley

7/07/14

To: Alhasan Ceesay

Cc: Becky Stephenson

Dr Ceesay,

Thank you for your final payment. I have already started to make the necessary arrangements in terms of collections. Please be advised that we will keep you updated with the progress and of course the various stages of sample collections.

Warmest regards,

Russ Cowley
Head of Development &
Communications

DNA Legal

Re: Quote for: AC/PRIVATEGPCHARGES

Mathew Gregory (mathew@dna-worldwide.co.uk)
7:54 AM
To: Alhasan Ceesay

Dear Alhasan,
Yes the collection site is in Serrekunda, we will contact the doctor for her to arrange an appointment with your family in Gambia and make her aware that you will not be paying directly. Instead we will transfer the funds paid by your self to the GP.

Kind regards
Matt Langdon
Business Development Team
DNA Worldwide
01373 800130

On 8 July 2014 20:49, Alhasan Ceesay <alhasanceesay@hotmail.com> wrote:
Dear Matt
Thank you for being so kind. I hope this is of one for Gambia. I will make that payment direct to your Uk HBCS account on returning from London by 17/7/14. I left my banking card in Manchester and I am at a course till 16/7/14.
I am the only one to be tested in the UK and have made bookings for it.. The others are in the Gambia. Please let me know sooner. Call me, 07556092403, if needed, Regards
Dr. Alhasan Ceesay

This information was immediately passed onto my family back in Gambia to keep them alerted to in coming call from the Serekunda Clinic authorized to the do the DNA sample collection from them. Two weeks later both Fatou and Rohey Ceesay had their DNA sanple collection done by Dr. Adama Sallah inSerekunda, the Gambia. The outcome showed me father of Rohey Ceesay.

Results ready for DNA Case: L019794 -

DNA Worldwide (info@dna-worldwide.co.uk)

7/25/14

To: alhasanceesay@hotmail.com

1 attachment (1127.1 KB)

25th July 2014

Case Ref: L019794

Client Ref:

Test Results - Legal

Dear Mr. Alhasan Ceesay

Please find enclosed a copy of the test results and supporting documentation if appropriate.

Please let me know if you have any questions about the results and we look forward to hearing from you in the future with new tests that you require.

We would be most grateful to hear how you felt about the service with a quick review along with any suggestions for improvements that may support clients better.

Yours Sincerely,

Michelle Underwood

DNA Legal *part of DNA Worldwide Group*

Results:

The results of the analysis are shown in the following table:

DNA-criteria

Alleged Father

Alhasan Sisawo Ceesay

DNA-criteria

Child

Rohey Ceesay

DNA-criteria

Mother

Fatou Koma-Ceesay

DNA-System

XY = male; XX = female

In all analyzed PCR systems, Mr. Alhasan Sisawo Ceesay does show the genetic markers which have to be present for the biological father of the child Rohey Ceesay. The biostatistical analysis of the PCR systems was performed according to the method of Essen-Möller.

The probability of Mr. Alhasan Sisawo Ceesay being the biological father of Rohey Ceesay is > 99.9999 %.

Conclusion:

Based on our analysis and the biostatistical evaluation of the results, it is practically proven that Mr. Alhasan Sisawo Ceesay is the biological father of Rohey Ceesay. The genetic data are in accordance with Fatou Koma-

Ceesay being the biological mother of the child Rohey Ceesay.

Dr. Burkhard Rolf, Dr. Stefan Knauss

Director Forensic Services Project Manager DNA-Forensics

Eurofins Medigenomix Forensik GmbH carries out all analyses with greatest care and on the basis of state of the art scientific knowledge. All results solely refer to the analysed samples. The results of the statistical evaluation can vary if a near relative (father, brother, uncle, cousin, etc.) could be also the possible father.

In the case, please specify the relative that could be the alleged father and we can perform a new statistical evaluation. Our expert's reports must not be duplicated in extracts without consent of Eurofins Medigenomix Forensik GmbH. My new legal representative,

Dr. Angela Stull of Llloyds Law Firm was sent the above and we now await the court setting date of the hearing; which I am told will be after 19 weeks to allow the visa office in Gambia present its case and reasoning behind the above dinyal to the refugee family union applied for by Mrs. Fatou Koma-Ceesay and daughter Miss Rohey Ceesay.

I had the following message two months later from my current solicitor Dr. Angela Stull of Llloyds Law Firm.

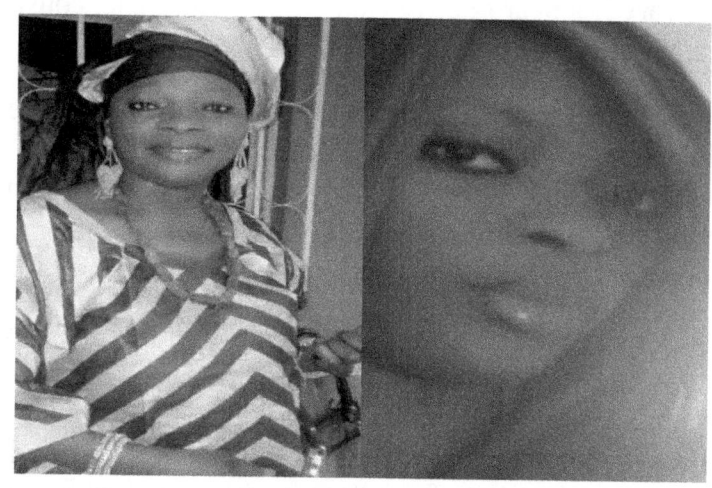

R-L: Mrs. Fatou Koma-Ceesay & Miss Binta Ceesay

Angela Stull

From:	Angela Stull
Sent:	05 September 2014 10:43
To:	'Accra.Visa.Appeals@fco.gov.uk'
Subject:	your reference: 819664 and 819667
Attachments:	Ceesay DNA results.pdf

Dear Sir/Madam,

Our firm has been instructed by Mrs. Fatou Cessay and her daughter Rohey Cessay to represent them with regard to their appeals.
Appeal numbers: OA/05926/2014 and OA/05922/2014

Their applications were refused because it was not accepted that the sponsor was married to his wife or that Rohey was his daughter. The family underwent DNA testing at considerable cost to them which clearly establishes that Rohey is the biological daughter of the sponsor and that Fatou is the biological mother. This also corroborates the fact that the Sponsor and Fatou are married.

We would ask that you please add these results to their file when reviewing the appeal.

Kindest Regards

Angela J. Stull, J.D.
Immigration Consultant
Lloyds Solicitors
angela.stull@lloydslaw.co.uk

For and on behalf of Lloyds Solicitors

angela.stull@lloydslaw.co.uk	Lloyds Law Ltd Trading As Lloyds Solicitors
0161 248 8050	580a Stockport Road
0161 225 8090	Longsight
	Manchester
www.lloydslaw.co.uk	M13 0RQ

The contents of this message and attached file are confidential and/or privileged and are for the intended recipient only. If you are not the intended recipient, any unauthorised review, use, re-transmission, dissemination, copying, disclosure or other use of or taking any action in reliance upon this information is strictly prohibited. If you receive this message in error, please contact the sender immediately and then delete the e-mail from your system. Copyright in this e-mail and attachments which are created by us belongs to Lloyds Solicitors. Any attachments with this message should be checked for viruses before it is opened. Lloyds Solicitors cannot be held responsible for any failure by the recipient to test for viruses before opening any attachments. Should you communicate with anyone at Lloyds Solicitors, you consent to us monitoring and reading any such correspondence. Lloyds Solicitors does not accept service of documents by e-mail or fax. If an attempt at service meets with a standard out of office assistant reply, consent to e-mail service is revoked because the intended recipient will see your message not earlier than the time set out in the out of office reply.

Lloyds Law Limited trading as Lloyds Solicitors is a company registered in England and Wales Registration No. 0753926.
Registered office 580a Stockport Road, Longsight Manchester M13 0RQ

AJS/IM/ 3636/Fatou

OA/05926/2014 & 05922/2014

05 September 2014

First-tier Tribunal (IAC)
Arnhem Support Centre
PO Box 6987
Leicester
LE1 6ZX

By Fax: 0116.249.4192 and post

Dear Sir/Madam

NEW REPRESENTATION

Fatou Koma Ceesay   OA/05926/2014
Rohey Ceesay   OA/05922/2014

We have been instructed by the Appellants to take over the care and conduct of their appeal case. Please make a notation on their records.

We also submit further evidence, paternity test results, that need to be sent to the Entry Clearance Officer in Ghana so that they can review this information and perhaps issue my clients their visas.

Kind Regards,

Angela J. Stull, J.D.
Immigration Consultant
angela.stull@lloydslaw.co.uk
Lloyds Solicitors

HM Courts & Tribunals Service

First-tier Tribunal
(Immigration and Asylum Chamber)
P.O. Box 6987
Leicester
LE1 6ZX

www.justice.gov.uk

Mrs Fatou Koma Ceesay & Miss Rohey Ceesay
C/o. Flat 1
96 Birch Lane
Manchester
M13 0WN

Tel: 0300 123 1711
Fax: 0116 2494 192
Minicom: 0300 123 1264
Email: customer.service@hmcts.gsi.gov.uk
(For General Enquires Only)

Your ref: Not Applicable

Appeal number: OA/05926/2014 & OA/05922/2014

11 September 2014

Dear Madam

Re: Your Immigration Appeals

We have received written confirmation from the below representatives dated 5th September 2014, informing HM Courts and Tribunals Service that they are now instructed to represent you with regards to your ongoing appeal.

Lloyds Law Limited
Lloyds Solicitors
580a Stockport Road
Manchester
M13 0RQ

You do not need to confirm this information, but if it is incorrect then please advise us in writing as soon as possible.

Yours faithfully,

Correspondence Section

Please give the appeal number, the full name of the appellant, their date of birth and the hearing date whenever you write to us or speak to us.
We can only give information to an appellant, their representative or the respondent because of the Data Protection Act 1998. We need the written and signed permission of the appellant to give information about an appeal to anyone else, including a sponsor.
You can ask for an interpreter in your language for your telephone call to us.
Please visit our website at **www.justice.gov.uk** for the answers to many regular questions.

Results ready for DNA Case: L019794 -

From: Angela Stull

To: Alhasan Ceesay

Dr. Ceesay

Hope you are well. I just wanted to update you that I have written to the Tribunal, the Presenting Officers Unit and the embassy in Ghana telling them that we have taken on the appeal. I also provided a copy of the DNA results to each of them in the hope that perhaps someone will take a look at the case now rather than waiting until the appeal hearing. Even if they don't at least I tried to get them to do something.

So, let us see what happens. Just to let you know. I will be in the US from October 22 to November 11. I haven't been home for 2 years and I am in need of some time off.I will have access to my email and the secretary will be able to get hold of me if necessary.

Regards
Angela

Mean while my mother in-law and daughter Rohey Ceesay, also known as Roeyata Ceesay each voluntarily sent following supporting statements to assist in the appeal case to come to hearing soon. My lawyer was delighted by DNS test vindicating from proof of parternity or Rohey Ceesay being my daughter.

Kindia Village
Guinea Conakry
20 September 2014

Witness Statement of Jalian Ture: Mother In-law

My name is Jalian Ture. My date of birth is 193. I am the mother in law of Dr. Alhasan Ceesay and mother to Fatou Koma-Ceesay.

I provide this statement in relation to the marriage of my daughter Fatou Koma-Ceesay and her husband, Alhasan Ceesay; to say that I was a witness at their wedding. My daughter was born in Gambia but we moved to Guinea though we are Gambian citizens.

When Alhasan and my daughter married, the ceremony took place in Guinea and it was performed by my husband Ansuman Koma who was also an Iman. Their marriage took place on 25th, December 1987. At that time, we did not keep any records of the marriages that my husband performed as no one ever saw any reason to do so.

I understand that times have changed and records are now important but in those days, it was not a common practice. Alhasan's mother was in her 80s at that time and too ill to travel and his father was already deceased.

My husband passed away in 1987 so he is not able to provide a statement. My daughter and her children have undergone a very long separation from Alhasan but Alhasan and Fatou have always remained devoted to each other. As the wife of a former Imam, it is my duty to tell the truth about what I have witnessed and what I know. I am telling the truth. I am an illiterate person but I have given this verbal account and have provided my thumb print.

Signed: Jalian Ture

Dated: 20/9/14

I, M Koma, hereby state that Mrs. Jalian Ture provided the narrative of the statement above. This has been written down and she has signed it with her thumb print.

Signed:

Dated: 20/9/14

STATEMENT OF DEMBO KUJABIE

I Muhamed Kujabie, son of Dembo Kujabie make this written statement on his behalf. Mr. Dembo Kujabie is paralyzed due to a stroke he suffered in 2000 and is unable to write. Mr. Kujabie says as follows:

I live at Bundung Mauretanie Bundung, K.M.C. My contact number is 7818907. I made this statement regarding the marriage of Fatou Koma Cessay and Dr. Al Hasan Ceesay. I truthfully state that I was a witness of the marriage between Fatou and Hasan on 25 December 1987 at the Bundung Mosque.

The Islamic ceremony was performed by Ansuman Koma, who is now deceased. The ceremony as I recall was very small and only parents and immediate family attended (?) I attended the ceremony as I was the friend.

In those days a marriage was not registered with the authorities as the marriage was conducted according to Islamic law. What I have stated is true and to the best of my ability and I ask that you will believe what I have said in this statement. A thumb print is provided as I am unable to write.

The facts as stated above are truthful and accurate.
Signed: Muhamed Kujabie
Dated: 20/9/2014

I Muhamed Kujabie, hereby state that the above statement was stated to me verbally by my father, Dembo Kujabie, and I have written it down. I read my father's statement back to him and upon being satisfied that it is correct, he has provided his thumb print. I sign below that the translation is a true and accurate wording as stated orally by Dembo Kujabie.
Signed: Muhamed Kujabie

Dated: 20/9/2014

We also had a witness startement from Ms Eliza Jones a Gambian I met in Colchester Esserx since 2000 who regularly visit my family whenever she travels to the

Gambia. My daughter Rohey Ceesay, alias: roheyata Ceesay also provided an additional statement indicated below.

Witness Statement of Rohey Ceesay
My name is Rohey Ceesay. I also go by the name of Roheyata Ceesay. My date of birth is 28 February 1997.. I am the daughter of Dr. Alhasan Ceesay and daughter of Fatou Koma-Ceesay.
I provide this statement to the court which explains the regular contact I have with my father. Rohey's father is a medical doctor and worked very hard to provide free medical assistance to the poor in Gambia.
My father is also an outspoken critic of the government in Gambia which landed him into a lot of trouble and was the reason he could not come back.
Even though my father has been gone, I, my mother, and sisters have always had a warm and loving relationship with our father. We talk on the phone regularly, he sends money when he can, we email.
Just because we haven't lived under the same roof for awhile does not mean that we are not close. On the contrary, we are very close and we all miss him. I am very proud of him for all that he has accomplished and will continue to accomplish.
My father has always been interested in my health, welfare and education. He always discusses my progress with me and my mother and he is concerned about my future.
We now have the chance to be together as a family and I would ask that you kindly consider my future and that you not keep me from my father any longer.
I have submitted to a paternity test that shows I am daughter of Dr. Alhasan Ceesay and Fatou Koma-

Cessay. My father is a part of my family and it is important that I be with him.

Signed: Rohey Ceesay

Name: Rohey Ceesay (alias: Roheyata Ceesay)

Dated: 20/9/14

This was followed by an update reply to the court.

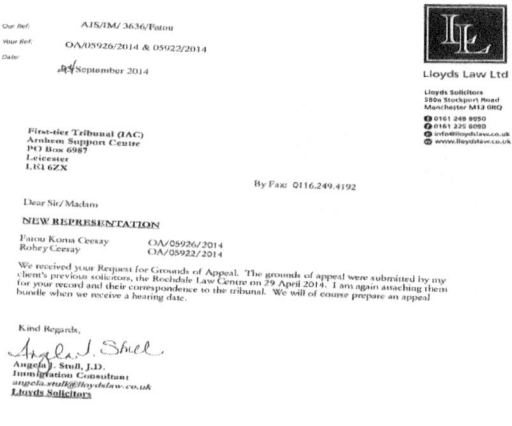

Grounds of Appeal
Fatou Koma Ceesay

We lodge the present appeal under Section 82(1) of the Nationality, Immigration and Asylum Act 2002. We are of the view that the Entry Clearance Officer's decision is not in accordance with the immigration rules and the decision to refuse entry clearance violates the appellant's human rights under article 8 of the ECHR.

1. Not in accordance with the immigration rules

The appellant lodged an application for entry clearance to the United Kingdom to join her husband Alhasan Ceesay. The sponsor has refugee status in the UK. The application fell to be considered under paragraph 352A of the immigration rules.

In the fifth paragraph of the determination dated 7 April 2014 the Entry Clearance Officer noted that the marriage registration record provided was signed in 2001 by the sponsor. The sponsor has instructed that he and his wife were married in 1987 in a small village ceremony and therefore no documents exist from this date. They took the decision to register their marriage once it became clear that the sponsor was not able to return to the Gambia.

In the sixth paragraph of the determination the Entry Clearance Officer notes that there is no documentary evidence of contact between the sponsor and the appellant. Paragraph 352A of the immigration rules does not require such evidence. Nonetheless, both the appellant and the sponsor have provided consistent evidence of telephone contact.

Additional evidence will be adduced to verify that the appellant and sponsor were married and shared a household before he had to flee his home.

2. Article 8 of the ECHR

We are of the view the determination violates the appellant's rights under article 8 of the ECHR.

On these grounds we lodge the present appeal.

25 April 2014
Rochdale Law Centre

Update: 1/10/14

From: Angela Stull

To: Alhasan Ceesay (alhasanceesay@hotmail.com)

Dr. Ceesay

I just wanted to update you that I received an email from the Ghana embassy asking for the grounds of appeal. I really don't know what is going on with the Home Office. I suppose the usual sorts of chaos disorganization. So, I sent it to them along with another copy of the DNA report. So, let's see if they change their minds.

Regards

Angela Stull

For and on behalf of Lloyds Solicitors

HM Courts & Tribunals Service

Immigration and Asylum First-tier Tribunal

✉ Customer.Service@hmcts.gsi.gov.uk
(For General Enquiries Only)
www.tribunals.gov.uk
✉ IAC Manchester
1st Floor Piccadilly Exchange
2 Piccadilly Plaza
Mosley Street
Manchester
M1 4AH
☎ Ph: 0300 123 1711
Fax: 0870 739 4164
Minicom: 0845 606 0766

Date: 11 November 2014

Dr Alhasan Ceesay
Flat 1
96 Birch Lane
Manchester
M13 0WN

THE IMMIGRATION ACTS

Appeal No:	OA/05926/2014	HO Ref:	
Appellant:	Mrs Fatou Koma Ceesay	Port Ref:	
Respondent:	Entry Clearance Officer	FCONumber:	819664
		Reps Ref:	AJS/IM/3636/Fatou

To the Appellant and Respondent

NOTICE OF HEARING

This appeal will be heard on **Monday, 19 January 2015** at **10:00 AM**, please ensure you arrive 15 minutes prior to the hearing at **IAC Manchester, 1st Floor Piccadilly Exchange, 2 Piccadilly Plaza, Mosley Street, Manchester, M1 4AH.**

The Judge will decide on the order in which appeals will be heard, so it may be that your case will not be heard until later in the day. Please make sure that you make the necessary arrangements to attend the Hearing Centre for the rest of the day.

DIRECTIONS

You must send the following documents to the Tribunal at the above address and to the other party, (to arrive) no later than 5 days before the date of Full Hearing.

App.	Resp.	
✓	☐	Witness statements of the evidence to be called at the hearing.
✓	✓	A bundle of **all** documents to be relied on at the hearing - these must be clearly page numbered, indexed and include a schedule identifying the essential passages. (The essential passages are any sections you consider highly significant in your appeal).

The **Appellant** must send copies of all the documents to the Respondent at Presenting officers unit, PO Box 509, Manchester, M16 6DX.

The **Respondent** must send copies of all the documents to the Appellant.

Copies of documents in a language other than English must be accompanied by a full certified translation.

Clerk to the First-tier Tribunal

ALL CORRESPONDENCE SHOULD BE SENT TO THE ADDRESS AT THE TOP OF THIS NOTICE QUOTING THE APPEAL NUMBER AND ANY HEARING DATE

IA30

Sponsor Copy

FIRST TIER TRIBUNAL (IAC)
MANCHESTER
APPEAL NO. OA/05926/2014 and
OA/05922/2014

MRS. FATOU KOMA CEESAY
MISS ROHEY CEESAY

Appellants

V

ENTRY CLEARANCE OFFICE, GHANA

Respondent

Witness Statement of Dr. Alhasan Sisawo Ceesay

I, Dr. Ceesay of Flat 1, 96 Birchlane, Manchester, M13 0WL will say the following:

1. My date of birth is 14.02.1946 and I am a national of Gambia.

2. I have always lived with my wife and children with the exception of 2001 to the current time.

3. I have always been in constant contact with my family by telephone as this is the easiest form of contact. My family does not have internet access in the home, they would have to travel 3 miles to an internet café.

4. I have only started emailing in the very recent months to sort out documentation for this appeal. We have limited our internet contact due to the fact that the government has unlimited access to anyone's personal information. So we have to be very careful about what we talk about.

5. On the 31st of December 2014 there was coup d'etat in Gambia which failed and the President accused the USA, UK and Germany of instigating it by using Gambians. My daughter Binta Ceesay was returning home and the city was on lock down. She was stopped by the security, her phone was taken off of her and she was beaten and released.

6. My daughter has 2 telephones and the one that I text her and talk to her on was safely at home and I believe that if it was in her possession at the time she would have been imprisoned.

7. My current leave is that of a refugee. I want to rectify what was written in an earlier statement about me initially "fleeing" from Africa.

8. I want to state that I started coming to the United Kingdom in 1990. I was issued a visa in 1989 but was unable to start my clinical rotation until 1990.

9. I did my rotation at the Colchester General Hospital. My wife came in a few months later and stayed with me until 1992. During this time she gave birth to our first child, Famatamanding Ceesay. (birth certificate attached).

10. Upon completing of my training I returned to Gambia. I then did a one year internship at the Royal Victoria Hospital in Banjul.

11. From 1993 to 2000 I was working as a Medical Officer in the field of General Practice at the Royal Victoria Hospital.

12. Then in 2000 my wife and I were invited to attend the wedding of a friend in the United Kingdom. My intention was to return home with my wife.

13. However, whilst here I looked into doing the MRPC which is a fellowship. I spoke with other doctors who suggested that I should just apply.

14. I applied to the General Medical Council and they accepted my credentials and on that basis I applied to change my visa status.

15. That application was refused on the basis that I could not switch from visitor to student. However by that time, the situation in my country had changed.

16. The issue for me was the fact that I publicly critized the government's rural health care delivery that brought me into disrepute with the government.

17. The attorney general, with the permission of the President, branded anyone who critized the government as a saboteur and upon arrival to the country they would be arrested at the airport.

18. The President himself during the opening of Parliament publicly stated that anyone who was against his government upon their return would be arrested.

19. I took this threat very seriously but I was still focused on trying to get my studies done and was writing the Home Office to allow me to study. I even asked my friends and the local MP to write on my behalf. I never hid from anyone and I was supported on and off by friends. This went on for years.

20. I did claim asylum and you have the record so I need not go over that again.

21. I also have 2 other daughters, Famatamanding Ceesay and Binta Ceesay. They are both over the age of 18 and are living in Gambia. My financial circumstances are such that I am not able to apply for them to join us.

22. I have been married with Fatou since 25 December 1987.

23. I married my wife in a small traditional ceremony in Latrikuda. An Imam officiated over the ceremony and his name was Ansuman Koma. That gentleman has since died. Our family attended along with the village elders. There was no requirement for couples to sign any form of marriage certificate or registry in those days.

24. However, I do have a statement from Dembo Kujabie who attended the ceremony. You will note that he is paralyzed and had his son Muhammed Kujabie prepare the statement for his him. Mr. Dembo provided his thumb print.

25. I also have a statement from my mother in law, Jalian Ture who was a witness to our wedding.

26. In 2001 my wife and I decided to have a marriage certificate because my position had been so precarious and if I would die, I wanted to make sure my wife and children had some sort of legal document to fall upon. I am a published author and I would want to make sure my wife receives any royalties from my work.

27. As for financial support, I would say that I have sent them money whenever it was available to me. I have provided proof of transfers. In the past I have also asked my friends to send money on my behalf to my family and you can see from the statement of Eliza Jones that she gave money to them.

28. All I can say is that the Appellants are my family. I am married to Fatou and have been for 27 years. Rohey is my youngest child and I am desperate for my family to join me.

STATEMENT OF TRUTH

I believe that the facts stated in this witness Statement are true.

Signed ....

Name: Dr. Alhasan Sisawo Ceesay

Dated: 15/01/15

With all the above preparation done my lawyer filed her defence package to the court ahead of the January 19th, 2015 hearing on the appeal for my family to be allowed to join me in the UK. The wheels of just turns very slow in matters like I found myself in.

The First Tier Tribunal gave 19 weeks to the Home Office in which time to respond why it refused visa to my wife and daughter to join me in the UK. When this request was not met my lawter, Dr. Angela Stull and I had no other asvenue of resourse except the court.

Hence on January 19th, 2015 I left my flat at 8:30 Am and headed for the court hearing due to start at 10:00 AM prompt as stipulated above. My lawter was confindent and she accompanied me to the court room smiling.

I kept saying to myself she must know something I do not know. Nonetheless, I prayed that the outcome be a positive one for the family. I t would sixteen years since I last saw my family and I miss those love girls of mine.

We were urshered into a brightly lit room with a youngish looking gentleman seating infrom a special chamber from were he introduced himself, after we were all seated, as

Judge hearing my appeal.

He reassured me that he has no connection with the Home Office or Immigration and that his determination would free of any of the Home Office. I was very surprised by the simplicity of his attire for I expected a wigged and red robe stern face fellow who hadly smiles to the one deciding the case. I turned out to be an angel with a humane heart.

Mr. McBride, a very kind and sympathetic officer represented the Immigration and the Home Office. On laying out the protocol the Judge allowed my lawter to present the case and any beif in support of the case.

Mr. McBride asked only asked me only two questions and told the Judge he has rested his side of his arguements as presented to him. Judge, asked if am in touch with my family back in the Gambia and if I do support them financially.

The answers to both questions were positive and few minutes later he asked Mr. McBride if he has any questions or any contention. To which Mr. McBride replied; "No yiur Honour." To mine and my lawyer's delight the Judge declared the hearing complete and closed.

He reassured me that even though he could not give a verdit at that moment he would certainly send me his determination in a fiorth night after the 19/01/2015.

0"05926/2014; 0"05922/2014

First-tier Tribunal
(Immigration and Asylum Chamber)
<u>THE IMMIGRATION ACTS</u>

| Heard at Manchester | Appeal determined following a hearing |

On 19 January 2015

Decision & Reasons Promulgated: 27th January 2015

Before
JUDGE OF THE FIRST-TIER TRIBUNAL CRUTHERS

Between:

(1) Mrs Fatou Koma CEESAY; and (2) Miss Rohey CEESAY
(ANONYMITY DIRECTION MADE)
Appellants and
ENTRY CLEARANCE OFFICER - Accra
Respondent

Representation:
For the appellant: Mrs Stull
For the respondent: Mr McBride

DECISION AND REASONS

As agreed at the hearing, this decision addresses both of the appeals referred to above. The decision is structured under five main headings: * introduction I issues; * evidence I submissions; law applied; assessment of evidence / conclusions and * decisions. Fuller summaries of the proceedings at the hearing appear in the typed record of proceedings on the file.

With reference to the tribunal's procedure rules of 2014, it is my judgement that the circumstances of this appeal are such that it is appropriate to make a direction for anonymity (because of the sponsor's situation in relation to the Gambian government).

Introduction I issues

1. The first appellant (date of birth 16 May 1960) is a citizen of Gambia. She appeals against a decision dated 9 April 2014 to refuse her leave to enter

I

OM05926/2014; 0"05922/2014 the United Kingdom as the wife of Dr Alhasan Sisawo Ceesay of Manchester 13 ("the sponsor"). The sponsor has status in this country as a recognised refugee.

2. The second appellant (also a citizen of Gambia) is the youngest daughter of the first appellant and the sponsor. In effect the appeal of the second appellant falls to be determined in line with the appeal of the first appellant. The remainder of this determination sometimes refers to "the appellant" (meaning the first appellant) but the conclusions reached should be read as applying to both appellants.

3. The decisions under appeal were made with reference to those paragraphs of the immigration rules, HC395, that deal with entry clearance for the family members of recognised refugees (as specified in the respondent's decision notices).

Immigration law issues

4. Primarily I have to decide whether the relevant requirements of the immigration rules were met at the date of the respondent's decisions.

5. The crux of the respondent's cases that the appellants had not shown themselves to satisfy the following parts of the relevant rules:

- the first appellant - paragraph 352A(iv): "each of the parties intends to live permanently with the other as his or her spouse civil partner and the marriage is subsisting"; and
- the second appellant — paragraph 352D (iv): "was part of the family unit of the person granted asylum at the time that the person granted asylum left the country of his habitual residence in order to seek asylum".

No separate human rights law arguments

6. For the appellants Mrs Stull realistically accepted that if they did not meet the relevant requirements of the rules, the appeals could not succeed on human rights law arguments.

Evidence I Submissions

7. In my assessment of this appeal I have taken account of all the relevant documents before me, and the oral evidence.

Documentary evidence

8. The relevant documents include those in the bundles from the respondent and the appeal notices (with grounds of appeal). In summary, the other documents for the appellants are: - Skeleton Argument
- sponsor's witness statement, 14 January 2015
- pages 12 to 60: various copy documents said to support the appellants' case
- Colour copies of relevant pages from the sponsor's passports - these copies put in on 19 January are simply better copies of pages already in the appellants' 60 page bundle (the original passports were also produced at the hearing).

9. In this determination, page references consisting only of a number are references to the appellants' bundle.

Oral evidence

10. The sponsor was the only witness. His evidence was given in English.

11. The sponsor confirmed the truth of his witness statement. He then responded to questions from Mr McBride and from me.

Submissions

12. Before reserving the case for further consideration and a written determination, I invited the representatives to make submissions. Mr McBride relied on the notices of decision - he had nothing to add to those notices. Mrs Stull relied on the Skeleton Argument for the appellants - she had nothing to add to that Skeleton Argument.

13. I set out below my assessment of the relevant evidence.

Law applied

General approach to the issues

14. In general the burden lies on the appellant to demonstrate, on a balance of probabilities, that the relevant requirements were met at the date of the decision under appeal.

15. By section 85(5) of the 2002 Act, because this is an appeal under section 82(1) (refusal of entry clearance or refusal of a certificate of entitlement) I am restricted to considering only the circumstances appertaining at the time of the decisions to refuse. However, paragraph 25 of the 'AT's starred determination in DR (ECO: post-decision evidence) Morocco* [2005] UKIAT 00038. notified on 9 February 2005 confirms that section 85(5) does not preclude subsequent evidence or subsequent actions being taken into account insofar as they cast light on what the position was at the date of the decision (for example, evidence of "intervening devotion" is admissible in spouse entry clearance cases such as DR). ©

Assessment of evidence I conclusions

16. I am satisfied that the evidence given by the sponsor was frank and honest.

The respondent's case — in context

17. In my assessment, there is very little of substance in the respondent's case here. As regards the appellants' case I the most substantial doubts expressed in the decision notices I make the following findings:

18,An issue common to both decision notices is the lack of evidence as to ongoing communications between the sponsor and the appellants.

I do find it odd that there is no paper evidence of communication at all (such as print outs of e-mails I birthday cards / similar). Apart from anything else, a statement in the name of the second appellant indicates that the sponsor does exchange e-mails with his family in Gambia (page 43). But I am prepared to accept the sponsor's evidence that he communicates with his family in Gambia mainly by telephone.

The sponsor explained that the appellants now live in a village some 25 miles from Banjul. He said that posting anything to the appellants would be a very uncertain undertaking, the communication could get "stuck in the city/' and arrive only two years later.

19. The grounds of appeal for the first appellant only partially address the specific point in the third bullet point of the related refusal decision. As per the grounds of appeal, I can accept that there may be no documentation from when the first appellant and the sponsor married "in 1987 in a small village ceremony."

But what the grounds do not address is the fact that the marriage registration document dated 17 May 2001 apparently shows the signatures of the sponsor and the first appellant, even though the sponsor would have been in the UK in May 2001. Although this point remains unexplained, I do not consider it to be of any real significance in the context of the evidence overall.

20. In the decision notice for the second appellant, the point is raised that in his Home Office interview of 3 December 2012 the sponsor gave the second appellant's name as Roheyata (not "Roheÿ') (the interview records are copied in the respondent's bundle for the first appellant). But the same paragraph of the decision notice indicates that the appellant gave the correct date of birth for the second appellant, therefore, even if there had been no explanation here, I would have been inclined to accept that it was the second appellant who the sponsor was referring to in December 2012. As it is, the explanation is also offered that "Roheyata" is in the nature of a family nickname (with the suffix "ata" meaning something like "beautiful") (as per the grounds of appeal for the second appellant).

The appellants' case

21. It is my judgement that such difficulties as there are with the case for the appellants are outweighed by the evidence tending to show that the appellants did meet the relevant requirements of the rules at the date of the decisions.

22. In summary, I accept the sponsor's evidence that: " . the Appellants are my family. I am married to Fatou and have been for 27 years. Rohey is my youngest child and I am desperate for my family to join me" (paragraph 28 of the sponsor's statement). Apart from the period 2001 to date, the sponsor has generally lived in a family unit with his wife and children (paragraph 2 of his statement). Through paragraphs 12 on of his statement, the sponsor explains how in 2000 he had intended to return to Gambia

with his wife after they had attended the wedding of a friend in this country.

He then decided to seek various extensions of his leave - as a medical practitioner/student - but eventually claimed asylum on the basis that he had publicly criticised the Gambian government's rural health care delivery (his paragraph 16).

23. Additionally, my reasons for accepting the appellants' case include:

24. I accept the sponsor's evidence that he rings his family in Gambia about twice a month (evidence on 19 January).

25. The decision notice for the first appellant acknowledges that the sponsor named the first appellant as his wife when he was interviewed by the Home Office on 3 December 2012. He also then stated that he had three children (ibid).

26. By a letter of 5 September 2014, the representatives for the appellants submitted a report dated 24 July 2014 from the "DNA Worldwide Group Ltd" (the respondent has not sought to cast doubt on the bona fides of this testing organisation).

The report indicates that the probability of the sponsor being the biological father of the second appellant is greater than 99.9999%. The conclusion of the report reads: "Based on our analysis and the biostatistical evaluation of the results, it is practically proven that [the sponsor] is the biological father of [the second appellant]. The genetic data are in accordance with [the first appellant] being the biological mother of the child [the second appellant]".

©

O"05922/2014

27. In the appellants' bundle there are birth certificates relating to the children of the sponsor. At pages 32 and 33 the certificates include two in respect of the birth of the appellant's first child in Colchester, Essex, on
17 September 1991 (as per 'paragraph 9 of the sponsor's statement). The certificates show the first appellant and the sponsor as the parents of the child born on 17 September 1991.

28. There is also the Gambian passport number 76032. In effect that is a joint passport for the first appellant and the sponsor.

29. It shows, amongst other things, that the first appellant and the sponsor entered the United Kingdom together (on a student basis) after appropriate visas were issued on 12 July 1989.

Decisions

The appeals in respect of the immigration rules are allowed.

Direction Regarding Anonymity — rule 13 of the Tribunal Procedure (Firsttier Tribunal) (Immigration and Asylum Chamber) Rules 2014

Unless and until a tribunal or court directs otherwise, the Appellant is granted anonymity. No report of these proceedings shall directly or indirectly identify him or any member of their family. This direction applies both to the Appellant and to the Respondent. Failure to comply with this direction could lead to contempt of court proceedings.

If an appeal fee(s) has been paid by the sponsor, I consider in the circumstances that it is appropriate for me to make an award of the whole fee(s).

This fee award is directed to the respondent and follows from my reasons for deciding that these appeals must be allowed. Apart from anything else, the original reasons for the decisions under appeal were relatively weak. And the respondent could have called the appellants in for interview (to discuss their claimed relationship with the sponsor).

And, as per paragraph 11 of the Skeleton Argument, the Review documents of the Entry Clearance Manager (dated 10 December 2014) proceed as if no further documentary evidence had been submitted, even though by 25 November 2014 the appellant's representatives had submitted to the respondent's office the DNA results referred to above and old passports of the first appellant.
Signed Date: 26 January 2015

Judge of the First-tier Tribunal PWC

HIVI courts
& Tribunals (For
customer.service@hmcts.gsi.gov.ukGeneral Enquiries Only)
Service www.tribunals.gov.uk
 Arnhem Support Centre
    P O Box 6987
    Leicester
    LEI 6ZX
       0300 123 1711

Fax 0870 739 5895
Minicom: 0845 606 0766

Date:27January
2015 Mrs Fatou Koma Ceesay c/o. Flat I
96 Birch Lane
Manchester
M13 0WN

THE IMMIGRATION ACTS

Appeal No:	OA/05926/2014	HO Ref:	Port Ref:	Reps Ref:	AJS/1W3636 Fatou
Appellant:	Mrs Fatou Koma Ceesay				
Respondent:	Entry Clearance Officer				

To the Appellant and Respondent
Enclosed are the First-tier Tribunal's decision and reasons in the above appeal. Either party may apply to the First-tier Tribunal for permission to appeal to the Upper Tribunal on a point of law arising from the First-tier Tribunal's decision.

Any application must be made in accordance with the relevant Procedure Rules and must be provided to the Tribunal so that it is received no later than 14 days after the date on which the party making the application was provided with written reasons for the decision, except where the Appellant is outside the United Kingdom; in which case any application must be provided to the Tribunal so that it is received no later than 28 days after the date on l,vhich the party making the application was provided with written reasons for the decision.

All Applications must be sent to:
First-tier Tribunal:
Loughborough Support Centre, PO Box 7866, Loughborough, Leics, LEI 1 2XZ or
by Email to: IAFT4@hmcts.gsi.gov.uk

DIRECTION ON AWARD OF COSTS RELATING TO FEES UNDER RULE 9(1)

To the Respondent

In determining the appeal, the judge has awarded costs to the appellant in the amount of £140.00.

You are therefore directed, unless you intend to seek permission to appeal to the relevant appellate court, to make payment of this amount to the appellant.

ALL
Appeflant Copy
HIVI courts
& Tribunals customer.service@hmcts.gsi.gov.uk (For General Enquiries Only)
Service www.tribunals.gov.uk
Arnhem Support Centre
P O Box 6987
Leicester
LEI 6ZX
0300 123 1711

Fax 0870 739 5895
Minicom: 0845 606 0766

Date: 27 January 2015

Miss Rohey Ceesay
c/o. Flat I
96 Birch Lane
Manchester
M13 0WN

THE IMMIGRATION ACTS

Appeal No	OA/05922/2014	HO Ref:	
Appellant:	Miss Rohey Ceesa	Ref:	
Respondent:	Entry Clearance Officer	Reps Ref:	AJS/1M/3636/Fatou

To the Appellant and Respondent

Enclosed are the First-tier Tribunal's decision and reasons in the above appeal. Either party may apply to the First-tier Tribunal for permission to appeal to the Upper Tribunal on a point of law arising from the First-tier Tribunal's decision.

Any application must be made in accordance with the relevant Procedure Rules and must be provided to the Tribunal so that it is received no later than 14 days after the date on which the party making the application was provided with written reasons for the decision, except where the Appellant is outside the United Kingdom; in which case any application must be provided to the Tribunal so that it is received no later than 28 days after the date on which the palty making the application was provided with written reasons for the decision.

All Applications must be sent to:

First-tier Tribunal:

Loughborough Support Centre, PO Box 7866, Loughborough, Leics, LEI 1 2XZ or

by Email to: IAFT4@hmcts.gsi.gov.uk

DIRECTION ON AWARD OF COSTS RELATING TO FEES UNDER RULE 9(1)

To the Respondent

In determining the appeal, the judge has awarded costs to the appellant in the amount of £140.00.

You are therefore directed, unless you intend to seek permission to appeal to the relevant appellate court, to make payment of this amount to the appellant.

ALL
Appellant Copy
'..-OUI LS FIRST-TIER TRIBUNAL
& Tribunals customer.service@hmcts.gsi.gov.uk
Service (For General Enquiries Only)

www.tribunals.gov.uk Arnhem Support Centre
P O Box 6987
Leicester
LEI 6ZX
0300 123 171 1
Fax 0870 739 5895
Minicom: 0845 606 0766

Lloyds Law Limited Lloyds Solicitors	Date :	27 January 2015

580a
Stockport Road
Manchester
M13 0RQ

THE IMMIGRATION ACTS

Appeal No:	•ON05926/2014	HO Ref:	
Appellant:	Mrs Fatou Koma Ceesay	Port Ref:	
Respondent:	Entry Clearance Officer	Reps Ref:	AJS/1W3636/Fatou

To the Appellant and Respondent

Enclosed are the First-tier Tribunal's decision and reasons in the above appeal. Either party may apply to the First-tier Tribunal for permission to appeal to the Upper Tribunal on a point of law arising from the First-tier Tribunal's decision.

Any application must be made in accordance N'ith the relevant Procedure Rules and must be provided to the Tribunal so that it is received no later than 14 days after the date on which the party making the application was provided with written reasons for the decision, except where the Appellant is outside the United Kingdom; in which case any application must be provided to the Tribunal so that it is received no later than 28 days after

the date on which the party making the application was provided with written reasons for the decision.
All Applications must be sent to:
First-tier Tribunal:

Loughborough Support Centre, PO Box 7866, Loughborough, Leics, LEI 1 2XZ or by Email to: IAFT4@hmcts.gsi.gov.uk

DIRECTION ON AWARD OF COSTS RELATING TO FEES UNDER RULE 9(1)

To the Respondent

In determining the appeal, the judge has awarded costs to the appellant in the amount of £140.00. You are therefore directed, unless you intend to seek permission to appeal to the relevant appellate court, to make payment of this amount to the appellant.

Clerk to the First-tier Tribunal

Copy issued to Appellant:

ALL

Representative Copy

'—oul LS FIRST-TIER TRIBUNAL

& Tribunals customer.service@hmcts.gsi.gov.uk

Service (For General Enquiries Only)

www.tribunals.gov.uk Arnhem Support Centre
P O Box 6987
Leicester LEI 6ZX

0300 123 1711
0870 739 5895
Minicom: 0845 606 0766

Lloyds Law Limited Date: 27 January 2015
Lloyds Solicitors
580a Stockport Road

Manchester
M13 ORQ

THE IMMIGRATION ACTS

Appeal No:	0"05922/2014	HO Ref:	Port Ref:	
Appellant:	Miss Rohey Cesay			
Respondent:	Entry Clearance Officer	Reps Ref:	AJS/M/3636/Fatou	

To the Appellant and Respondent

Enclosed are the First-tier Tribunal's decision and reasons in the above appeal. Either party may apply to the First-tier Tribunal for permission to appeal to the Upper Tribunal on a point of law arising from the First-tier Tribunal's decision. Any application must be made in accordance '"ith the relevant Procedure Rules and must be provided to the Tribunal so that it is received no later than 14 days after the date on which the patty making the application was provided with written reasons for the decision, except where the Appellant is outside the United Kingdom; in which case any application must be provided to the Tribunal so that it is received no later than 28 days after the date on which the party making the application was provided with written reasons for the decision.

All Applications must be sent to:

First-tier Tribunal:
Loughborough Support Centre, PO Box
7866, Loughborough, Leics, LEI 1 2XZ or
by Email to: IAFT4@hmcts.gsi.gov.uk
DIRECTION ON AWARD OF COSTS RELATING TO
FEES UNDER RULE 9(1)
To the Respondent
In determining the appeal, the judge has awarded costs to the appellant in the amount of £140.00. You are therefore directed, unless you intend to seek permission to appeal to the relevant appellate court, to make payment of this amount to the appellant.
Clerk to the First-tier Tribunal
Copy issued to Appellant:
ALL
Representative Copy
Alas! I thank God and my solicitor Dr. Angela Stull, at Llyods Law Firm, Manchester City for this relief. I wait to hear from the Home Office and British High Commission in Ghana, West Africa regarding issuance visas to enable my family to join me after sixteen years of separation and loneliness. I am eager to have my children start schooling to give them a fighting chance in this world. I relayed the good news to wife and children who were very happy and looked forward to our reunion.

It would take five weeks before my wife was contacted by the British Consulate in Banjul and told that they would be issued visas upon providing results of TB test.

This was done in a week and the wait continued until after a forth night before their passports with family reunion visas affixed to last up to December 2017. In this welcoming mode I book flight fares with Air Iberia to fly my wife and daughter from Banjul via Barcelona direct to Manchester, UK on the 25th July 2015.

The joyous union occurred on 26/7/15. It was a unique state which on one hand welt with joy while on the other sorrow for leaving my two elder daughters stranded in the Gambia. Both Binta Ceesay and her sister Famatanding were in tears for being left behind to face the political instability of the day.

With my wife and daughter, Rohey Ceesay putting a break to my sixreem years of solitude we proceeded to Flat 1, 96 Birch Lane where I lived in Manchester. It was a warm feeling disturbed by the small bedsit we were. Luckily I was finally able to secure a two bedroom flat in Withington, Manchester on the 12/8/15.

The ice being broken I embarked on getting Rohey Ceesay into school. This too took onexpected turn as her age on arrival would not let her attend Prinary School in the UK. We had to settle with her starting at college level intead.

Manchester College opened its doors enabling her start her UK educational adventure at its Shena Simon Campus in Manchester. So far her teachers are pleased with her progress. She is adjusting to life in England and at school. My wife's expecatation of getting an instant job despite my urging for patients at times tightens the screws. She is catching up with the requirements, such as a National Insurance number and employers willing to giver chance to a post.

Nonetheless we are faring on well and are grateful to Kemo Ceesay and his wife Awa, an inspirational Gambian couple that actually lodged my wife and daughter the first three days in Manchester. They are both eager to experience winter in Manchester. The first snow shower will certainly dampen their current enthusiasm as happed to all of from the tropics.

Chapter 13

Manding Medical Center

When God wants to destroy someone, He first made him an unusual dreamer. So Gandhi had his dream of people solving social deference none violently and Rev. Martin Luther king, jr. held onto his admirable dream of children of Jews and Gentile, black and whites holding hands and living in harmony spearheading peaceful cause for mankind.

There are the Albert Schweitzer's and mother Theresa's of the world dreamers who spent their lives believing in their dreams for mankind. My dream, since 1956, was the simple goal of providing medical aid to those far and in remote villages. The villager, who is forced to walk miles on end to seek medical aid for his already dying child, wife or friend, deserves a better health system.

Something I saw in 1956 left an indelible mark in my mind and I have since then asked and prayed that God help me bring part if not full to the kind of tragedy that was passing right before me. I was hopelessly unable to give relief except to comfort those involved.

In 1956, while on my way to Saba village, I met an anxious father carrying his son and his almost dead pregnant wife on the back of donkey heading for the health center at Kerewan village, three or more miles from where I met him.

The child was vomiting yellow stuff, he was sweaty, his eyes were reverted backwards and the pregnant lady groaning every time the mule moves. There was some greenish fluid dripping off her lapper.

She could barely hold the ropes controlling the donkey. I went to Kerewan later that evening and asked about the status of that family, only to be told that the boy passed away half a mile to the dispensary and the lady was referred to the central hospital in Banjul but the family had no money to pay for her transportation nor was the River ambulance available as it was undergoing maintenance at the Dockyard.

To cut a long story short, both child and mother died because of lack of medical facilities or modern medical aid to the villager. One or all of those lives could have been saved and remain beneficial to the country than the fate that befell them.

I prayed and grieved with the family for months and redoubled my efforts at school in other to solve such development in future. I committed myself to medicine from that day on and never regretted making such a challenging decision in my life. Hence, when on the day I was taking the Hippocratic Oath,

I not only swore to uphold all therein but to make sure that God help me not to ever deviate from my commitment and promise to be part of the solution in the health services of the Gambia, to foster health education for the villager, and to complement the existing medical facilities in the Gambia as well as ease the shortage of medical service personnel.

To many, except the dreamer, such Erewhons leads to failure as they turn to be white elephants. Some friends tease me by flatly promising to rise from their graves on the opening day of such an Alice in wonderland project.

Let me make it crystal clear that I had no elusions about what was needed, or to be done and that the building of the hospital would indeed be a lifetime challenge I am fully ready to grapple with. There would be a lot of well-wishers but very few will ever want to join until the opening day ceremonies.

So first things first, I met an attorney friend Mr. Ousainou Darboe, a villager like me, on September 24, 1992, and pleaded for his assistance with the legal aspects of setting up a charitable foundation, Manding Medical center at Njawara village in the provinces for the sole purpose of providing much needed medical aid to the villager.

He was very obliging and requested no payment in return for his services. In the mean time I got a board of governors elected while he prepared the memorandum and articles of association of Manding Medical Centre at Njawara village.

Also, I met with the Lower Badibou district chief, Kitabou Singateh, who by the way was my primary school class mate at Kinte Kunda from 1953 to 1957, the District Authority, Commissioner and the kerewan Area Council.

All of whom were more than delighted and did all they could under the law to help me set up a grassroots local advisory committee, which was headed by the commissioner, to assist the board and also let the villagers feel being part of the ongoing project.

At my home village, Njawara, a group organized itself and formed a pioneering committee to formally ask the Alkalo (village head/mayor) and the people of Toro Bahen village to donate the earmarked land between it and Njawara for the sole purpose of establishing the Manding Medical Centre on it.

The land issue was partially cleared by the first week of the appeal. In October 1992, Alkalo Omar Koi Bah of Toro Bahen, along with alhaj Musa (Njabi) Bah and Sirimang Bah called my brother, Doudu Ceesay, the elders of Toro Bahen and I to officially inform us that the earmarked land of two plots have been donated to me for the sole purpose of erecting a medical center and hospital facility for the villagers of the region and Gambia.

We thanked him for his foresight and kindness towards future generations. I went back to my lawyer, Ousainu Darboe who by then had finished all work needed for the registration of Manding Medical Centre. We are forever indebted to Alkalos Omar Koi, Arfang Bah, Musa (Njambi) Bah and resident Sirimang Bah, and the people of Toro village. Lastly but not the least our venerable able lawyer Mr. Ousainou Darboe, without whose kindness and legal mind the registration of Manding Medical Centre would have taken longer that it did assisted me.

I also express profound gratitude to the Chief of Lower Badibou district, Kitabou Singateh; the commissioner, and the local district authority for their understanding and willingness to contribute positively towards our goal and growth.

I submitted the registration application material to the Attorney General's Chambers at the Justice Department, Banjul, on October 22, 1992 and Manding Medical Centre was officially registered as an incorporated charitable organization under the companies Act, 1959 by the 27th of October 1992.

Manding Medical Centre' certificate of incorporation is number: 224/1992. With the completion of the paper work and registration of the center, I embarked on a blitz of letter writing informing philanthropists and organizations world wide about Manding Medical Centre and the need for assistance or donations of medications, equipments, medical videos with which to teach our cadre and villagers to become health worker or evangelist, or nurses and to help us build the center. To complete the establishment process, after the land was officially ours, I wrote to the following letter to the Ministry of Health informing them of the formation of Manding Medical Centre, a self –help health organization at Njawara, Lower Badibou, North Bank Division, the Gambia. Our temporal address was at 5B Ingram Street in Banjul, capital of the Gambia.

Manding Medical Centre

5B Ingram Street

Banjul, The Gambia

March 2, 1993

Permanent Secretary

Ministry of Health

The Quadrangle

Banjul, The Gambia

West Africa

Dear Permanent Secretary

Re: Application for the establishment of a Medical Centre at Njawara in the North Bank.

We are pleased to bring to attention the setting up of a self-help Health organization in the North Bank Division at Njawara village. The directorates and members of the organization would be more than grateful if the Ministry of Health would allow us establish Manding Medical Centre at Njawara village, Lower Badibou District of the Gambia.

Manding Medical Centre, when fully operational, will provide medical, surgical, gynecological and obstetrics, Pediatrics and other facilities to the villagers. It will also help ease the shortage of medical facilities in that region. Manding Medical Centre will have health education secessions in the villages as an effort to enlighten our youths.

Again, thank you for taking time to consider our application and we certainly look forward to a positive recognition of the need for such a center in the rural sector of the Gambia.

I am anxiously waiting to hear from your office at your convenience. Regards

Yours sincerely

Dr. Alhasan S. Ceesay, MD

Director/Coordinator

Meanwhile the villagers grew more enthused and throngs of them attended our monthly health field trips or clinics. The attendance grew so large that we ended up listing the villages to attend in turn of nine villages per trip. This usually totals to a bit above 1,000 patients at a given visit.

I normally go on weekends with three doctors and at times four volunteer doctors along with Nurses aid Mrs. Mbee Sonko and Ida Njie to assist us do the job. The field trips/clinics start with an announcement by Radio Gambia giving the names of villages expected to attend and at which village health center.

The clinic day starts with an early morning breakfast by the team and then a ride to the village health center where we would find the villagers and their sick ones assembled. Every occasion starts with the offering of prayers and then the various village heads, in attendance help us in organizing the flow of people wanting to be see by one of our team doctors.

In most cases the day goes trouble free but at certain localities the political tension does make it very difficult to have such large groups of people without little arguments. Thanks to the Commissioner (s) for deploying the police or making them available to quell trouble and help us maintain order during these clinics.

Commissioner Lamin Koma can tell you how rough things can be at some of these clinic centers. He was trapped in one of these bad moments of people rushing to be in the front line of the queue to see one our doctors.

The Ministry of Health finally sent us the following affirmative reply as thus: -

Ministry of Health & Social services

The Quadrangle

Banjul, The Gambia

Ref.P510/289/01(95)

Dr. Alhasan Ceesay

Manding Medical Centre

5B Ingram Street

Banjul, The Gambia

RE: Application to establish a Medical Centre at Njawara

I acknowledge receipt of your letter of the 2nd March 1993 on the above-mentioned subject. I wish to inform you that this Ministry has no objection to your application to establish Manding Medical Centre at Njawara.

This initiative is in line with our national health policies and we would render our support in our joint efforts to improve the health of the people.

Signed: N. Ceesay

For Permanent Secretary

After several more field trips it was suggested we apply for a None Governmental Organization (NGO) status. It was believed that if we become and NGO, help would come our way quicker.

I went to work on this suggestion and arranged for Tango Secretariat Centre to send one of the United Nations voluntary program officers to come and evaluate our performance relative to the objectives of Manding Medical Centre.

This was accepted and a field trip was set up for September 12 to 22, 1995. Radio Gambia made the announcement well ahead of the time for our arrival and the following was the outcome of that august gathering of September 21 &22, 1995.

Dr. Alhasan S. Ceesay, MD

Dr. Ceesay and wife Fatou Koma-Ceesay

Chapter 14

TANGO SECRETARIAT TRIP REPORT ON MANDING MEDICAL CENTRE, SEPTEMBER 21 – 22, 1995

A field trip to Kerewan at the North Bank Division was organized by the Manding Medical Centre Executive Director Dr. Alhasan S. Ceesay in conjunction with Tango Secretariat Centre to see the organization's activities and meet the members before recommending the organization as a member of Tango.

On September 21, 1995, two meetings were organized in two big centers where members gather to air their views and experience from the organization. Alkalos, chiefs, imams, women, men and youths attended these meetings. The key leadership from five villages in their speeches showed interest and support for the project and organization.

Alkalo of Toro Bahen Omar Koi and chiefs donated the land for the constructing of Manding Medical Centre, the hospital and its ancillaries. The two meeting were highly attended and successful.

The Tango (UNV) program officer Mr. Muloshi on behalf of Tango gave a keynote speech on Tango's operations and activities as an umbrella organization and urged members to work hand in hand with the organization in their efforts to develop their villages and North Bank area. The three meetings with the commissioner during the field trip on our courtesy call were successful and encouraged the executive Director of Manding Medical Centre, Dr. Alhasan Ceesay, to cooperate with the strict, especially the commissioner who is one of the advisors in the local committee.

The commissioner thanked Tango for making the purpose of the mission clear to him and promised that he will try by all means to cooperate with Tango in the area of Technical advice and institution capacity building. Clinic day was organized on September 22, 1995 at Njawara and 150 people attended and got treatments.

RECOMMENDATION

Looking at the caliber of leadership and development activities compared to some NGO tango members in comparison to Manding Medical Centre, the organization need consideration since they have already activities with a promising future.

Looking at the composition of the Board, they have people with a great vision. They have strong membership and backup at the grassroots levels. The organization has chosen to do what is right at the right time and their concentration in one area is vital and a good starting point.

Any success achieved by any organization depended on good leadership and discipline. Manding Medical Centre has quality leadership and deserves NGO status.

Signed: M. Muloshi

UNV Program Officer

We were delighted by the recommendation made by the United Nations voluntary Program Officer in the Gambia. We redoubled our efforts to contact organizations seeking help worldwide. In between letters and monthly field trips to different select health centers we were blessed with visits from interested friends and groups or representatives of similar organizations in the globe.

I had several telephone calls to Dr. Edward Brown, an official of the World Bank in Washington, D. C. responsible of the bank's health affairs at the time. He was very receptive and had several added discussions with Dentist Melvin George, then Director of Medical and Health Service for the Gambia, on how the bank could help in the financing of the building of Manding Medical Centre.

These talks went on well and Dr. Edward brown gave me his promise and personal commitment to helping the project and that we have to start in a small scale and the building will have to be done in several well planned phases.

Dr. Sidi C. Jammeh, a former Armitage School colleague, promised to help me by constantly reminding Dr. Brown of the need to help us with the project. This kept the momentum at the World Bank alive for Manding Medical Centre.

Among our guest were a couple from Colchester, Essex, UK, Lorna V. Robinson and husband Keith Robinson were very impressed by our project and enthusiasm of the ordinary villagers about Manding Medical Centre.

They fell in love with the idea and objectives of the self-help health organization and promised to help as much as they could. We had by this time submitted application for NGO status and ACCNO Secretary replied thus:

ACCNO Secretariat

Dept. of Community Development

13 Mariner Parade

Babjul, The Gambia

September 12, 1994

Ref.CD/ACCNO/Vol3/(183)

Dr. Alhasan S. Ceesay

Director/Coordinator

Manding Medical Centre

P. O. Box 640

Banjul, The Gambia

Dear Sir,

RE: application for an NGO status within the ACCNO framework

Please find enclosed a self-explanatory letter from the Ministry for local government and lands concerning the approval of your application for NGO status. ACCCNO Secretariat congratulates your organization for successfully completing the registration process and wishes you a fruitful relationship in the field of development.

Thank you for your cooperation

Yours Faithfully

Musu Ngujo

For: ACCNO desk Officer

Cc: file & R/File

Replies from our worldwide appeal letters did not pour in money nor did these materialized beyond promises to help in due course.

Hence, I decided to open up a pharmacy at my expense at my residence in the Bundung area of Serekunda using the proceeds from its sales to finance the health field trips and activities of the organization.

This meant spending an extra three to fours at the pharmacy daily after eight hours at the RVH before rejoining my family. All drugs used for the treatment of patients at our field trip clinics were purchased from sales I made at the Bundung Pharmacy.

A local agency, known as IBAS, lent me D8000, interest free, which was used in buying drugs and paying for transportation for the project's activities. The loan was completely repaid well ahead of the allowed sixteen months period given by IBAS. We are obliged and grateful to Aja Ndey Oley Jobe and management of IBAS for their kindness to assist us at the time.

Just when things were about to be financially complete for us to start the first phase of building the various sections of the hospital, came the unexpected coup d'etat of July 22, 1994. The reaction from would be our donors and supporters or sponsors were swift and equally unexpected.

All those who were considering giving the project a chance sited likelihood of sudden national unrest and instability as reasons for their withdrawal of promised aid and participation while some suggested my waiting until after the transition phase of the coup d'etat before they would reconsider reopening our files with them. Again it resorted to legend or case of the chicken the egg, which came first as no one, knew when the transition would end and we kept our fingers crossed hoping that daylight will be ours in not far distance.

It was a severe blow to our hope and for getting the type of interest and support that was engendered for Manding Medical Centre would be difficult to match after such crisis that occurred in the Gambia. Many were acting in conjunction with their governments, which were not sure of what the future under military rule would be for the Gambia.

All prospective and possible international sources earmarked for Manding Medical Centre were either frozen or evaporated into thin air with the coup leaving me floating in the middle of the ocean of despair without a life jacket except God's merciful hands.

I knew the villagers would grow restless if nothing happens in the direction of building the center. I called an emergency general meeting with members from most of the villages and told them of the new challenge and development and this information not only fell on deaf ears but left their spirits dampened.

Interest waxed and waned at some quarters but I kept on trying my best not to be despondent like the others have shown. I kept the organization alive under very limited funds raised from the pharmacy at Bundung until my trip to the UK in January 2000.

Before leaving the Gambia, the Commissioner for north Bank Division and chairman of the local advisory committee for Manding Medical Centre, Mr. Lamin Koma, gave me the following letter to assist me in my fund raising drive while in England and possible other European countries. It read thus:

The Commissioner

Kerewan Village

North Bank Division

The Gambia, West Africa

June 15, 1998

TO WHOM IT MAY CONCERN

I hereby write to testify and confirm that Manding Medical Centre is a self-help health project situated at Njawara village, North Bank Division. As the Commissioner of this division I was elected as the Chairman of the local advisory Committee of the Manding Medical Centre.

As I am concerned, I am aware of this self-help project since it took off the ground, by the able hands of Dr. Alhasan S. Ceesay, a born citizen of Njawara village.

The purpose of the establishing of such a medical centre is to provide medical attention/care to all Gambians irrespective of religion, tribe, nationality or gender and age within the country and sub-region.

It is in these regards that this office writes to seek for your assistance in providing support in cash/kind to make this medical center a reality. I look forward to your continued support and cooperation.

Signed: V. Baldeh

For Commissioner

North Bank Division

The new millennium started with good omen for Manding Medical Centre. I have been invited to go to Europe and America on a found raising trip for the center but could not because of my commitment with the Royal Victoria Hospital (RVH).

I needed a longer vacation period to be able to travel and keep my job at the sane time. Above all my family needed the monetary support, which would fade away if I lost the post at the RVH.

Hence, to my delight and greatest timely occurrence I heard from my long-standing friend in Colchester, Mrs. Lorna V. Robinson, inviting my wife and I to come to the UK to attend the wedding of their younger daughter on

January 9th, 2000. Coincidentally, I had just started my annual leave, which was to finish on the 26th of January 2000. The excitement mounted when we received a fax from the visa officer at the British High Commission in the Gambia requesting that we report to the visa processing office with our passports on Tuesday 8.30 am January 4th, 2000 for processing of our visas for our pending travels to the UK.

This took me by surprise because of the casual way we had discussed the possibility of such a trip. So when we got the telephone call followed by the said fax from the visa section I was caught off guard and had to rush through all the preparations for my wife and I to travel to UK without a second thought on whether adequate arrangements were being made for my eventual pursuit of a postgraduate degree (MRCP) in internal medicine.

Hind side has it that I needed to discuss this aspect with the visa councilor and request for eventual student visa status or leave to remain until my completion of the post graduate degree I wanted to pursue.

Miss Famatanding Ceesay, Daughter

God's ways and timing are best for every occasion. I was yearning to get a way out of the financial limbo the center ran into since the change of government in the Gambia. Now that opportunity was suddenly thrown on my laps by Lorna Robinson's open-ended invitation for my wife and to attend their daughter's wedding ceremony in the UK.

Interested donors started being weary about Military rule and possible restlessness that may ensue. Hence, Manding Medical Centre literally lost all its prospective overseas support as well as sponsors most of who had cold feet after the July coup d'etat of 2004.

I ended up running the center from my meager salary of D1500 or seventy-five pounds sterling per month and of literally hard labor with long hours at a time. The other source was from what little I could make from sales at the Bundung pharmacy.

To cut a long story short we were granted visas to travel to the UK. We left the Gambia on the 6th of January 2000 on a new footing and challenge to bring back some life into Manding Medical center while in England. I got on the ball as soon as the wedding ceremony was over. I obtained a three–year study leave from the Management Board of the Royal Victoria Hospital in Banjul.

This gave me all the time I needed to try to rekindle interest in the center and thereby inject into Manding Medical center cash flow it needed to help us meet or our targeted goal and objective for the farming community in the North Bank Division of the Gambia. It was more like a miracle entering this new concrete and direct ways.

Help from my host Lorna Robinson of Colchester, Essex, UK further anointed my hands. Lorna and I wrote several letters to various places, including celebrities and organizations, most of who replied in the negative because of perception they had about the political climate in Gambia since the coup d'etat of July 22nd 1994.

Nonetheless some hinted being interested at a later date, meaning when the solders return to camp. A few donated small amounts plus hospital items. By now it became clear that we have to counter the perception most, on this side of the isles feel or had about the Gambia at the time.

This dreadful start did not alarm me much for I am fully aware of the wrong information about the average African in the village, who like most, is just a descent human being trying to earn an honest living for himself, family and community.

Villagers are least interested in all the political gimmickry shrouding and clothing their lives. I do not at all blame the rest of world for getting sick and tired of helping and not seeing any tangible good come out of it and worse some African politicians and regimes show no interest in helping move the African people onto better and modern rewarding modalities of life.

They offer more lip service than opening avenues for progress. How many knew that the Ethiopian starvation was politically orchestrated by the then Mangestu regime? Genocide regime and the heartlessness of some African politicians made me feel sick.

To remove any possible skeptics regarding Manding Medical Centre and its objectives we decided to have it registered as a charitable organization in the UK under the name of Colchester Friends of Manding charitable trust. The Robinson knew a solicitor who would be so kind to help us with the legal aspect of the registration process with UK charity Commission.

They spoke to Mr. Bruce Ballard of the Birkett long Solicitors to come to our aid. This kind gentleman, like my lawyer friend, Mr. Ousainou Darboe, gladly agreed to help and sent us a draft of the Trust deed.

After a series of changes were made on the draft he forwarded our request to be registered in the UK as a charitable organization helping its twin partner or parent group, Manding Medical Centre at Njawara village in the Gambia, West Africa. Meanwhile, we concentrated our activities through media campaign effort to call attention to existence of Friends of Manding and their desire in building a hospital for Manding Medical Centre at Njawara, the Gambia.

Again we ran into a very gentle heart in the person of Miss Helen Anderson of Colchester who was the Community website editor for Essex County. She went head over heels regarding the idea of helping others so far away when approached by Lorna Robinson.

Helen thought the idea wonderful and at the same time helped us have our own website and also had an article published by the Evening Gazette which had a large reader circulation.

In the same vein I got the interest of Dr. Linda Mahon-Daly, Dr. Peter Wilson, Dr. Laurel Spooner, Dr. Richard Spooner, Dr. Philip Murray, Dr. Barbara Murray, Dr. Fredric Payne, who by the way was our Medical superintendent under who I worked at the RVH during the later part of colonial Gambia, along with many surgeries in the Colchester area.

These were my Good Samaritans of the day who worked acidulously to make Manding Medical Centre become a reality for the villagers in the Gambia. Dr. Linda Mahon-Daly helped distribute letters about Manding Medical Centre to nearly all her colleagues in the Colchester Borough and so did Dr. Laurel Spooner.

Bless their hearts for kindness and job well done. The news article published by the Evening Gazette brought us another very helpful and kind person, Mr. Malkait singh who is an ophthalmologist and had made several trips to the Gambia before knowing about the Friends of Manding.

He was delighted to join Neville Thompson, Connie Thompson, Lorna Robinson, Keith Robinson, Loenard Thompson, Mark Naylor, Barbara Philips and others as pioneering members of Friends of Manding. Mr. Malkait Singh and I grew to be very good friends and he had since given me lots of personal monetary help to cater for my exams and family back in the Gambia.

I am very grateful for interest and kindness, and concern he showed about my family. A few months after the formation of Friends of Manding, Dr. Laurel Spooner spent a week in the Gambia vacationing and doing some fact finding about the center.

During which time she visited Manding Medical Centre at Njawara in the North Bank Division. The villagers were happy to meet her and thanked her about good work being done in Colchester regarding Manding Medical Centre.

Everyone was happy about the news that people in the UK were poised to assist Manding Medical Centre goes forward in its drive to provide medical aid to villagers. A meeting of member of the Friends of Manding was scheduled for the first week of February 2001.

Mean while our solicitor continued pressing for registration of Friends of Manding, which is the arm and Manding Medical Centre's Colchester branch support group, as charity in the UK.

Dr. Laurel Spooner suggested we start with small-scale form of the center and then gradually expand as funds become available. This consideration would be studied in full and deliberated upon by the committee during the forth-coming February meeting.

Keith, Dr. Ceesay, and Mrs. Lorna Robinson

Miss Binta Ceesay, Daughter

Chapter 15

WHAT IS MANDING MEDICAL CENTRE?

Manding Medical Centre, located at Njawara village in the North Bank Region, Gambia, West Africa, is a self-help village health organization founded by Dr. Alhasan S. Ceesay. Its objective is to provide medical service to the villagers by providing efficient and affordable medical aid to all people in and around the Gambia, especially the rural sector.

We are dedicated to relieving suffering and ensure effective treatment for villagers and all attending Manding Medical Centre at Njawara, NBR.

ESTABLISHED

The Manding Medical Centre is founded by Dr. Alhasan Sisawo Ceesay, a native of Njawara village in 1992, because of sheer shortage of medical service to the region and the preponderance of premature deaths by children from Malaria, malnutrition, diarrhea, and worm infestations.

These childhood maladies account for almost 25% of Gambian children's death before the age of five years. The Gambia Ministry of Health officially recognized the Centre in 1995 and prior to which it became a None Governmental Organization (NGO) on September 12th, 1994.

In addition, the Manding Medical Centre now has Friends of Manding Charitable Trust, Colchester, Essex, UK as its arm and liaison in the UK and the European Union countries. The Friends of Manding is a registered charity in England and Wales. Its registration number is 1088136 since August 21, 2001.

In similar development and purpose, Dr. Avery Aten heads the Friends of Manding Alpena Charitable Trust, Alpena, Michigan, UAS since May 2005.

MISSION STATEMENT

Suffering in another human being is a call to the rest of us to stand in fellowship. It requires us to be there and it is a mystery, which demands the spirit of caring, sharing and our presence.

Our duty as healthcare professionals is providing medical care, which is a fundamental right of all human beings. This village health organization is dedicated to providing medical aid to the rural sector and farming community in the Gambia. It will compliment the health service in the Gambia in addition it will promote preventive medicine in the hinterland of the Gambia.

MEMBERSHIP

Well over twenty thousand villagers, comprising of farmers, village heads, and chiefs, the Kerewan Area Council, Commissioners and local District Authority are now fully active enthusiastic members of Manding Medical Centre. All are welcomed to join the endeavors of the center. People from the rest of the globe are more than welcomed to participate or share with us our dream in bring much needed medical service to people in desperate state because of lack of medical facilities.

ACTIVITIES

Manding Medical Centre tries to alleviate some of the above mentioned health problems and situations by having bimonthly health field trips/clinics to villages teaching them about health, preventive medicine and hygiene that would help reduce the number infected and the vectors responsible for these diseases.

We encourage antenatal and postnatal attendance of clinics by mothers and we treat the sick amongst them with minimum charge to not so elderly and pregnant young ladies.

The service is free to children, the very elderly, and the indigent needing emergency treatment. The rest pay amounts well below tat in private practice. Money accrued is subsequently used to buy drugs with which to treat the patients and for other projects of the center. When in cession the center treats well more than 1000 patients per field trip to the villages.

We provide free information and advisory service on aids and sexually transmitted diseases (STDs) to the young, all patients, their relatives and friends. We also plan to have a Nursing School in due course to augment not only staff but also the government health centers when the need arises.

IMMEDIATE GOAL AND APPEAL

The villagers are very enthused about the center and Toro Bahen village, next to Njawara village, has donated two plots of land for the building of the center and its ancillary units, which is now leased to manding medical center for ninety-nine years. More than 2000 children die tragically from malaria and other childhood ailments stated above for shortage of health services.

We are eager to start building the children' and maternity wings of the proposed Gambia General Hospital at Manding Medical Centre and do need raise the required 900,000 pounds sterling to accomplish our goal.

Ten bags of cement cost thirty pounds sterling or $60 (sixty us dollars). Also we would be most grateful if we could be assisted with medicines and equipment to facilitate our work. Hence we implore you to kindly support our yearning to build the children' and maternity wings of Manding Medical Centre.

We are dedicated to providing medical aid to the villager, especially children. We are investors in people and you are invited to join the endeavors of Manding Medical Centre at Njawara village, the Gambia, West Africa. Help us make a difference and beacon of hope for the villagers. Please give generously.

Today's hope can be tomorrow's reality. We want to contribute positively towards the health services of the Gambia, and with this center in place it will create greater health awareness and privation by the villagers. Cash contributions of any amount should be sent in the name of Manding Medical Centre, to the Friends of Manding charitable Trust, 82 Finchingfield Way, Blackheath, Colchester, Essex, CO2 0AU, and England.

It is vital to be certain that Dr. Alhasan S. Ceesay is informed of your contribution via email thus: alhasanceesay@hotmail.co.uk. Your kindness and humane consideration to help save lives will always be deeply appreciated and grateful for by the villagers, the Gambia and I.

OVERSEASES LINKS

The Friends of Manding in Colchester, Essex County, UK, is formed by a local group of residents, doctors, and nurses who regularly visited the Gambia and is in support of Manding Medical Centre. Manding medical center through the auspices of the Friends of Manding recently received recognition and registration by the UK Charity Commission. They serve as support and our liaison in the Europe Union. The Friends of Manding in behalf of Manding Medical Centre at Njawara has been entered in the central Register of charities with effect from August 21, 2001; the registration number is 1088136 for England and Wales.

Also, a similar charitable trust, the Alpena Friends of Manding Charitable Trust of Michigan, USA, has been established in Alpena, Michigan in June 2006.

It's headed by Dr. Avery Aten a resident physician chairman of the Women and newborn of the Alpena region Community Health along with the medical community of Alpena.

Ntoro Bahen village, Badibou, NBR, The Gambia

Dr. Ceesay & Mohamed Sherrif Azan, kind landlkord 2003

Chapter 16

MANDING MEDICAL CENTRE MILESTONES

Manding Medical Centre has been in my mind's drawing board since the early 1950s but it took off in earnest when I returned to the Gambia, after graduating from medical school in 1992. The Centre is registered as a charity with the Attorney general's Office, Department of Justice, Banjul, The Gambia, since 1993.

The Gambia Ministry of Health also recognized it in the same year. Toro Bahen village, Lower Badibou, NBD, Gambia, donated two huge plots of land for the location of the center in 1993.

Our None governmental (NGO) status was approved in 1994. On September 21, 1995 Tango Secretariat sent a United Nations voluntary program Officer, Mr. Muloshi on field trip to evaluate the organizational and extent of support for Manding Medical Centre at Njawara village.

Mr. Muloshi's recommendation after two days field trip to the region stated thus; "Looking at the caliber of leadership and development activities to some NGO Tango members in comparison to Manding Medical Centre, the organization need consideration since they have already activities with a promising future.

Looking at composition of the Board, they have people with a vision. They have strong membership and backup at grass root levels. The organization has chosen to what is right at the right time and their concentration in one area is vital and good starting point.

Any success achieved by any group or organization depends on good leadership and discipline. Manding Medical Centre has high quality leadership and deserves NGO status."

It was not until my travels to the UK in 2000 that the Friends of Manding Charitable Trust was formed and registered as charity in England and Wales by the UK Charity Commission. Friends of Manding are the extended arm of Manding Medical Centre at Njawara, The Gambia.

They serve as our liaison in the UK and the European Union. Please browse on our website thus: http://friendsofmandinggambimed.btck.co.uk, to learn more or for further information about our work and organization.

We are still on fund raising activities to earn enough to enable us build the children' and maternity units of the hospital at Manding Medical Centre at Njawara. In May 2005, 11 American students and their instructor Mr. Thomas Ray visited Manding Medical Centre at Njawara.

Additionally, input from has now resulted in Alpena City, Michigan, USA, twining by proclamation with Njawara and Kinte kunda villages in Gambia respectively on the 5th of December 2005.

In June 2006, Dr. Avery Aten, Chairman of the Women and Newborn of Alpena Region Health Community along with the medical community of Alpena commenced processing application for a charitable Trust to be named Alpena friends of Manding Charitable Trust, Michigan, USA.

This will soon be finalized and up and running to help Dr. Alhasan Ceesay in the provision of medicine and educational assistance to schools in the Lower Badibou district, the Gambia, West Africa. In August 2008, Dr. Alhasan Ceesay and the Badibou Cultural Dance Troupe will visit Alpena and other cities in Michigan for fund raising drive to enable the building of the Manding Medical Centre children and maternity units at Njawara village.

Dr. Richard Bates, an Obyng, and a number of medical professionals involved in obstetrics and gynecology at Alpena, Michigan joined Manding Medical Centre's crusade on 17/08/07.

Chapter 17

TEMPLATE FOR REGIONAL DEVELOPMENT

Manding Medical Centre became a template for districts elsewhere and villagers to nurture, develop further and handover to the next generation. This None Governmental Health Organization epitomizes a developmental watchtower for the region.

Manding medical center is a pulsating source of hope, jobs training and superb medical service at Njawara village the Gambia. Every one knows that government alone does not move things fast enough. Society must be radical and pragmatic to pitch into its development.

We know all too well that the developed world got where its because private efforts were self prophetic and projects like Manding Medical Centre goes long ways to initiate and stimulate community to work together for a positive agenda for its people.

Hence after many years of foot dragging and vicissitude by society I decided I will build the hospital if I have to single-handed. I worked years receiving no government assistance and without grants from the great of the Gambian community. Manding Medical Centre is a positive good that help our regions to cross the road to a better healthcare delivery.

We thank every one for making it possible that our center became a platform and guide in rejuvenating our regions. We now provide medical service to all Gambians and none Gambians domiciled in the Gambia. We will create more jobs as need arises.

This was the reason why I gave my life's comfort for reward that will benefit most needy villagers. It came through determination and kindness of many people worldwide. There are some things only governments can do but together communities through collective initiatives can achieve at least fifty percent of their developmental needs in addition to government effort.

Today some see Manding medical centre as perpetual monument of good, an honor to the country and a general benefit to villagers and children in the North Bank of the Gambia. Manding medical centre is an inspiration and cause for thankfulness and celebration.

Miss Roheyata Ceesay, Daughter

Chapter 18

AN APPEAL TO INTERNATIONAL COMMUNITY

Dear Readers,

The above information about Manding Medical Centre is included in this work only hoping that it will help spread the word more extensively and draw awareness to a greater community of people and readers of my work.

It's my belief that lots of good people out there may want to participate or give to the cause and goal of the center should they be aware of its existents for the villagers.

Hence, I am appealing for help and participatory support from all able to extend their hearts to make this much needed medical endeavor to come to fruition for the rural sector of the Gambia. Who knows you might even end up coming to bask in our beautiful seaside and relish Gambian generosity.

Music for me is reaching out to help others and my patients are yearning for your kind participation and donation in cash/kind. Thanks a million for considering our appeal. God blesses your heart(s).

I write with believe that by it money can be generated to provide a much needed medical service to the rural sector. Writing about the Manding Medical Centre may course some Good Samaritan and any wanting to leave foot prints on the sand of time for a good cause to come to our assistance to help us meet the goals of the center at Njawara village, the Gambia, West Africa. My head, heart and soul are devoted to my family, the Gambia and Manding Medical Centre.

It is not a God given calling but a mere conviction that our rural folks deserve better health service than currently available and hence human calling to want to contribute positively to bring resolution of some of our rural health service inadequacies.

I never had an angel come down to me nor have I ever heard the voices of God saying, "Ceesay, you must do so and so" as many mocked Manding Medical Centre emanated from sheer conviction that it is a dutiful way of doing the right thing for curbing premature deaths of children before reaching 5 years of life from malaria, water born diseases, and warm infestations; and in the same vein providing both pre and postnatal care to the pregnant.

Hence, portions of proceeds of sales in all my work go to help meet the center's operational costs and in providing scholarship to indigent indigenous rural candidates due course return to serve rural Gambia wishing to read for a medical degree or agriculture and Medicine.

Signed: Dr. Alhasan S. Ceesay, MD/Email: alhasanceesay@hotmail.com

Chapter 19

LORNA ROBINSON, AN ANGEL OF MERCY

Keith, Dr. Ceesay, & late Lorna Robinson

There are certain moulds God broke them moments after He finished making them. Mrs. Lorna V. Robinson was one of these unique, caring, sharing and rare angels of mercy. Mrs. Lorna Robinson and I met through her job as general nurse at the then Essex County General hospital in Colchester, Essex County in 1990, when I was a trainee doctor at the hospital.

She and husband Keith Robinson became my friends as far back as in the 1990s and one of their annual pilgrimages is visiting my family in the Gambia, West Africa. This benevolent couple has since been my Colchester if not my England.

Together we set to catch a dream of providing medical aid and service to Gambian villagers. I left at the end of my training to serve my country in 1992. In December 1999 Mrs. Lorna Robinson sent an invitation for my wife and I to attend wedding of Miss Fiona Robinson, her younger daughter, to gentleman Reeves.

We have since 2000 worked acidulously to make the above goal come to fruition, especially for those in the rural sector of the North Bank Region of the Gambia. It was Lorna's joint effort with, nurses, Doctors Laurel Spooner, Barbara Murray, Richard Spooner, Phil Murray, Linda Mahon-Daly, Peter R. Wilson, Malkait Singh and residents of Colchester, which lead to the formation of the Colchester Friends of Manding Charitable Trust. It was registered as a charity in England and Wales in 2001. The charity number is 1088136.

This charity acts as liaison in the European Union countries for Manding Medical Centre at Njawara village in the Badibous of the North Bank Region, the Gambia. Since its conception, the Friends of Manding Charitable Trust had busied itself on weekly or bimonthly Gambi-barzaars in an effort to help raise money for building of both the children and maternity units of the center.

Mrs. Lorna Robinson spent countless week-ends either selling material such as toys, coats and anything she could lay her hands on as long as she believes it will generate money for the building of the children and maternity units of the center. She spent most of her retirement time organizing activity for the center to help promote our cause. She sent books, spectacles, pens and pencils along with medication for the center's use.

The influence of this Good Samaritan group in Colchester reverberated and lead to the formation of a similar charity group in America, which is lead by Dr. Avery Aten, Alpena Friends of Manding Charitable Trust, Michigan, USA, was formed in May 2005.

All this came about because Mrs. Lorna V. Robinson, the lady of mercy behind the wheel, would not rest while the indigent goes without the most basic things in life. Here is how Lorna views her part during one of many conversations we had about the need to share worth and ourselves with other less fortunate than us.

She simply said, "Ceesay, I feel delighted and warm at heart in helping others, like the villagers. I strongly belief good used could be made from my work and experience I had at the NHS over years. I will try to recruit as many retired nurses to our cadre as long as they listen to my please.

The other secrete is that such activity keeps me young, participating and contributing to the needy. I feel alive and forever growing. In life we most extend our hearts to others and with compassion reach the needy."

This tit bit tells about the unselfish nature of Mrs. Lorna V. Robinson who through the years since her retirement gave her all to help others, especially the villagers, breath a sigh of relief and to have hope and knowledge that someone far away they never met cared about them.

Lorna continued saying, "It brings joy to my heart when I share the little I have with the needy. It helps to uplift the despondent. Millions suffer needlessly for not having means of proper health care, clean and safe water, good shelter and chance to attend schools. I want to help you get the villagers from a downward spiral of deepening health deprivation.

I certainly take hope in people like you and your stand to help your folks back home in the Gambia." It was this unique caring angel that I lost on the third of March 2010 for she returned peacefully to her maker on this day. The above was my Lorna and now I cry, when shall we be blessed will another like her? Losing Lorna Robinson left me feeling that I lost the best person, outside of my family, I ever known.

She was a kind soul of unswerving determination to share the little She had with the little guy needing her help. She stood by my cause in thick and thin moments of my stay in the United Kingdom.

Dr. Alhasan S. Ceesay graduating from the American University of the Caribbean, West Indies, 1992

The provision of medical care to villagers is more than a responsibility; it is a sacred trust for me. I will not the villagers or memory Mrs. Lorna V. Robinson down because I believe in looking to the well being of the less fortunate. One carries on trying on reflecting on all the children and villagers who need this health care. Hence no trepidation will hold me back.

My family, the villagers and I miss and deeply mourn her premature departure from mother earth. May she rest in peace with her maker and may we the living without fail or fear able to follow the high shining examples of indefatigable Good Samaritan she was in life. I hope you will join me to keep her memory and legacy alive for other to copy while we continue taking medical aid to villagers in rural Gambia. Lorna V. Robinson thanks a million and goodbye for now.

Signed: Dr. Alhasan S. Ceesay, MD

Manding Medical Centre, Njawara

The Gambia, West Africa. E-mail: alhasanceesay@hotmail.com

Ishfaque Ahmed, Dr. Alhasan Ceesay & Yusuf Mohamed

Chapter 20

MY SAMARITAN MEN OF GOOD WILL

Every successful person had Samaritan angels who Offered their shoulders for him or her to stand on and see further than most. Compiled herein are my Samaritan men of goodwill. Hence, I beg leave to indulge in a bit of sentimentality about a few rare human angels who played major part in today's success and help for my villagers. Believe me their moulds, as you will soon find, are beyond those of simple people.

These men help me reach today's pedestal. In medicine for the villager, I profiled ladies who championed my cause. Now, bear with me for just a few lines on the Samaritan men of goodwill. They like the previously mentioned ladies al not only believe in my dream and objective for the villager but also gave all they could to help make that dream come to fruition.

These men gave unparalleled needed help and friendship to me when I was distressed and in utter despair and darkness. Some even shed a few tears with me because the pain and set back certain roadblocks caused my goal. One of these was the day I received GMC' e-mail of the 17th June 2008 recanting recognition of my primary medical qualification based on frivolous website enter.

Hell brewed to its hottest temperatures, as it took time to unravel the misunderstanding, before GMC rectified the error. However, with your indulgence let us start from the beginning of the geneses.

It was with God' anointing hand in conjunction with Sisawo Bajo Ceesay, alias Sisawo Salah) that my twin partner I landed on this Garden of Eden. Father gave us love and good guidance throughout his life with us. He and I had deferent perception about western Education and culture but we reconciled after my completing primary school at Kinte Kunda.

My father's experience from the hands of colonials made him never to entertain idea of his progeny deviating from the farmers' mold. Nor would he allow me pursue Western Education and ideology, which at the time was alien to my father and his peers.

He once told me: Son, my wish for you is to be a hard working good farmer and not indulge in the quagmire and sleaze world of spin-doctors. I do not want you tinkering with ideology that would infuse into you wrong philosophies about life and God.

My father came from a different generation with totally different perceptions about invaders ruling them. Let us for a moment step into their shoes to find out why the resistance for their progeny to attend school.

In my father's days men believed in God, the sanctity of life and peaceful coexistence of the communities they lived. About the invading longhaired men he calls devils, father said: "Son the way these men, meaning the colonialist, took over our countries can only be the work of the devil.

They came from the blue sea and seized our land and minerals, and remaining on the best parts while leaving us the worst places to farm and for our animals to grace. To pour oil on fire they requested that we change our religions and ways to their dark and indiscipline life styles.

To top up, our people were forced to live under laws promulgated by the invaders on top of which we must pay to learn their languages while they make systemic concerted efforts to distorted and destroy everything that was dear to us.

They massacred, disgraced, and dethroned all our kings and chiefs. These shameful acts were reinforced with policies of divide and rule by pitting tribe against tribe and even bribing those bad elements willing to do their dirty work.

Wages paid to workers were not worth the coin they were minted on. They made certain no organization, political or professional civil service existed in our countries." He said, "They filled the jails with those of us who refused to be indoctrinated or accept the supremacy of the foreign invaders. So Son, because of kindheartedness and gentled nature of the African our ways are undermined and thrown out by invaders who replaced it with greed, unkindness, spin-doctoring, and lack of respect for man and nature.

He concluded by saying, these are just a few reasons why I would not let my blood attend school". The above is a pinhole view of father's radicalism and patriotic views. He did recap late later in his old age and finally gave full blessings to my efforts and future goals.

He passed away peacefully to his maker in 1991 while I was a trainee doctor doing my clinical clerkship rotation at Colchester General Hospital in Colchester, Essex County, England. Notices no matter how simple were just bundles of scribbles on worthless paper to the farmer. The illiterates who cannot decipher the prints are cheated of their rights and land.

I was not going to be among those who cannot decipher the print and hence found my way to Kinte Kunda Primary School where I met with the head Master, Mr. Louis Albert Bouvier, who hales from Banjul, our capital city.

This benevolent teacher was my first real contact with Western Education and we gelled instantly and became inseparable. He allowed me to stay at his home and treated me as his own son. He was kind and firm and wasted no time teaching me about life and on how to compete without strangulating the competitor.

Dr. Alhasan S. Ceesay, MD holding Africa

He told me repeatedly that competition was a healthy fund and stressed that one must be honest and have integrity and tolerance in life. He counseled hard work at everything one did.

Above all, it was incumbent on me to have faith and to serve God daily, if not more but never less. Also he allowed me all the freedom a growing child needed without pampering me.

He did lay certain straightforward and simple rules for me. I was to study at a designated time, return home in time whenever I went into town, unless given an extension by him, and to be in bed by 10:00 pm, with lights off whether sleepy or not. He insisted that I perform my five daily prayers as expected of my religion even though he was devoured Catholic.

Mr. Bouvier would only help with my homework when he felt that I have done my best at it and that I was not trying to have him do the work. Otherwise, he would let me go and make a fool of myself before the class before I deserve his coveted help. Hash you think but this strict beginning or treatment, as you would call it, made me do well at school and do things with confidence independently at very tender age.

I remain profoundly grateful to Mr. Louis Albert Bouvier for being educational springboard, for being a sincere and true friend and mentor. Something said by Francis Farmer summed up the relationship between L. A. Bouvier and me. She said, "To have a good friend is the purest of all God' gifts, for it is a love that has no exchange of payments.

It is not inherited, as with family. It is not compelling, as with a child. And it has no means of physical pleasures, as with a mate. It is, therefore, an indescribable bond that brings with it a far deeper devotion than others."

Mr. L. A Bouvier continued to help and mold my academic life until when I started Armitage School in 1957. Leaving a friend like Mr. Bouvier was difficult and emotional for both of us. We have become one and are now to say farewell and perhaps separate forever.

He prepared me well but like any parent or true friend he worried about the difficulties that lay ahead. I just wished they had transferred him with me to Armitage. On the day I boarded the land rover to Armitage tears rundown Mr. Bouvier's cheeks and mother turned her head away to hide her own.

L. A. Bouvier was my best friend, after the loss of my twin brother, fate had it that I was now about to be far away from all I knew and loved. Mr. L. A. Bouvier kept cautioning me to, "keep your head up and do your school works. You have never been a failure, and even if such a sad experience occurs, keep trying over and over to overcome it.

We send you to Armitage with prayers, pride and above all with our deepest love. May God keep you in good health. Goodbye, Mr. Ceesay." It was very moving for this was the first time he addressed me as Mr. Ceesay. We boarded the Land Rover and as it started to move Bouvier followed for some distance exhorting me not to fear to ask for help when need arose.

He kept saying he would gladly help or would ask my parents to pitch in whenever possible. Mr. L. A. Bouvier and I kept in touch despite the distance poor mail service of those days. The link continued while I was in the USA. I lost my friend in a motorcar accident, six year before returning from America in 1974.

His vehicle is said to have ran off the road went over a hill. Another part of me went with him. The evil that men do lives after them and the good is interred with their bodies.

Well rest assured that L. A. Bouvier's good deeds did remain alive and intact on earth. At Armitage it was a newly qualified teaches from Kaur, Mr. Keko B. A. Manneh, who then doubled as our class' English and Mathematic teacher that filled in gap left by my leaving L. A. Bouvier at Kinte Kunda.

He was soft-spoken Chaucerian, a nickname we gave him because he crammed the entire work of Chaucer. He too loved me and was a good guide at Arbitrage. I am grateful for encouragement and help he gave and for really being there when I needed an honest person to open up to about difficulty or academic aspiration.

I left for New York on the 24 August 1967 and arrived at Alpena Michigan 1:30 Am on the 25 August 1967. Mr. Henry V. Vali, a counselor and foreign student advisor at Alpena Community College, was at the bus station to pick me.

After the formality of welcoming to Alpena he drove me to 251 Washington Avenue the home of Mr. Howard Riggs where it had been agreed I stay until start of the semester in September before moving to Russell Wilson Hall at the Alpena Community College campus. Not surprising Mr. Vali and I became friends and remained so ever since.

Mr. Howard Riggs and family welcomed me home as late as it was on that glorious day when I set foot in Michigan. They were all delighted to have me in their lovely home and they gave me princely meal to nourish my body and milk to quench my thirst.

Howard owned Ice-Cream Pallor down Town. He was very modest, delightful man and above all a very generous person. Soon Mr. and Mrs. Riggs became mom and dad through out my American stay for their overwhelmingly kind people deserving such salutation from a poor villager.

Howard's warmth and generosity to other made his family unique company to foreign students coming to Alpena. The Riggs were the ideal Americans to me.

They were average working family who readily shared the little bit God gave them with others less fortunate. I remained grateful to these kind-hearted friends. Mr. Vali and Mr. Thomas Rither, Director of Foreign students at Alpena Community College, and I met several time to discuss my financial nightmare.

Mr. Rither was too concerned that the college might face INS censor if he allowed my staying without a sponsor or means to pay fees and cater for myself. He was adamant and made it very clear to me that failure to get help for the first semester will leave him with no other option but to advise the immigration to consider deporting proceedings against me.

He gave a week ultimatum for me to sort things out before our next meeting 18 September 1967. Copies of letters from my future sponsor, Mr. Isdor Gold, never move or evoke sympathy from him as he epidermises a true inelastic bureaucrat.

Mr. Henry V. Vali convinced Mr. Thomas Rither to hold on while get in touch with some residents about my case. He was on the telephone to different would be possible sympathizers to my cause.

Most of who agreed to contribute toward the cost of my first semester at Alpena Community College. Vali also spoke to the president of the college in my behalf to prevent Mr. Rither from hastily and unilaterally contacting the INS for frivolous fears in his head. My plight soon became a house whole affair and many residents pitched in to help resolve the case.

The appeal by Mr. Henry Valli and Mrs. Viola Glennie snowballed letting me start my first semester at Alpena Community College, Alpena, Michigan. Fr. John miller at St. Bernard Rectory in Alpena not only lent me $250 but evangelized my state in every sermon for three weeks netting me much needed financial help.

God bless his heart. He left Alpena before my transfer to Olivet College in Olivet Michigan in 1979. Judge Philip Glennie was head of the 26th circuit Court of Michigan at the time. His wife, Mrs. Viola Gennie, was professor of foreign language at Alpena Community College.

Both not only contributed substantial amounts towards my tuition but also became my adopted parents in Alpena. They continued to link with me like wise support my goal until their return to heaven in the late nineties.

I remember these friends with joy mingled with sadness that they are not here to share reward they showed but also I remember them with intense gratitude for role and kindness shown me while a student at Alpena Community College, Alpena, Michigan, USA.

In another vein Alpena Community College gave me part time job at the Library and a summer job at the Salmon

Experimental Fish hatchery. Thanks to grand efforts of Mr. Henry V. Vali and residents of Alpena I was able to overcome the financial crisis of my first semester at the college.

I met Mr. Cloyd Ramsey while seeking a summer job at the Medical Arts Clinic in Alpena. He was then manager of the unit at the time. Upon hearing my plight he promised to see what he could do even though the clinic itself had no jobs openings for that summer. I left him impressed and very moved by what he heard.

He too became an integral part of my time and sojourner in America than any through contributions and loans he took from the Alpena bank in my behalf to support my studies throughout my stay in the USA and short stay in Liberia, West Africa.

It was through kindness of Mr. Ramsey and his sponsorship that enabled Michigan Technological University at Houghton to accept me do a Masters program in Biological Sciences from 1971 to 1973.

Mrs. Rasheen Ahamed, Punjab Collection Shop

L – R: Dr. Alhasan Ceesay, Prof. Sulayman Nyang, Mr. Clloyd Ramsey and Prof. Francis Conti

It was Mr. Cloyd Ramsey who came to my rescuer when things went very bad and unbearable and practically unsafe for me after the military coup d'etat against William Tolbert' administration of Liberia in 1981. He provided a round trip Air ticket to the USA and supporting it with invitation for me as their guest at Sandusky, Michigan December 1981.

The invitation secured me a B-2 Visa to Detroit, Michigan. I arrived in New York 1:15 pm 20 December 1981. I prayed on disembarking and I was grateful and thankful to God and Cloyd Ramsey having set foot once more on US soil. I thank Cloyd ceaselessly in my heart for having helped me escape to America despite the ignominy of being in exile and to seek asylum soon.

I caught my flight to Detroit, Michigan around 3:45 pm same day. The Ramseys were at the Detroit Metropolitan International arrivals terminal waiting to receive me. They must have noted the fatigue in my face, if not the sorrow of leaving my beloved Gambia and people behind for an indefinite time.

They welcomed me graciously and we headed for Sandusky, a small village in Michigan. I therein and then became part of the Ramsey family. Life has it that when some of us were created the mould broke. Most give their time and money to their own families or to work that brings them some happiness and some money.

Cloyd Ramsey is among a few who give themselves wholly and unselfishly to others. I can never be able to repay or tell how devoted Ramsey is in sharing life with the needy unless you meet him. In brief, Mr. Ramsey and wife Narrate fed and sheltered me when I needed food and place to stay until I get my feet back on earth.

He was my salvation voice in the wilderness of life's rugged road. I stayed as their guest in Sandusky until it was time to seek asylum at the Immigration and Nationality Service (INS) in Detroit. There was no other situation less tense and so empty of hope than this next phase in my life.

Life became an abyss of despair which only God and good friends, like the Ramseys, pulled me out from underneath. Shakespeare said, "Between the acting of a dreadful thing and the first motion; All the interim is like a phantasm, or a hideous dream. The genius and mortals instruments like to a little kingdom, suffers then the nature of an insurrection."

Indeed an insurrection has been going on in my head during those horrible days of the coup d'etat of April 15th 1980 I became aware of the need to muster courage, strength and endurance to prepare myself for the coming exile days and form it may take. Again, Mr. Ramsey contacted the Gambia several time to no avail to verify and correct a possible misunderstanding that may have occurred. Several friends and legislators Ramsey contacted advised that I seek asylum from the INS. Senator Carl Levin sent us a package of three copies of Form 1-589 for my use on 6th January 1982. We took the bull by the horns, completed the forms and Ramsey and I proceeded to INS office at Mount Elliot Street, Detroit, Michigan on the 22nd February 1982, were I was subsequently interviewed separately and told action will be rendered in four months earliest.

If wishes were horses beggars would gallop to heaven for it took well more than eight months before any reply came and only after numerous INS court hearings did we get some semblance of partial positive direction. The final act was left with the State Department and vice president's office.

Things were so delayed and difficult that I asked Ramsey to take me to the Catholic Mission for me to seek Sanctuary or more public help and support. We landed at St. Paul's' Cathedral, Diocese of Michigan, where Hugh Davis led me to the refugee office of the Diocese.

On hearing my story the refugee co-ordinator, Mrs. Patricia Koblinsky called rev. Hugh C. White, advisor to then reigning Bishop of the Diocese, Bishop Coleman Mcgehee Jr. The Diocese received and let me stay at 44 Ledyard Street in Detroit.

In the mean time Ramsey sent the following appeal to the INS office at Mount Elliot in Detroit, Michigan:

TO WHOM IT MAY CONCERN

This letter is to acknowledge my association with Alhasan Ceesay, over a period of fifteen years. During that time I have found him to be a young man of very high ideals. His only interest in life has been to obtain an education and return to serve his home country and help his people.

I have personally invested thousands of dollars in Alhasan Ceesay because it seemed to me to be a very efficient way to help the impoverished people from his country that has had a great deal less than I have.

If anyone were to follow the course of his life, he would see that his motives most certainly were not to simply escape the futility of his home country and live that, good life here. There is no doubt in my mind that the dangers that he describes do exist for him.

Even if these were less than perfect proof, would you like to take the chance of being wrong and find out that he had been imprison or worse killed for no reason at all? Please save this man. If you cannot do it for his sake, then consider the investment made by concerned individuals, other organizations and myself. Thank you for your serious considerations of this matter.

Signed: Cloyd Ramsey, Sandusky, Michigan, USA

My next Alpena Samaritan and brother in Chris as well as profession was Dr. Charles T. Egli, who I met almost about the same time I did with Ramsey. He was a Surgeon working for the Medical Arts Clinic at the time of our meeting. He came into the radar after a speech I gave to the Alpena Medical Association.

He too has contributed prominently and was instrumental in having the medical Association comes to my aid with a donation of $400 towards my second semester fees at Alpena Community College.

By this miracle I was able to complete payment for the second semester at college. Charles, as he prefers being called, is a surgeon and devoted Christian who also became very close friend and had done a lot to encourage my efforts.

His rallying for assistance continued through out his days at the Medical Arts Clinic. For you to note Dr. Egli's closeness here is a letter he sent in my behalf during my petitioning for asylum in the USA. It read:

Medical Arts Clinic

Alpena, Michigan

November 14, 1986

RE: Deportation Notice on Alhasan Ceesay

Dear Senator Levin,

Alhasan Ceeesay was a college student in Alpena many years ago when I first met him and was very much impressed by his sincerity and enthusiasm. He went onto graduate school at Michigan Technological University in Houghton, Michigan, in hopes of getting into medical school.

He tried very hard to get into medical school in Africa. He was receiving no support from his own country because it considered him a political agitator and tribalist. Alhasan Ceesay on his own initiative was able to get into medical school in Monrovia Liberia and succeeded in taking two years medical education before he fled for safety to the USA. He later sought political asylum in the USA for fear of persecution due to the aftermath of an attempted coup in July 181.

It has always been his desire to complete his medical training and return to the Gambia when the climate warrants. For almost five years now, Alhasan has been trying to receive asylum, during which time his chances at medical school are affected.

Most recently he received a letter from INS judge ordering his deportation. The deportation of Alhasan Ceesay back to the Gambia would result in his certain death or imprisonment and would constitute another tragedy in the way our government handles people like Alhasan.

In a country where there are so many illegal aliens it seems that there must be some place for one more refugee. I beg you to personally consider Alhasan's case.

Sincerely

Dr. Charles T. Egli, MD

Mr. Homer Shepard, resident of Flint Michigan, was also very kind to me while at Flint. He offered to lodge me during the summer of 1969 on securing a full time job at the St. Joseph Hospital on Flint, Michigan as nurse assistant.

Homer and wife offered to help defray rent expenses, which were taking a quarter of my earnings. With this help I was able to return to Alpena Community College at the end of the summer and pay my dorm and food bills and still had some pocket money to buy pens and other sundries during the semester.

God blesses his heart. We lost contact since my return to Africa. All letters to his address were redirected, as addressee no longer leaves here. Bishop Coleman Mcgehee had already blessed efforts of the hastily formed CEESAY COMMITTEE.

It became the Adhoc committee and my Pegasus wing. Like any normal human gatherings we had our different ideas as to how to approach the asylum problem but all of it steered towards or sought better ways to meet the challenges and enigma about to end all that I stood for and worked hard for in life. The brain storming sessions were very pragmatic if not practical and well-intended discussions. One of the exploratory searches for solutions led us to Mayor Harvey Sloan of Louisville, Kentucky.

I met Mayor Sloan in 1976 when I was trying to get into medical school at the University of Louisville. Also we used to write each other while I was in Monrovia, Liberia, West Africa. I was invited to his office early February 1983, and was given opportunity to talk with key aids at the Louisville City Hall while he attended other state affairs.

His executive aids, Sharon Wilbert and Mrs. Blanche reviewed my case along with information already in my file open in my name. They concluded that I did deserve help and I was asked to speak to Mrs. Joyce J. Rayzer, Director, and Health Affairs for the Mayor.

Joyce contacted the Dean of the Medical School and gave him an in-depth briefing of my background and precarious situation I was faced with. Two weeks later on February 28th 1983, I received the following letter from Joyce in behalf of Mayor Harvey Sloan. It read thus:

Office of the Director of Safety

City Hall

Louisville, Kentucky 40202

28 February 1983

Dear Mr. Ceesay,

It appears, as the old saying goes, that I have good news and bad news. I have been in contact with the University Of Louisville School Of Medicine with regards to your admission at the fall term. I have spoken to Dr. Donald Kemetz, Dean of the Medical School, and Mr. Harold Adams, Special Assistance to the president of the University of Louisville.

Both of these administrators upon reviewing the information you sent me feel that you are a very good candidate for the minority admission program. There is however, one issue, which must be resolved favorably before your admission to medical school, or the financing and packaging necessary to begging this endeavor can be given serious considerations.

The issue, which must be resolved, is the financial determination base on whether you would be granted asylum in the country. Without the asylum being granted and hence financial aid the university cannot proceed with your request for admission this fall because your legal status would be too tenuous for them to invest hard cash in your future medical development under such nebulous state.

It appears that you must begin medical school anew. The two years completed at Liberia, cannot be accepted for transfer. You will start as freshman upon being granted asylum in USA. Again, try and find resolution to granting you asylum. I have been assured that everything that can be done for you will be done immediately upon a favorable notice of your asylum. Every body in the Mayor's office says hello, and we are sending you our prayers.

Sincerely

Joyce J. Rayzer

Director, Health Affairs

This was the impact Mayor Harvey Sloan had. In addition Mayor Harvey Sloan sent the following directly from his desk to the INS pleasing for them to grant me asylum.

City Hall

Office of the Mayor

Louisville, KY 40202

November 7, 1983

Alhasan S. Ceesay of the Gambia has contacted this office in an effort to gain political asylum in other to complete his medical education at the University of Louisville. I know that he is dedicated individual and is more desirous of providing needed medical aid to his fellow man. Mr. Ceesay petitioned for political asylum in February 22, 1982 due to a purge, which followed a failed coup in the Gambia.

The Medical school at the university of Louisville is currently processing his application for the 1984/85 academic years. It would be most helpful if you could assist him in expediting his papers. He will not be admitted unless a written statement confirming his residency status is available.

Since he has already lost two years awaiting residency confirmation, it would be deeply appreciated if you could assist this young man in any way possible. If my staff or I can be any further assistance in the matter, please do not hesitate to contact this office.

Sincerely

Harvey L Sloan

Mayor Louisville

Let us for a moment revert to Bishop Coleman McGehee at the Episcopal Diocese of Michigan in Detroit Michigan. Below is letter sent to the INS director, Edwin Chauvin at Mount Elliot in Detroit, Michigan

Office of the Bishop

4800 Woodward Avenue

Detroit, Michigan 48201

24 October 1983

Dear Mr. Chauvin,

As Bishop for the Episcopal diocese of Michigan, located in Detroit, Michigan, I write you this letter on behalf of Alhasan S. Ceesay, a petitioner for political asylum in the United States.

As you may note from the file Mr. Ceesay seeks political asylum base on his fear of political persecution and danger to his physical safety and well being by the government, were he to be returned by the INS to his country the Gambia.

Mr. Ceesay's life will disclose to you, he was active opponent of the political regime in the Gambia. After protesting incarceration of his friends, Mr. Ceesay was placed on a list of individuals who were allegedly involved in criminal activity and who were involved with the Movement for Justice in Africa (MOJA) and were sought for interrogation by the Gambia government.

The Gambia government has singled our Mr. Ceesay because of his political opposition and has prevented him from continuing his medical education in Liberia by cutting off his financial assistance and by asking the Liberian government to return Mr. Ceesay to the Gambia. I am personally acquainted with Mr. Ceesay, and believe him to be an individual who is worthy of support of the Episcopal Dioceses of Michigan.

I feel that it took great courage for Mr. Ceesay to stand up for human rights and to publicly oppose the political regime in the Gambia. I am convinced that Mr. Ceesay is an altruistic individual who deserves to pursue his medical training to benefit, both in the United States and perhaps elsewhere, those individuals who might be helped by his medical ability.

Mr. Ceesay has already establish his medical science aptitude in his studies at Medical School in Liberia, and he has applied to and been accepted by the School of Medicine at the University of Louisville, Kentucky, with tuition to be paid by that institution, upon his authorization to remain in the United States.

Mr. Ceesay has also sought authorization to engage in employment pending the outcome of his asylum request, he proposes to assist in medical research at the university should his employment authorization be granted by your office.

Therefore, on behalf of Mr. Ceesay as well as the members of my Diocese, I would urge you to give favorable consideration to Mr. Ceesay's petition and expedite his request for employment and his political asylum petition in every possible way so that his efforts to enter the University of Louisville School of Medicine may not be delayed any longer than may be necessary by legal and administrative procedures which you office follows.

Please feel free to contact me if I can be of any assistance in helping you to reach your determination on this matter. I fervently believed that, upon your investigation of Mr. Ceesay's case, you would reach the conclusions that he would be an asset to the United States, and that his fears as to his persecution and personal safety should he return to the Gambia, have firm foundation in fact.

Very truly yours

(The Rt. Rev.) H. Coleman McGehee, Jr.

Bishop of Michigan

The Bishop of Michigan, H. Coleman McGehee followed the above with a letter to then vice president George Bush Sr. Who sent the following tars reply.

The Vice President

Washington, D. C

April 25, 1984

Dear Rev. McGehee,

Thank you for your recent letter concerning Alhasan S. Ceesay. It was thoughtful of you to write and I appreciate your having taken the time to bring Mr. Ceesay's case to my attention.

I have asked the State Department to review all asylum cases and human rights violations, which are brought to my attention. I have, therefore shared your letter and the enclosures with officials at the Department of State and asked that they review Mr. Ceesay's request and write to you directly.

I have also asked that a copy of their response be forwarded to my office. With best wishes

Sincerely

George Bush

Bishop McGehhee, Bishop Mason, Rev. Hugh C. white, Rev. David Brower, Rev. Bill Woods, Rev. Virgil Jones, and Rev. Mark D. Meyer all touched my heart in similar fashions Hence here is my collective feeling and experience in a nut shell about these devoted men of Christ.

All of the priests lived in Detroit, Michigan except Rev. Mark D. Meyer, who lived in Plane view, Texas, USA. I lived with Rev. Mark Meyer in 1989 after hurricane Hugo devastated our campus at Montserrat, West Indies. The rest of the above I met while trying to defray deportation notice from the INS. Those were challenging and nerving political moments for m family and I. These men of God never docked when told about my nightmare. These true believers became unique brothers I would like to share few outstanding things they did in style engraved in simple devotion to Christ's dictum.

I write because these men impressed me in their interpretations and devotion to the Gospel of Christ. Hence forgive me if I became a bit sentimental in relaying help they gave to me at various challenging times of my life. They were personal pastors for me.

These were the beacon of hope and faith that stood by me when it was all doom and gloomy for me. They were simple people, humble ones at that, I can confide with, debate with, and had shoulders on which to cry my heart out without being embarrassed and above all expect a little prayer at the end of it.

Then guess what? We would be on tract trying to get hold of friends of theirs and people that might lighten my burden. Their devotion to justice and fairness was magnanimous and are my brothers in Christ. Rev. Mark Meyer, on being told the hardship I endured in Montserrat from hurricane Hugo gave me a room and gifts more than ten thousand u.s. dollars to help me complete my pre-clinics at the American University School of Medicine.

I learnt from these men of God that there is a special strength that can sustain us through almost any difficulty. That strength comes from God and from kind hearts like these Samaritans of good will. The strength comes from partly within but even more, it comes from faith and love of those close to us.

These men gave themselves wholly and as unselfishly to others in need when I met them at the Episcopalian diocese of Michigan. They devoted time to my cause and dropped selfish interests aside to help me fight my case against the INS while I was up to my neck in legal and political mud.

I found nothing in these men but admirable integrity, honesty and unswerving commitment to leading life devoted to God, the Bible and in helping the downtrodden. I always feel elated whenever I get chance to speak to these kind hearts from afar. Meeting them makes me feel reunited with my best friends.

I rather have a million more like then than multi millionaires that do not care about the plight of the common man. Again, I applaud contribution and friendship these men touched my heart and life with. God blesses them.

My family, villagers and I are extremely indebted to them. These men translated their concerns, and love of humanity and continued to be my good Samaritans and a bridge over trouble waters. These believe in the worthiness and sanctity of life.

And above all they ascribe to the power of knowledge and justice over ignorance. We look forward to the day we can serenade them amongst us in the smiling coast of the Gambia. We pray they keep fit to be able to join us in the opening ceremony of the Manding Medical Centre at Njawara village, the Gambia, West Africa.

These men translated their deep faith, concerns, and love of humanity. I opted to do my clinical rotations in Colchester, Essex, UK in 1990 and chanced to meet the Robinson's. Keith Robinson vested my newly born baby girl, Famatanding Ceesay, at the Colchester County Hospital, which marked our first meeting.

This slightly shy bloke impressed me a lot. He was all smiles and fund. He titled the little ears of my daughter and told her not to be as bad as her daddy. We all laughed over it. We from that moment liked each other and he became one of my inseparable unique Brits. Keith and wife would visit the Gambia and my girls loved them to bits.

Not for the presents he takes to them each time but because of his amiable personality, altruistic, very caring human he is. He had spent boxes of monetary aid towards my NGO, Manding Medical Centre at Njawara village, and the Gambia. On the forming of the Friends Manding Charitable Trust, he was unanimously voted chairman of the charity by the members.

He had since inspiration of the Friends of Manding Charitable Trust worn the cap admirably and did a job well done for the charity. Also he had been instrumental in the Gambibazaar held every fortnight in Colchester to help raise funs for Manding Medical Centre's goals back in the Gambia. He is committed to seeing the center come to fruition for the villagers of the Gambia and any that would need its service.

Personally, he and his wife had been my lifeline and support. They have always come to my aid the call of expectation and I remain profoundly grateful to him and his wife Lorna V. Robinson. Ten years ago I was on the verge of preparing becoming a consultant and return to serve the Gambia.

Today an untold anguish my life went through in these years was dampened by kindness of Lorna and Keith Robinson and many other kind and generous Brits.

They are my Colchester Samaritans and Njawara villager's angels with golden hearts. We are working hard to seeing that Manding Medical center transcends the dream it was to reality for the Lower Badibou region. Its service is much needed by the villagers.

God blesses their hearts. In Manchester many helped but few match Elhaj Asfaque Ahammed, Neville Brown, Kofi Awudo and Ahmed Nizami. Elh. Asfaque Ahammed is proprietor of Punjab Collection located at Wilmslow Road in Manchester.

A lot has already been revealed about the kindness and generosity of this gentile heart and family in my first book, "The legend again all odds." Asfaque Ahammed has since my early days in Manchester to today been benevolent towards me.

He gives me food and money any time he thinks or feels that I am on the brink of collapsing because of joblessness, hunger, and worries about the state of my equally beleaguered family back home. Only God can reward such humble good people. I first met Neville in Montserrat, West Indies, while I was a medical student at the American University of the Caribbean.

We have ever since been cordial and upon finding me out in Manchester he had steadfastly kept that friendship ablaze. He in various ways would come to my aid with small but significant donations at the time.

He even helped in securing a job at Belfry House Hotel at Hands Forth in 2006. He is kindhearted fellow and my Montserrat. Kofi Awudo is Toggles gentleman I also met through his link with Neville Brown. He turned to be very kind and generous to me. He bought me shoes and shirts to allow me start work at the above hotel.

Years later on my return from Glasgow, Scotland he was the one that lodged me free of charge for three winter months. He is of exceptional quality and humane person. I remain grateful both fellows. I met Mr. Ahamed Nizami in 2008, an angel in human flesh, at Waseem's work place in Manchester.

This lawyer turned Editor and I gelled from that hour to today. He is currently the Chief Editor of the Khalish Magazine, an Urdu language magazine in UK and worldwide. He also doubles as one of the Pakistani group leader in Manchester. On knowing my predicaments his benevolence surfaced.

There nod then he promised to help me with some the problems pulling me down and also indicated interest in helping my NGO Manding Medical Centre get financial aid to get a head start on the provision of its goals for the villagers. In addition he proposed a fun raising idea using his medium and other avenues that may come to light.

We tentatively initiated, depending on approval and provisos set by Keith Robinson, Chairman of Friends of Manding Charitable Trust in Colchester been met, formation of the Manchester manding Medical Center Annex to be office at 9 knowley Street in Manchester. To further demonstrate his kindness and interest in my goal Ahmed Nizami donated fees for all three PLAB exams I took in 2009.

Gentle hearts like Ganem Hadied and others felt sorry that my life became an unkind and rough ride for me. He said, "Ceesay, I wish I can help more to get you out of the limbo you found yourself. Just believe in God and this pain will one day pass like history." Mahmud Adam also marched Ganem's effort by collecting money from the Liverpool mosque.

Both monies were used for my exam fees and for which kindness I remain eternally grateful to all donors. Mohamed Salam of Greenhey business in Manchester was another Good Samaritan that came to my aid when I was left to sleep in cold weather at Alexandra Park. Upon contacting him he kindly offered me room in one of his flats in Manchester.

He was very kind and generous towards me. We have many times prayed together for my eventual breaking out of nightmarish bad luck life had been to me in recent times.

Last but not the least is Sami Bati from Algeria who I stayed with at 245 Great Western Street and who relentlessly called and ask people and friends to come to aid. He raised a bundle to help me pay school fees for my daughters in the Gambia and feed my bones.

My brother Abdullah Hashim and wife Asiya Qadri were very kind Bangladesh cum Pakistani couple I met during the most challenging times of my life. Their kindness is yet to be matched by their peers. I met the couple while sleeping rough in the street of Manchester as Mohamed Salam' offer of a place came to an abrupt end.

The place was rented to a family leaving me homeless with no place to go except spend the nights at cold and treacherous Alexandra Park. It was very risky but being jobless it was the only option left to me. Hence, it was a miracle when this God fearing Good Samaritan couple came to my rescue.

They not only lodged me temporally at their other flat at 2 Sway field in Manchester but also continued to shower me with gifts and food. I certainly look forward to hosting and having my villagers and family serenade this unusually kind and generous couple from Bangladesh. Yankuba Samateh and dear friend Abdal Nasser deserve a mention with gratitude and thanks for kindness and generosity they showered me with during these dark days and for constantly reminding me that I am more than capable of bringing my dream to fruition for the villagers. Mrs. Roheyata Corr-Sey, a cousin, remained the most supportive and one that kept encouraging me more than any family member had done during this sojourn of mine. God blesses her and her family.

I look forward to being able to thank her in person for insisting that blood is thicker than water and for being with me in thick and thin of this murderous trail. I just have to have continued faith; confidence to do it and the universe will cooperate to justify these days difficulty.

My life being as mythical as Pelebstine fever, it was full of ups and downs and again it was Ahamed Nizami who offered to lodge me when I was asked to leave my previous address where I was renting. His kindness is phenomenal and transience's mortals.

I look forward to him being my guest in the Gambia. Worth mentioning is Abdullah Shahim, a young Bangladeshi fellow who practiced his believe that we are all God's children and do need to help the miskin whenever we can.

He has graced my life with kindness and brotherhood that any human being yearns to get. He and his wife Asiya Padri have been one of the bright experiences of my UK sojourn. God bless their hearts. Asiya is a shining beauty and sunshine of Abdullah Shahim.

Each day became a specific thrill that lead to that exhilarating moment of victory for mankind. It was a hard challenge and a march placed before me. It is a march I will pursue towards the day I would once again be able to serve the Gambia as a physician.

Friends such as Lorna Robinson, Eliza Jones, Mahmud Adam, Ganem Hadied, Abdinnisir, Faisal, Yusuf Ali, Ishfaque Ahmed, Ahmed Nizami, Abdullah Shahim, and countless angels all suffered my pain and felt way into my heart through compassion as I plied through financial inadequacies.

Angels like Faisal, Abdul Rhaseed, Abdinnisir, Yusuf Ali, and Mahmud Adam deserved to be classed as paragons of kindness. These Somalis are among many who refused to let me bit the dust because of foot dragging visa problem. They encouraged by sharing food and they had with me and made certain that I persevere for a bright day for family and country.

These are people who help lift my feet when my wings could not remember how to fly away from hardship. Faisal would on week ends prepare hot and well spiced Spaghetti and meat, or buy food for me from the next door restraint.

Abdinnisir Hassan in almost tearful manner would push me into going to get food. On top of this generosity these folks let me stay in their flat at 284 Great Western Street,

Manchester while my lawyer fight not only to untangle but to get the Home office act on change of status request I made to that office back in 2004. I feel favored, if not blessed having to face these inhuman challenges without loosing my sanity.

Being in the belly of a ferocious beast is more comfortable than life I am currently saddled. I feel like being at the interface between Purgatory and hell on earth. Simply put, my experience was no domain for the weak. The dilemma in this life remains ceaselessly changing. These few, this band of altruistic brothers kept me going through many a dark hour of my life in America and Great Britain.

They stood tall for me among many in caring for the plight of those who they never met in poverty stricken parts of the world. Friends like these are angels who lift us to our feet when our wings have trouble remembering how to fly. In this almost inhospitable life friends like these are a great gift indeed.

Tinged with trepidations for what the future can sing I picked up courage and inspiration knowing that good comes out of fighting for what one believes in. Life has taught me how to look after myself and that things do not just happen, people make it happen. And so the villagers and I appeal for your help and participation with Manding Medical Centre.

Together we can walk on water and make this dream of providing medical aid to villages become worthy cause for generations. I have learnt not to rest on my oars else I fall into a deep and turbulent sea of troubles.

I have to keep running in order to be with the best or where I am. I will continue to not only learn to improve my performance but to work hard to see that this dream of providing a much needed medical aid to villagers is brought to fruition.

Dalliance said, "Say of me what you will and the morrow will judge you, and your words shall be a witness before its judgment and a testimony before its justice. I came to say a word and I shall utter it. Should death take me ere I give voice the morrow shall utter it. That which alone I do today shall be proclaimed before the people in the days to come."

Dr. Alhasan Ceesay at the Manchester Central Library

Chapter 21

Devils or Eliphants in the Room

First, I have to admit that sixteen years that my family and I were apart was bound to cause changes in behaviour, expectations and social emancecipations. Rohey Ceesay, my youngest of three daughters was the only one fortunate to be allowed to join me in Manchester under the family reunion act.

I left her when she was just 2.5 years old and saw next as a blooming beauty grown up lady of 18.5 years. She and her mother arrived on the 27th of Luly 2015 and we bunked together in a one bedroom suit for three weeks before finaly moving into a two bedroom flat at Mauldeth Road West in Withington, Manchester.

Two weeks after the dark devil started showing its ugly head in various forms. The last thing an African father can stand is a child that talks back in the most crude and unacceptable vercabulary.

Despite all that I went through to give my daughter chance to not only to be with me but to have fighting chance in life by accessing educational facilities in the UK, she turned a night mare that insist that I was not her father and in so believing she would refuse doing things when asked by me. Her reply on asking her to pray was: "No one must tell me to pray for only I will be in my grave; or my braids cannot be soaked." As it looked; my daughter Rohey Ceesay seemed bewitched to rebel against me. Like most teenagers she cannot wait to get home and be on the internet.

Once on the internet, this eliphant in the room would careless about her environment or need to do any chores in the flat. Her mother does everything from laundry, cleaning to cooking while our teenage lady remain glued to either the TV or mobile texting or having foolish chats with equally hopeless contacts.

At times my tolerance get so low that I end up turning the internet Wi-Fi off to allow her have some conversation with family or tell about her day at school. Rohey hates reading but is enearmored by ipods, dresses others wear, texing and audio chats for hours on end.

In the end she became a bee in my bornet for we quarrel more frequently than love dadies and daughters are sopursed to have. She is exceptionally sturbun. I missed her, when she was in the Gambia, the most among the three girls but as at writing this chapter she is making herself a pain in the shocks for me.

She is very aguimentative and one is almost certain she would refuse command or will do the request at her own sweet time regardless and caringless wether it was important. I have always prayed she turn into new leaf before it becomes late for her current reactions and behaviour will not be tolerated at job places. As a dad this worries me a lot for these girls are dwels and pearls to my heart. I want them be the best and sail through life in smoother path than mine. If wishes were horses beggar would be galloping to glory.

All my expectations after 16 years of being apart were a joyful and rejuvenating family reunion. It was to be fresh start for the heart and to remove scarring solitude separation causes. On their arrival to Manchester I managed to help them get their National Insurance numbers, be included in the Electoral Roll, Schools and the NHS.

What surfaced in reaction you about to find is that neither wife nor my daughter actually fathomed or accepted difficulties I under went and extent I went through to have them join me in the United Kingdom. Hence my wife Fatou's expectations were shattered on finding that I was living poor and jobless.

Her head, on arrival, was filled with grandeous plans and on finding that there was no money to fulfil her dream and aspiration she lost her bearings in the marriage. Two months into her arrival Fatou became a new FATOU I never expected in my life.

Sher started being very difficult and matters got worse when she made friends who urged her to free herself by pushing or urshering in a remote control rusty idea of a

50/50 in the Flat. As far for her; it is sacrilegious and heresy to be cooking breakfast and worse saying good morning to me tantamount to enslavement. This is new is the so-called developed world for African men have always stood by their wives and never waited to be told what chores to do.

She would leave the flat as early as 8:40 Am and return as late as 7:45 pm. When asked were she had been her tarse reply was mostly; "School. Do not you know?" So I ask which adult school in Manchester opens as late as you want me accept?

By the time we were seven months together in the UK the unholy alliance she fell for almost cause our marriage to go to sleep. Wife became so desolutioned and challenging that some times I feel like crying out loud; "Et tu Brutus!"

Wife at one time under external influence did believe that saying morning or cooking breakfast tantamise to enslavement. The verbal aguiments, unbearable constiliations of daily tongue bashings and insults became so pasistant that I asked myself if it were not a tragic mistake bringing these two uncontrolled in addition to my difficulties in the UK.

I would lie if did not confess being angry and bitter at the whole trend, especially my having yearned their rejoining me.

I had to give the marriage a lifeline by involving or sharing my difficulties with few trusted Gambian friends Like Kemo Ceesay and Yankuba Samateh to seek advice out of love for this duo elephants in my flat.

Both were taken by surprise and expressed profound disappointment on hearing my complaints regarding my family in the UK. They agreed to review the tape made during one of our many verbal encounters before intervening.

I met Kemo Ceesay (Immigration Solicitor) on a face to face basis on Monday the 26th of September 2016 at a nearby McDonald Francis on Whimslow Road Mosside Manchester to allow me vent as well as present my deligma. Hence after a brief chit-chat over delicious chips and chiken about situations in the Gambia I brought reason why I wanted the meeting.

Lawyer Kemo Ceesay, a trusted Gambian friend in deep thought, Manchester 2016.

I told him about the dailly tongue bashing and insults I lived under since March 2016. I based some of her actions being nudged by outside influence her lady friends drum into hear ears. I even sat on my pride and played section of voice recorded version of wife going at me with the most abusive language in Mandinka and Wolof.

Kemo Ceesay was shocked and never thought wife would be that swayed after such a short sting in the UK. He used lot of Quranic verses and what village elders admornished about problem resolution.

After twenty minutes of reviewing the ramification of taking drastic actions to stop the undignified tirate we agreed on a shared wisdom of letting peace take its cause at present.

I agreed not to react to any more provocations by her, my daughter or likely friend of hers. We drove back home with full understanding that I will not denigrade myself no matter how hard she or any of her armchair advicers pushed to end my marriage with women I love and that gave me three gorgeous daughters; whose hearts would be broken if I ever separate from their mum.

Yankuba Samateh also came Tuesday 27th September 2016 to see how he can verify as well as bring an amicable end to an onslot of unexpected disgraceful manner wife adopted in so short a time in England.

He made it just intime when I received delivery from Viking Office Depote in UK. Like Kemo he was dymared and could hardly believe what he heard on voice recording of my wife mercilessly tongue bashing at me. Yankuba Samateh like Kemo urged restraint and discussion to rout out doubt and outside influence whose dirty hearts and fingers are about to ruin a good marriage and friendship cum companionship of well over twety five good years.

I gave hime my word os honor that I will seek peace; whatever it takes enable that goal's fruition and tranquillity in my marriage. All is well that ends well. The abscence of hope in anything causes fear to rule the heart. I had put all of me in an effort to give my family a fighting chance in this undulating life and in addition to bring healthcare relief to rural Gambia.

Grand Bajoja Ceesay admornished that; "Those who stood for truth have fearless endings. And that it is always worth sacrificing for family and community wherever one may find oneself."

We all know Turkies do not vote for Christmass nor did I ever expect the challenge that befell me in Manchester and now with my wife and daughter; a people I loved so much. Hence I felt incredibly sad and wanting to howl foul to the firmaments but instead I picked myself up and dusted all rubbish away for a better future for all in the new ever tolerant me. I yearn for progress and will fight for love and peace in my family. My experience revealed a multilawer plot that only true love helped me scale it unscurched.

Yankuba Samateh: "Gambia Badibunko!"

Alasan Mballow, Famata Ceesay, & Alasan Mballow Jr

Chapter 22

I REST MY CASE

Paul in a letter to Timothy 2 said, "I have fought a good fight, I have finished my course, and I have kept the faith." I hand this work for publication for you to be judge of the ravages of the years and how my life was that of extreme ups and downs. In reality,

I am very grateful to God even though my life met with various misfortunes, the most unbearable being the delay in my becoming a physician. My life as witnessed in these pages was an assembly of trials and tribulation emanating from roadblocks placed on my path by inhuman laws and unfortunate dark circumstances.

Life has taught me to submit to divine decrees, whatever they may be from God. I feel on the whole overly rewarded and delivered even though I had no family here in England nor was I as lucky as others who can feel and experience the warmth of their wives and children on daily basis.

I succumbed to it as the way things were going to be for me and lived with this state of affairs while in Manchester, England. I experienced various turns of fate, enough for ten elephant loads, while on the little moat of the silver sea called England.

With my travels I was able to see Europe, the Americas and have learnt a great deal from it as well as experienced numerous unforeseen adventures thrown on my path. My life in England was pain; fear of deportation, hunger, extreme poverty due to joblessness, solitude and missing my wife and children I loved dearly.

I had a huge sense of duty in relation to the villagers and was not ready to fail them because of personal comfort or pleasures. Consequently Manding Medical Centre and benefits to be accrued from it became my most if not the only occupation and direction in life. Here is Manding Medical Centre if managed well it will do justice to rural health service for the next generation of Gambians to build upon.

The medical centre is now a recognized charity in both the United Kingdom and America. I am committed to serve the villagers so that life of the children and young people would be better than mine when I was young.

I hope Manding Medical Centre becomes a model testimony of the boy from Njawara village who doggedly struggled to become a doctor and despite various twists of life is able to provide medical aid and service to villagers in rural Gambia.

May be this will strengthen some other fellow to strive to do better than I did to bring health and happiness to the region. I hope my adventure persuades youngsters that man is capable of a lot more than he thinks he is capable of.

Our footprints must be inspirational to give heart to new coming Gambian generations. Twenty years ago none would dream of thinking me becoming an author or to challenge powers as I did in this little frame and life of mine. I met a beautiful Maraka girl while I was in Monrovia, Liberia, West Africa. Fatou Koma is daughter of Elhaj Ansuman Koma and Jalian Ture of Kindia from Guinea Conakry.

Her positive attitudes towards me lead our meeting on weekends at Cousin Sainabou Jobe's home. We started going out together and very soon I had the courage to ask her hand in marriage.

There was no bone of contention with regards for my love for her. She was the darling of my heart at first sight and I was not going to let a fly land on her from that day onwards.

We had a simple wedding because her father did not quite approve of me because of fear for his uneducated but very pretty daughter being dump at one stage of the marriage for another educated city girl.

I, in the long run, allied his fears and he ended up being one of my best friends and confidants I had up to the day he went to his maker. Fatou Koma-Ceesay and I are blessed with three beautiful daughters namely, Princesses Famatanding Ceesay, Binta Ceesay, and Roheyata Ceesay.

All of who, unlike me, had their schooling start at the age of five. The elder girl is aspiring to become a doctor and had been admitted to start her premed courses at Alpena Community College in Alpena, Michigan, USA.

Together Fatou Koma-Ceesay, the children and I went through all the tragedy of hunger, poverty and other sad experiences my sojourn in the quest of the Golden flees for the villager brought to us.

Fatou Koma-Ceesay initially hated Manding Medical Centre for she felt it consumed me and took me away from her and the children. The call got me entangled in a web of unfortunate circumstances and laws. The marriage had at one point almost spiralled to its end as wife' move became questionable.

Nonetheless she remained a good mother and wife who took care of the girls in my absence. My mother in-law was battered by confusion and as to why Fatou stuck it out with me under such immense hardship. Love is stronger glue!

We loved each other and so we were able to stand by the other in good or bad times and my trip to England was the worse ever in our connubial life. It caused great turbulences in the marriage but I stuck with it for love's shake and the children who I love dearly.

Today, we are back together as family under the same roof while planning and supporting future of our darling girls. God bless Fatou Koma-Ceesay's heart and be reassured of endless love I have for her.

For now Dalliance said it best for me when he said, "Say of me what you will and the morrow will judge you, and your words shall be a witness before its judgment and a testimony before it justice.

I came to say a word and I shall utter it. Should death take me ere I give voice; the morrow shall utter it. That which alone I do today shall be proclaimed before the people in days to come."

I wrote with the hope the life enshrined herein will serve not only as an inspiration to the despondent but a lesson never to allow this sort of experience it passed through this planet.

I wrote in the hope that life enshrined in my books will serve not only as an inspiration to the despondent and downtrodden but a lesson never to allow this sort of experience it passed through this planet.

I wrote because I felt that my life has something worth revealing to the world to engender tolerance and understanding between people and their governments.

I risked revealing today for all of us to learn from it and move to a better and rewarding future.

Among the forces of life is one that stands a certain lofty peak a few is endowed with or able to explore its heights. Ambition urges us to leave the lower surface of earth where the ordinary people live and ascend to heights that pierce the heavens. This mission has led to numerous Erie paths but for me this Pell-mell towards a better medical service for the neglected villager was a worthwhile adventure.

I am profoundly grateful and indebted to my wife Fatou Koma-Ceesay and our daughters, princesses Famatanding Ceesay, Binta Ceesay and Roheyata Ceesay for enduring all the pains that we went through in thick and thin times during my sojourn to America and England.

Also my deepest gratitude goes to Cousin Yata Sey-Corr for helping keep my family hopeful. God bless her heart eternally. I forgive my own brothers and sisters who refused to cater for my family in my absence. Hello, hats off to Sey kunda!

Dr. Alhasan Ceesay, holding Africa

Chapter 23

MY ENDEARING LIFE & FATE

For a while in my native innocence all I had was erudition and wit, which always misfired. Everything I touched came to nothing but failure, whatever I tried to achieve came crashing down on my head.

At any given moment some mishap befalls me and nothing surprised me any more. **I took my current plight with stride and smiled as fate taunts me. I remain poor but my in extinguishable strong will enabled me face life squarely and took me through these dark days. The twist of fate abated but my age had advanced beyond retrieval.**

The above apocalyptic life is indeed trying moments for my family and me. The only passion I have is providing medical service to villagers through Manding Medical Centre. My dream spawns better future health service for future generations.

I never set to write a bestseller but to inform and share ideas. Also I enjoy reading it as it's not found in any bookstore. It is hoped that in writing another will be spared of experienced I endured before being able to provide medical service/aid to Gambian villagers.

Browse: http://friendsofmandinggambimed.btck.co.uk **or contact** alhasanceesay@hotmail.com

To view/purchase books: Google search Dr. Alhasan Ceesay/ books.

Dr. Alhasan S. Ceesay, MD

Chapter 24

THE WAY OF A DREAMER

Back in the Gambia a friend decried my efforts as nothing but a dream that I persistently chased. I let such observers know that it only takes time before my dream become fruitful. Here are a few examples:

I left the Gambia in 1967 as a nurse and returned; after insurmountable roadblocks as a medical doctor. While practicing in the Gambia I further created two worthy entities, namely

(1) The Gambia Health Credit Union, which today provides needed financial assistance to all health workers i.e. Nurses and Health Inspectors country wide.

(2) In addition I created NGO Manding Medical Centre at Njawara village, Lower Badibou to help provide a much needed medical aid and service free of charge to villagers who could not afford to pay private clinics. With the help of visiting doctors the centre has treated more than 9000 villagers free of charge since its inception in 1993.

On returning to the UK, I again with help of resident nurses and doctors in Colchester Essex setup the Friends of Manding Charitable trust in Colchester UK. This was recognized and registered as a charity in England and Wales by the UK- charity Commission in 2002.

In the midst of which I published my first book 'The Legend Against all Odds' and now has published more than thirty eight novels. To further cement my goal for the villager I was able to convince the Alpena City Council to form a sister city link with Njawara and Kinte Kunda villages in the Lower Badibous of the Gambia in 2005. This was made easier after my being awarded on May 5th, 2005 'Distinguished Graduate Award' by Alpena Community College. My web site: friends of Manding gambimed continues to lure people to Njawara to see what help they could give the villager.

Today, I am not only an author of several books; Google search: Dr. Alhasan Ceesay/books to view of purchase as contribution to rural healthcare; portions or sales from these books go to support goals of Manding medical Centre at Njawara. I am indeed a dreamer and will continue to dream fir my people.

If the above is dream then here is another step to help see through me. I am humble to let you know I am now a Publisher and my company in the UK is 'PUBLISH KUNSA LTD' and one can have their work published by logging on to our web site; www.publishkunsa.com .

Again two pounds sterling from any book published by my company goes towards scholarships and rural healthcare as stipulated in terms of contract we would work on manuscripts. Dreams must be activated and not wasted. I cannot fly without wing but can make artificial wings to let reach higher hits that loafers never can dream of.

Allow the dream to force you into action. Yes, I too have a dream, which is simply that every hamlet in the Gambia be bequeathed good healthcare, safe drinking water, enough food and chance to a solid education for every child. Yes. Education is power and a mover. I sacrificed my life to endure depravity, humiliation and solitude in other to bring medical aid to villagers. With all these I am busy trying to get more medical skills and experience before heading to Gambia, home , sweet home.

With this tit-bit I can freely and willingly encourage you to dream but not to let it remain at that. A life with trials or challenge is like an orchestra without conductor and it very defeating if not boring indeed. One must act for the good of self and any community we find our selves.

An old village sage once advice that 'A good person and at best a leader never yield to failure but only learns from it to move forward. Grand Pa Bajoja Ceesay told me that; "One willing to do good should not expect people to remove obstacles or stones from their path; but such leaders must accept it calmly in the event these place more boulders on our way."

This is what a dream turns out. At first it becomes a lonely avenue full of heartaches, which eases gradually as the good things unfold from one's relentless efforts to make the dream becomes fruitful and rewarding.. Simple its life 99.9% very hard work full of stumbling.

Do not we all dream of going to heaven? Well the path to such respites need challenging theological and spiritual discipline. Hence we earthly dreamers dabble with ideas of landing on Mars and eventually colonizing it. So allow me ask, what is your dream for mankind, especially Africa?

Can Africa ever be free of ignorance, self subtenant, corruption and misuse of the tribe? These just few multipronged toxic dragon heads African must dream to remove from our midst. With better education and discipline Africa can overcome and progress. Dreamers are doing utmost to slay the pestilent dragon hindering life in the villages of rural Africa.

We must remove the monster of retro ration for the shake of the future generation. Again grandpa Bajoja Ceesay advices that we stay the good cause and never be taken by detractions. I am no millionaire but have a million dreams worthy of pursuing for my people. Would you dream along with me? Glad to let you know hard work yields rewarding fruits.

Dream and be in control of not only your own life but be a source of hope and inspiration while contributing positively to your community. Do not be carried along by current get rich quick and live selfishly. Life is to be shared even with dreamers. Time is not mine and life will continue for the villager. Success comes slowly and brings with it contagious hope that serves as blue print for other.

The fate of mankind is up to each of us. Do not succumb to idleness. Use youthful opportunity to develop out of ignorance, and corruption by having courage to bring change to the people. Be the change you want in others. Expect resistance on your path to bring change. A useful proxy in fulfilling a dream is not letting it wane away. Always think it possible and work hard at its realization.

Be warned to think what could be done and not that which cannot be archived. Matrix of success lies in hard work with guided ski full knowledge. I will work on my dream and morrow will be my judge along with benefits accrued from it. I hope my last footprints of my journey on earth will inspire people towards doing well and sharing their worth with others. From one villager to another may this wish be true for rural Gambia.

The Gambia: home sweet home; land of smiling coast

Chapter 25

ABOUT THE AUTHOR

I was born at Njawara Village, Lower Badibou District in the North Bank of the Gambia. I am a scion of a Mandinka and Fulani tribe and am one of five siblings. I had my education at Kinte Kunda, then Armitage High School, ending up as a registered nurse at the Royal Victoria Hospital, Banjul, before embarking to the USA on my medical degree quest.

I graduated from the American University School of Medicine in Montserrat, West Indies, in 1992 and returned to the Gambia to start setting up a self-help village health NGO Manding Medical Centre. The Gambia Government and the Badibou local authority register NGO Manding Medical Centre. The centre has treated more than 9000 patients free.

I Also crearted the Gambia Health Credit Uniom which serves all health personnel. I am married to Fatou Koma-Ceesay and we are blessed with three beautiful girls, Famatanding Ceesay, Binta Ceesay and Roheyata Ceesay. Unlike me, all of them started school early without the roadblocks I had to cross in my early years. I am currently a medical officer at the Royal at the Royal Victoria Hospital on study leave. It is my hope that this work will inspire others and bring much needy help to providing medical service to rural Gambia.

You are urged to log onto: www.friendsofmanding gambimed.btck.co.uk; to learn more about my work with villagers. Dear reader I hope you enjoyed navigating through the piece of work I am contribute for all of us makes case for change in attitudes of government and the governed.

For now, Dalliance said it best for me when he said, "Say of me what you will and the morrow will judge you, and your words shall be a witness before its judgment and a testimony before its justice. I came to say a word and I shall utter it. Should death take me ere I give voice, the morrow shall utter it. That which alone I do today shall be proclaimed before the people in days to come."

I wrote with the hope the life and position enshrined herein will serve as not only an inspiration to farmers, the despondent but also a lesson never to allow these shameful international jigsaw games continue as experience to pass through this planet.

I felt that it is worth writing about the above because it is something worth revealing to honorable men and women to engender change, tolerance and understanding between people and governments. I risked speaking out for all of us to learn from it and move forward to a better and rewarding future.

Chapter 26

Mourning Mother America!!

Alhasan Ceesay (alhasanceesay@hotmail.com)

The Editor

Alpena News

Michigan, 49707

Dear Editor

I am Dr. Alhasan Ceesay, native of the Gambia and alumni of ACC 1979. I write seeking permission to shed tears, offer prayers and express my condolence on passing of my American mum.

The sad news reached me a few weeks ago. I write with a heavy heart for loss of Mrs. Rita Elizabeth Riggs. She today joined her maker and I like to reiterate my sincere gratitude to her, her family, and Alpena residents.
In 1967 and on arriving in Alpena, almost dazed for never having left the Gambia mum Rita and Dad Tubby Haword Riggs brushed my fears aside to the wilderness by showing such human kindness I never expected from some one so distant and different.

Yes they opened their home and hearts to me and remained my friends.

God bless them and America!

Rita and I have always been in touch and I am certain she is hovering above admonishing me to keep on fighting for downtrodden Gambian villagers. In this vein I also want to remember other friends such as late Viola Glennie, Judge Glennie, Magreett Cruise, Bill/Richard Cruise, Tubby/Howard Riggs, and Dr. Strom of ACC etc. Yes, most of those who hosted me in Alpena have left.

May their kind souls rest in peace at the best place in Heaven. Today Gambian villagers, my family and friends bow in gratitude and in sadness for having lost a very exceptional lady. Yes, my 91 year old lady has left me. Tobby and Rita have been ambassadors of American kindness and rare breed ready to share the little they have with others despite origin, creed or believes.

They only saw humans like them. Hence Rita's life is one we need to celebrate and learn from it for the silent good she gave to many setting foot in Alpena in the 1960s. She gladly housed Gabber from Ghana, Emanuel from Peru and many more including me Dr. Alhasan Ceesay from the Gambia. In short my villagers and I will always remember Rita as icon of goodness. God bless to all of you. Regards
Dr. Alhasan S. Ceesay, MD
Email:alhasanceesay@hotmail.com

In our journey through life we once on a while come across some human angels like the above American adopted mum of mine. She always had broad beaming smiles anytime I visited her home.

She would rush to the Kitchen and bring the most delicious dish or cake she had for me to fill myself. This was not all for she normally donates to help in payment of my fees at ACC when I got stranded in 1968. She became mum to me on day one I set eyes on her. She was sincere and not aloof and loves listening with empathy to our home stories.

On one of her visits to the ACC Fish Hatchery, where I worked party she said, "Son, this is not weather for a tropical fellow. Come to the house. I will prepare hot soup and some matting's and thermal wear for you." Such was her kindness and concerned for others.

On transferring to Olivet College, this lady would call every two weeks checking how I was faring and if I had friends to help when needed. She spoke to a friend of theirs who had a gas station in Marshall City, Michigan and pleaded with them to offer me summer and where possible week end job to help supplement my financial needs.

She took me just as she did for her own. I will never forget her and way Mrs. Viola Glennie help me since setting foot in America. Glennie continued being in touch even while at Medical Schooling at the University of Liberia in Monrovia, Liberia, West Africa.

These twin sisters are angels that never for one moment rest on their laurels when it comes to me. I now have lost all of them but vow to keep their good work indelible and cherished.

William Shakespeare reminds us that evil men do lives after them and the good is interred with their bones. Never have I been touched by so many all of who wanted nothing in return. Their acts were predicated on helping the downtrodden in Africa and contributing to my success meant fulfilment of that dream. Big inspirational foot prints indeed!

IN LOVING MEMORY

Rita Elizabeth Rigg

1920-2013

Chapter 27

PROFILES OF HEROINES WHO CHAMPIONED MY SUCCESS

I pray that my readers would kindly allow me indulge in a moment of sentimentality in writing about the following magnanimous ladies who not only shaped my life but sacrificed all they had to let me succeed in this life.

First and foremost of all is my mother, Mrs. Famatanding Tarawaleh, without whose love and devotion my twin brother and I would never been on this planet nor about all that you now know about me to have come to light.

To us Africans every day is mothers and fathers day for one cannot repay the love, guiding and education parents gave while we were but fledglings. Mother epitomizes, love, caring, kindness and ability to share with others. She believed in teamwork co-operated with all the wives in the compound.

Her warmth and charm made it comfortable for others to relate to her as well as confined in her. I have already said a lot about mother in my first book, "The legend against all odds". So I will not bore those who already have a copy of afore mentioned book.

However I would like to reiterate that mother was an excellent one we would not exchange at any time for any reason and she had fulfil beyond doubts all that was expected of a mother.

She contributed immensely to my primary school education and helped me ply through battle I waged against my father' perception with regards to schooling and Western morals. She was instrumental in making it possible for me to have the right to Western education.

I am grateful that the world welcomed me through loving heart and endearment of my mother. I am certain she is not the least disappointed on my stance in this life's sojourn. I am my mother as much as my father is. They were good springboards from which to take off in today's world. She sadly departed this life at the age of 89 years of glorious village life. Mother's passing left us very lonely and missing her dearly.

The second lady of note and indeed one that had influenced my medical aspiration was none other than Grandma Sallah Hanti Sey. She was a renowned herbalist of her time from the Fulani region of Bundu in Senegal. I was her protégée and lieutenant at work at the tender age of six. We would go deep into the bush harvesting herbs, roots, leafs and backs of trees from various plants to be used for medicinal purpose.

I now wished that I was, at that tender age, able to compile the names of the plants she used to treat yellow fever, measles, diarrhoea, malaria and dengue fever. Boy! Her portions would stop most diseases as soon as the patient took them.

I barely recall the concoctions but their results remain vivid and clear in my memory of those years. I had no idea of the importance of what she was engaged but the crystal ball becomes clearer and obvious when one recalls the sheer numbers of people from far and wide who would walk hundreds of miles to seek treatment from her.

The amazing thing about this unique lady was that she was so accommodating and never charged a penny or cent for service rendered to her patients. Some would insist that she accept the goat or sheep they brought along with them. Her final act to such requests would be to kill the beast and let the patients feed on it while under going treatment.

Her home was always packed with patients arriving at different times of the day. She would today be nick named mother Theresa because of her ability to cope with these influxes. Grand ma was a reference book' a bundle of joy and love to young ones like me. She sang lullabies to soothe children.

And told endless spell bounding stories about African Kings, their wealth and the way they extended their realms that left the listener envious. These stories kept many listening children at times petrified, scared or cry out of sympathy for the fate of the characters in her stories.

She even told of stories about Africans carrying loads of gold on horse, mules and slaves across the Sahara to Egypt and also of how they help the great king of that land build colossal building pointing to the sky. We now assume these to be the wonderful pyramid adorning Egypt.

Her embrace was a welcomed relief and sought panacea that sends the toddler to sleep. It was just too cuddling and comfortable and we used to run to be with her as soon as she appears.

People, lately, used to tease me that grand ma Sallah's kindness might have rubbed on me. They just would not understand that I am no clone of her but want to good and share my life and skill with others. They see my local village health organization being not only an off shoot of her herbalist days but also a fulfilment of her wish for the region. She had three sons and a girl.

None of who took interest in her herbalist career. She died peacefully in her sleep at the age of 92 years of fruitful life indeed. Her daughter, Mrs. Fatou Sallah Ceesay, was the youngest of grandma's children and lived in Banjul, the capital city of the Gambia.

It was at this untiring lady's place that I stayed after my high school days and part of the time when I was doing my nursing training at the Royal Victoria Hospital, Banjul. She was kind and protective of me out fear that city life would ruin me. Seven of us crowded her room and the okay kraal was much fun to be at. This lady would get up at 5 AM and prepare our breakfast, pull out the uniforms of those still going to school for me to ready the children for school. Fatou Sallah Ceesay would be at the school gate selling food or fruits to the children for breakfast.

And during break hour she would sell pancake and locally made soft drinks etc to those who could not have breakfast at home because of distance and transportation problem to and from the school grounds. Her earning tops of the money needed to feed the troops in her house.

She too had influenced me greatly and I miss her greatly. She died three years before my 1979 visit to Gambia. The other female member of the family that had profound effect on my life is my elder sister Binta Ceesay. She was credited for spectacularly rescuing me from the dead when I was left in a basket outside of the house to be buried as stillbirth the next day.

As folklore has it I was born lifeless and only made feeble cries after 5 Am which led my sister to pick me from the basket and return me to mother to be breast fed. By so doing this lady saved my life and I remain eternally grateful to her. She cared and helped me bond with the other siblings after the death of my twin brother. We got even closer as grown-ups did.

I still confide in her and Binta Ceesay remains an integral part of the day to day life of Njawara Ceesay Kunda. She has always been supportive of my goals and advises when needed. When it comes to having things done then the scale tips toward Binta Ceesay.

The principle of love and respect towards others make her relationship with the family, friends, and villagers admirable. As a result of which she became the magnet towards which everyone is pulled.

Proverbs 16:32 in the bible says, "He that is slow to anger is better than a mighty man, and he that is controlling his spirit than the one capturing a city." It is fair to freely say that Binta Ceesay belong to this mould.

Her cool and calm nature brings her many friends anywhere she goes. Binta once told me that having an insight and understanding of a situation makes you see the likely reason (s) for confrontation and one can prevent anger from flaring and distorting the main cause of a row. She always warns me against becoming lazy.

She paraphrased it by saying that "God works in mysterious ways but one must be willing to help God's hand and desire for you." She stressed that I must work hard to earn my own living and that I should never give deaf ears to criticism. It helps us see what others could not and thereby turns us into better and wise achievers.

Finally she advised that I remain steadfast with my faith at all times. The pillar of my success goes to none other than my wife Mrs. Fatou Koma-Ceesay who changed the course of life for the better. She is the jewel and coronet of the crown of a host of heroines that reach the summit of the highest peak of mountain life.

She is the unique person that gave me romantic love without asking for guarantees of benefit in return for her commitment to being my wife. Fatou is radiant at heart and deed. Fatou is my soul and she is mine even in death. Ours was love from first sight that never faded but grew daily for both of us to the present.

Romantic fantasies of life reconcile in this lady. She stands out in my heart and emotion and is the beauty of the world in my eyes. Fatou is stunningly beautiful, young, sexy, intelligent and all I wanted in a woman. She is much more than a feeling, which removes protective barriers one may have erected.

She was unquestionable the love I yearned for and she made me finally realise a soothing or comfort and sharing I hardly experienced since reaching manhood. As time went on we developed and matured into twins that loved, share everything and struggled in life. This beauty lived through thick and thin of my seesawing life. One look at Fatou will allow you class her as the queen of the palace of queens.

With her beauty goes an exceptionally well-mannered sociable and intelligent lady. We now have three beautiful daughters, Famatanding Ceesay, Binta Ceesay and Roheyata Ceesay, who are as brilliant as their mother. I am yet to hear anyone making objectionable remarks about my dream girl.

Having Fatou Koma-Ceesay as my wife and mother of my children makes me feel very happy like wise born lucky. I am just hoping to be able to compensate her impact on my life by being a worthy husband to her at all times.

The rest of my heroines are from lands beyond the Dark Continent. They each were left at awe upon learning about my struggles and the path my desire to have Western education led. So I present to you my American and British heroines starting at Alpena Community College (ACC) in 1967.

I arrive at this college having lost my sponsor and the college was about to send me back to the Gambia for lack of financial support. It was then that Mrs. Viola S. Glennie, then a professor of foreign language, came to my rescue without my knowledge of her benevolence. She was also my teacher for I had enrolled in her French class. She and her husband, late Judge Philip Glennie, were the first to response to appeals to make it possible for me to continue at the college.

She was very instrumental in having Alpena ladies Association donate £400 towards my studies at Alpena Community College. We became even greater friends as time went on. She and her husband would take me out on weekends and tried everything they could to soften the blow of disappointment I ran into as a first entrant to America.

She was very sorry and flabbergasted on hearing the unbelievable effort I put in other to have the right to Western Education. My relationship with the Glennies grew and she remained in touch with me at all my world travels.

She has now returned in peace to her maker happy that I kept my covenant with my people in Africa. I left them to complete my studies at Olivet College and at Michigan Technological University in Houghton, Michigan. The Glennies were my American "mum and dad" and I miss them very much." God rests their souls in heaven.

Amen! The first American family at whose home I stayed the first two weeks in Alpena was at the Riggs. They lived at 240 Washington Avenue in Alpena in Michigan. Mrs. Ritha Riggs and husband owned an Ice-cream pallor down town Alpena. I was the second of two Africans that ever lodged at their home while attending ACC. The First was Mr. Eric Gabba from Ghana and did engineering courses at the college.

Even though my bus arrived very late, around 1:45 AM, Rita Riggs was there waiting to welcome me at her plush home. I was ushered into their mansion and offered a glass of fresh milk to quench my thirst.

At the same time a table was set for me to have some food before retiring to bed. I stayed with the Riggs from 19 August to the 9th of September 1967 when I had to move to Russell Wilson Hall as then required of all foreign students attending ACC.

Mean while Mrs. Rita became "MUM" for short. She was a wingless angel in a human body. Always smiling and ready to offer assistance any time one needs it. She treated me as one of her own from day one of my meeting the family in 1967. And she and her family were marvelous friends to me.

She and her husband Howard Riggs helped a lot with part of my tuition for that term at Alpena Community College. I felt sad that I had to be at the dormitory my first year at the college. The Riggs moved out of Alpena six months after I met them. We kept in touch until my return to the Gambia when

I lost contact as all letters to them were returned by the U. S. post office. I learnt from a friend that one of their younger daughters is now a nurse at Alpena General. I shall follow this lead to re-link with my past and first American family. Mrs. Rita and Her husband Howard

Riggs I learnt are no longer with us. Next is Mrs. Magritte Cruise, a resident of Alpena, Michigan and one of the schoolteachers. I met her when my financial state had plummeted to zero level with all my former supporters having left the college.

Upon hearing about my circumstances she volunteered to lodge me for rest of my studies at the college. Her husband works as an engineer with the Jesse Beset foundation in Alpena. Magritte love debates and so we used to discuss about Africa, politics, education, conservation, family planning and the pill, among other topics into the wee hours of the night.

Her children also used to bombard me with all sorts of question about the African way of life and especially those of their age group. Sometimes these kids sound more like the entire continent comprised of only the Tarzan images they picked up from misinformation by the telecast entertainment on adventure into the jungles of Africa.

At times, I just let them know that Africa was a vast land far bigger than the USA with thousands of cultures and tribes. No one knows all about everyone they may come across in books. This made them believe that I might just come from Detroit, Michigan for according to them I do not dress like the typical pictures of Africans they see in moves or on television.

And to make matters worse I spoke English well and understood it without the "afro-American" accent. So Magritte and I had to do much better job in convincing those youngsters that I was indeed the real thing from the Mandinka tribe in Gambia.

Let me come back to Mrs. Magritte Cruise who in her own right was a generous and very forthright person. She too organized groups for me to talk to about the Gambia and how I got into primary school and eventually landing into Alpena Michigan.

She said, "We could not ever dream of having someone so far away to choose to start college at so remote a place like Alpena. You must be very daring after all the stories about the KKK and blacks etc.

Did this ever cross your mind?" I replied that a mountain climber never fears falling because the possibility is there; besides if we do not go out and seek for our people who will do it for us. Did Christopher Combo felt scared using the Nina Santa Maria and the Pinto to set sail in search trade in East India?

I can tell you I had a unique experience with Cruises and was very happy to dispel a lot assumed believe about African and Africa. Magritte and her husband Bill Cruise were very much the push that led to my having a partial scholarship from the Jesse Bessie foundation to help me continue drive to take the golden flees back to the

Gambia. Another unique heroine who helped me while the going was very unbearable was a nurse, Mrs. Geraldine Shepherd; I met while working as an assistant nurse on a summer job at St. Joseph Hospital, Flint Michigan in 1970.

She became involve out of sheer sympathy upon learning about the sorry state my life succumbed in the summer of 1970. It was then that she learnt from friends that I spent nights at rat infested basement someone rented to me for ten dollars a week and that rats have been nibbling my feet while I am asleep.

There was great fear that I might get infected from such encounters. There was no shower facility so I used to sneak into the hospital and have quick wash before someone notice.

My meager weekly pay was not going to support luxury and I needed a bundle to pay for the $6000 tuition fees and this excluded the cost for the dormitory, books, meals, and transportation fees.

She got me out of my misery after discussing my state with her husband Mr. Homer Shepherd. They agreed to offer me one of their empty rooms free of charge for the rest of that summer. I remain thankful for their kindness and understanding which helped me raise money for my schooling that year.

The summer; although started with hard and difficult moments, ended joyfully with the Shepherds. This benevolent family even asked nurses to contribute to a secrete package present they were preparing for me to take along at the end of the summer.

We have since been constantly in touch and their home became my home anytime that I pass through Flint. Again, I remain profoundly grateful to the Shepherds for being so kind and helpful to my mission in 1970. They helped me cross the challenge I faced in Flint, Michigan in 1970.

I fell into trouble on returning to Africa to start medical schooling in Liberia. Political disturbance in both Gambia and Liberia led to my return to the USA December 1981. Lot about this has been documented in my first book so to cut a long story short; the INS in Detroit refused my request and gave me fifteen days in which to leave the U.S.A.

Faced with this pending denial of my request back in 1982, I walked into the hallowed halls of St. Paul's Cathedral diocese of Michigan in Detroit searching for sanctuary and help with litigation against the INS. I actually miss took that cathedral as being a Catholic mission in Detroit.

My reasons for coming to Detroit were very clear. It was the days of doubts about not only my future but also those of Africa. It was in those sorrowful hay days when politicians and military men and their juntas wreck innocent lives thoughtlessly.

American sense of justice was the only humane salvation, if not the only avenue of hope left to me. After a few hurried flights, on April 15th 1982, I was on the second floor where Hugh Davis introduced me Mrs. Patricia Koblynski, Pat for short, the then refugee co-coordinator for the Diocese of Michigan in Detroit, Michigan.

Over a grim blackness of an impending denial of my request Mrs. Koblynski as you will soon find out was god sent angel to soften my fall. Once in her office, Pat stopped her typing and asked what help she could offer me. I narrated my experience and mission in such nervous way that she had literally held me to reassure me that she cares.

I showed her the INS letter notifying me it intention to deny my request for asylum in America. I gave her all news clippings we had about the coup in the Gambia and the Government's reaction upon reinstated back to power by the Senegalese Forces.

Pat read everything given her and then called Rev. Hughes White, advisor to the Bishop, who came to join us right away. Pat, Hughes and Virgil Jones and I went over all details of my plight and the eminent dangers ahead if forced to return to the Gambia prematurely.

At times I broke into tears and later pick up my sanity and continue telling my sad experience and loss I encountered since 1981. That very day Pat, with the blessings of Bishop Coleman McGhee, set up would become the Ceesay Committee to help me fight my pending denial case at the Detroit Immigration and Naturalization Service (INS). This committee became the brains behind my fight with the INS courts.

Without Pat's initial involvement life would have turned for the worse. She relentlessly fought for my freedom until her untimely death, which left me sad, shocked and bewildered. Patricia Koblynski was a good friend who cried with me and at the same time wiped my tears.

She gave me hope of freedom and assisted entire villages and me several thousand miles away. She knew none of these people but like the rest of Diocese of Michigan was more than dedicated in seeing that we all breathe the air in peace and walk together side by side in freedom on mother earth.

Pat, thanks a million for living a full Christian life and for all of us. Our profound gratitude and indebtedness goes to you for being our Good Samaritan. The only benefiting legacy I have for you and my villagers is returning to serve the Gambia and especially the villagers for whom you fought so hard during these last minutes of a true Christian and wonderful life of giving to others.

My villagers and I will never forget you or kindness you bestowed us. Let us now reflect a bit on Mrs. Lois R. Leonard, Editor of the Diocesan Newspaper the Record. Lot was said about this wingless American Angel in my first book.

Let me reiterate that Lois is a human rights advocate and a dedicated journalist interested in the struggles of the under developed world and the downtrodden. She was one that would stand between a giant and midget to protect the latter, if she felt the midget being right, weakling from being crushed.

Lois Leonard does not hesitate to call a spade a spade or pay attention to mis use of authority or responsibility wherever it occurs. Despite this stance, Lois was a kind-hearted lady more than willing to share with others. She champions freedom of expression and human rights for all of us.

She came on board the Ceesay Committee as soon as she heard of my troubles and never missed a single meeting of the committee's four years of life. Mrs. Lois Leonard was an asset that kept our meetings lively and balanced. She never hesitated for one moment in putting her point across or that in suggesting new approaches she feels convince would push our goal forward.

In short, Lois was one of our respected think tanks in those days and it was through her that we were able to engage the services of Professor Francis Conti of Detroit College of Law. She wrote lots of articles about my plight spear heading appeals for support and asked for help both to the committee's drive and me to bring relief to my predicaments.

She remained loyal to the cause until her death in 1989 when I had moved to Montserrat in the West Indies. Before then she kept the lines of communication between us open and would once on a while send me money to help with the little mundane needs as she called them.

Meet Mrs. Lorna V. Robinson, Britain's crown-less queen. I met this angel through her nursing job in 1991 at the Colchester General Hospital while I was a trainee doctor doing my clinical clerkship at the hospital.

We have been friends since then and for those who read my first book will understand the uniqueness of the giving lady. Lorna Robimson and her husband Keith are regular visitors to the Gambia and have been to my place in Gambia on several occasions. Lorna helped christen my first child, Famatanding Ceesay, while we were in Colchester, Essex County in 1991.

She also was the first to show interest in the self-help village health organization (Manding Medical Centre) I set up at Njawara village in the Gambia. She and her husband were key to the formation of the Friends of Manding, which is an off shoot of Manding Medical Centre at Njawara. Doctors, nurses, and residents of Colchester who frequently visit the Gambia form the Friends of Manding.

Two of the most prominent trustee of Friends of Manding have been to Njawara village and returned convinced that the centers stand was for a worthy cause and service to the villagers. Lorna frequently sent me small packages of medicines and equipment to help our service at Njawara.

Mrs. Lorna Robinson serves as the secretary and Keith as Chairman of Friends of Manding. Lorna never stopped from being in touch with us when we returned to the Gambia. She was very kind to invite my wife and me to attend weeding ceremonies of her younger daughter, Miss Fiona Robinson to Mr. Reeves Watson.

I stayed at the Robinsons after the wedding and started the trail you just read about in previous chapters. I left for London when the health of the Robinsons was not able to endure. I was just comfortable watching break their backs day after day to keep me sheltered and fed.

So I had to leave Colchester voluntarily for London February 2002. Lorna a unique, kind-hearted, hard working tireless heroine one never forgets. She is an early bird that burns the midnight oil daily in an effort to seek help for the Manding Medical Centre and the villagers at Njawara in the Gambia.

As a nurse she carries her duties with diligence and tact that only Angels like her can deliver. Lorna is charming, likeable, cheerful, free spirit and a friend one yearns to have. Most are home with her within few minutes of coming to know her.

She is well versed politically about event in the developing and developed world and a socially amiable lady. Lorna goes beyond all expectation to reach out and help the needy, especially Gambian villagers.

She is my ray of hope in the dark bowels of a foreign land. Pope John Paul (Albino Lucciano) said "A wise man does not allow him-self to be dogged by appearance and by praises; he sees the temperament and ambitions of others in their faces and gestures." Lorna shunts praises and she just continues to do her good deed without any television fanfare.

She has been having Gambia nights collecting materials to take to the villagers since I met her in 1991. As for me, my family and remain grateful to this couple of wingless angels in Colchester.

The Orthopedic Unit of the proposed hospital of the centre would surely be named after her when in full gear. God bless her and keep her in fit and sound on the opening day ceremonies of the Centre so that villagers would be able to serenade them for their relentless contribution to our dream of providing medical aid to the region and for generations of Gambian villagers.

Finally meet Ghana's sunshine Mrs. Faustina Forkouh. I met this unique lady upon arrival in Manchester last September 2002. Mr. Kinte, a friend and Gambian brother of mine, had arranged that she shelter me for three months while I sort myself out regarding my exams and job feasibility.

It was assumed that my current nightmare would have by then abated. Anyhow she welcomed me with open heart and hands to her abode and refused to charge any fees after hearing my plight. She only said, "I was in serious situation and I am happy to help as much as I can possible cope with it." I promised to be a gentleman after she warns that I be good to both of us.

As fate would have it took up to end of July 2003 before I can move be on my own. Living with her throughout this elapsed time was lively and very much an education. She and I lived like sister and brother from the same parents. Faustina is altruist, Ghana's philanthropist and Good Samaritan to all that come seek her help.

She would cook and bring food to if she notices that I have had a meal for a day or two. She spends the night awake when my asthma flares I use to feel so guilty putting her through such scary moments. Simply, she was heaven sent to me for I needed understanding and kindness she showed in accepting to stay at her place until my state improves.

When Mustapha Kinte finally reached the "end of his roped" she told him that she would continue to lodge as well as feed me until November 2003 at which time she hopes my difficulties or state would have resolved. She is the shining star from the Gold Coast that epitomizes a typical Ashanti personality.

Faustina is gracious, caring and fair when dealing with others. I found her warm, friendly and deft indeed. Her friendliness is contagious plus she holds tenaciously onto African culture. Finally, it is said that behind every successful man is the love and managerial effect of a good woman; for me it is these heroines to whom I am profoundly grateful for all the good that happened in my life.

They gave their all and dogged their heels so that I succeed in my endeavors for the Gambian villager and humanity.

Mrs. Fatou Koma-Ceesay: Rose of my heart

Chapter 28

MY SAMARITAN MEN OF GOOD WILL

Every successful person had Samaritan angels who Offered their shoulders for him or her to stand on and see further than most. Compiled herein are my Samaritan men of goodwill. Hence, I beg leave to indulge in a bit of sentimentality about a few rare human angels who played major part in today's success and help for my villagers. Believe me their moulds, as you will soon find, are beyond those of simple people.

These men help me reach today's pedestal. In medicine for the villager, I profiled ladies who championed my cause. Now, bear with me for just a few lines on the Samaritan men of goodwill. They like the previously mentioned ladies al not only believe in my dream and objective for the villager but also gave all they could to help make that dream come to fruition.

These men gave unparalleled needed help and friendship to me when I was distressed and in utter despair and darkness. Some even shed a few tears with me because the pain and set back certain roadblocks caused my goal. One of these was the day I received GMC' e-mail of the 17th June 2008 recanting recognition of my primary medical qualification based on frivolous website enter.

Hell brewed to its hottest temperatures, as it took time to unravel the misunderstanding, before GMC rectified the error. However, with your indulgence let us start from the beginning of the geneses. It was with God' anointing hand in conjunction with Sisawo Bajo Ceesay, alias Sisawo Salah) that my twin partner I landed on this Garden of Eden. Father gave us love and good guidance throughout his life with us.

He and I had deferent perception about western Education and culture but we reconciled after my completing primary school at Kinte Kunda. My father's experience from the hands of colonials made him never to entertain idea of his progeny deviating from the farmers' mold. Nor would he allow me pursue Western Education and ideology, which at the time was alien to my father and his peers.

He once told me: Son, my wish for you is to be a hard working good farmer and not indulge in the quagmire and sleaze world of spin-doctors. I do not want you tinkering with ideology that would infuse into you wrong philosophies about life and God. My father came from a different generation with totally different perceptions about invaders ruling them. Let us for a moment step into their shoes to find out why the resistance for their progeny to attend school.

In my father's days men believed in God, the sanctity of life and peaceful coexistence of the communities they lived. About the invading longhaired men he calls devils, father said: "Son the way these men, meaning the colonialist, took over our countries can only be the work of the devil. They came from the blue sea and seized our land and minerals, and remaining on the best parts while leaving us the worst places to farm and for our animals to grace.

To pour oil on fire they requested that we change our religions and ways to their dark and indiscipline life styles. To top up, our people were forced to live under laws promulgated by the invaders on top of which we must pay to learn their languages while they make systemic concerted efforts to distorted and destroy everything that was dear to us.

They massacred, disgraced, and dethroned all our kings and chiefs. These shameful acts were reinforced with policies of divide and rule by pitting tribe against tribe and even bribing those bad elements willing to do their dirty work.

Wages paid to workers were not worth the coin they were minted on. They made certain no organization, political or professional civil service existed in our countries". He said, "They filled the jails with those of us who refused to be indoctrinated or accept the supremacy of the foreign invaders. So Son, because of kindheartedness and gentled nature of the African our ways are undermined and thrown out by invaders who replaced it with greed, unkindness, spin-doctoring, and lack of respect for man and nature.

He concluded by saying, these are just a few reasons why I would not let my blood attend school." The above is a pinhole view of father's radicalism and patriotic views. He did recap late later in his old age and finally gave full blessings to my efforts and future goals.

He passed away peacefully to his maker in 1991 while I was a trainee doctor doing my clinical clerkship rotation at Colchester General Hospital in Colchester, Essex County, England. Notices no matter how simple were just bundles of scribbles on worthless paper to the farmer. The illiterates who cannot decipher the prints are cheated of their rights and land.

 I was not going to be among those who cannot decipher the print and hence found my way to Kinte Kunda Primary School where I met with the head Master, Mr. Louis Albert Bouvier, who hails from Banjul, our capital city. This benevolent teacher was my first real contact with Western Education and we gelled instantly and became inseparable.

He allowed me to stay at his home and treated me as his own son. He was kind and firm and wasted no time teaching me about life and on how to compete without strangulating the competitor.

Dr. Alhasan S. Ceesay, MD holding Africa

He told me repeatedly that competition was a healthy fund and stressed that one must be honest and have integrity and tolerance in life. He counseled hard work at everything one did. Above all, it was incumbent on me to have faith and to serve God daily, if not more but never less. Also he allowed me all the freedom a growing child needed without pampering me.

He did lay certain straightforward and simple rules for me. I was to study at a designated time, return home in time whenever I went into town, unless given an extension by him, and to be in bed by 10:00 pm, with lights off whether sleepy or not. He insisted that I perform my five daily prayers as expected of my religion even though he was devoured Catholic.

Mr. Bouvier would only help with my homework when he felt that I have done my best at it and that I was not trying to have him do the work. Otherwise, he would let me go and make a fool of myself before the class before I deserve his coveted help. Hash you think but this strict beginning or treatment, as you would call it, made me do well at school and do things with confidence independently at very tender age.

I remain profoundly grateful to Mr. Louis Albert Bouvier for being educational springboard, for being a sincere and true friend and mentor. Something said by Francis Farmer summed up the relationship between L. A.

Bouvier and me. She said, "To have a good friend is the purest of all God' gifts, for it is a love that has no exchange of payments. It is not inherited, as with family. It is not compelling, as with a child. And it has no means of physical pleasures, as with a mate. It is, therefore, an indescribable bond that brings with it a far deeper devotion than others."

Mr. L. A Bouvier continued to help and mold my academic life until when I started Armitage School in 1957. Leaving a friend like Mr. Bouvier was difficult and emotional for both of us. We have become one and are now to say farewell and perhaps separate forever. He prepared me well but like any parent or true friend he worried about the difficulties that lay ahead.

I just wished they had transferred him with me to Armitage. On the day I boarded the land rover to Armitage tears rundown Mr. Bouvier's cheeks and mother turned her head away to hide her own. L. A. Bouvier was my best friend, after the loss of my twin brother, fate had it that I was now about to be far away from all I knew and loved.

Mr. L. A. Bouvier kept cautioning me to, "keep your head up and do your school works. You have never been a failure, and even if such a sad experience occurs, keep trying over and over to overcome it.

We send you to Armitage with prayers, pride and above all with our deepest love. May God keep you in good health. Goodbye, Mr. Ceesay." It was very moving for this was the first time he addressed me as Mr. Ceesay.

We boarded the Land Rover and as it started to move Bouvier followed for some distance exhorting me not to fear to ask for help when need arose. He kept saying he would gladly help or would ask my parents to pitch in whenever possible.

Mr. L. A. Bouvier and I kept in touch despite the distance poor mail service of those days. The link continued while I was in the USA. I lost my friend in a motorcar accident, six year before returning from America in 1974.

His vehicle is said to have ran off the road went over a hill. Another part of me went with him. The evil that men do lives after them and the good is interred with their bodies. Well rest assured that L. A. Bouvier's good deeds did remain alive and intact on earth.

At Armitage it was a newly qualified teaches from Kaur, Mr. Keko B. A. Manneh, who then doubled as our class' English and Mathematic teacher that filled in gap left by my leaving L. A. Bouvier at Kinte Kunda. He was soft-spoken Chaucerian, a nickname we gave him because he crammed the entire work of Chaucer. He too loved me and was a good guide at Arbitrage.

I am grateful for encouragement and help he gave and for really being there when I needed an honest person to open up to about difficulty or academic aspiration. I left for New York on the 24 August 1967 and arrived at Alpena Michigan 1:30 Am on the 25 August 1967.

Mr. Henry V. Vali, a counselor and foreign student advisor at Alpena Community College, was at the bus station to pick me. After the formality of welcoming to Alpena he drove me to 251 Washington Avenue the home of Mr. Howard Riggs where it had been agreed I stay until start of the semester in September before moving to Russell Wilson Hall at the Alpena Community College campus.

Not surprising Mr. Vali and I became friends and remained so ever since. Mr. Howard Riggs and family welcomed me home as late as it was on that glorious day when I set foot in Michigan. They were all delighted to have me in their lovely home and they gave me princely meal to nourish my body and milk to quench my thirst. Howard owned Ice-Cream Pallor down Town.

He was very modest, delightful man and above all a very generous person. Soon Mr. and Mrs. Riggs became mom and dad throughout my American stay for their overwhelmingly kind people deserving such salutation from a poor villager. Howard's warmth and generosity to other made his family unique company to foreign students coming to Alpena. The Riggs were the ideal Americans to me. They were average working family who readily shared the little bit God gave them with others less fortunate. I remained grateful to these kind-hearted friends. Mr. Vali and Mr. Thomas Rither, Director of Foreign students at Alpena Community College, and I met several time to discuss my financial nightmare.

Mr. Rither was too concerned that the college might face INS censor if he allowed my staying without a sponsor or means to pay fees and cater for myself. He was adamant and made it very clear to me that failure to get help for the first semester will leave him with no other option but to advise the immigration to consider deporting proceedings against me.

 He gave a week ultimatum for me to sort things out before our next meeting 18 September 1967. Copies of letters from my would be sponsor, Mr. Isdor Gold, never move or evoke sympathy from him as he epidermises a true inelastic bureaucrat. Mr. Henry V. Vali convinced Mr. Thomas Rither to hold on while get in touch with some residents about my case.

He was on the telephone to different would be possible sympathizers to my cause. Most of who agreed to contribute toward the cost of my first semester at Alpena Community College. Mr. Valli also spoke to the president of the college in my behalf to prevent Mr. Rither from hastily and unilaterally contacting the INS for frivolous fears in his head. My plight soon became a house whole affair and many residents pitched in to help resolve the case. The appeal by Mr. Henry Valli and Mrs. Viola Glennie snowballed letting me start my first semester at Alpena Community College, Alpena, Michigan.

Fr. John miller at St. Bernard Rectory in Alpena not only lent me $250 but evangelized my state in every sermon for three weeks netting me much needed financial help. God bless his heart.

He left Alpena before my transfer to Olivet College in Olivet Michigan in 1979. Judge Philip Glennie was head of the 26th circuit Court of Michigan at the time. His wife, Mrs. Viola Gennie, was professor of foreign language at Alpena Community College.

Both not only contributed substantial amounts towards my tuition but also became my adopted parents in Alpena. They continued to link with me like wise support my goal until their return to heaven in the late nineties.

I remember these friends with joy mingled with sadness that they are not here to share reward they showed but also I remember them with intense gratitude for role and kindness shown me while a student at Alpena Community College, Alpena, Michigan, USA.

In another vein Alpena Community College gave me part time job at the Library and a summer job at the Salmon Experimental Fish hatchery. Thanks to grand efforts of Mr. Henry V. Vali and residents of Alpena I was able to overcome the financial crisis of my first semester at the college.

I met Mr. Cloyd Ramsey while seeking a summer job at the Medical Arts Clinic in Alpena. He was then manager of the unit at the time. Upon hearing my plight he promised to see what he could do even though the clinic itself had no jobs openings for that summer. I left him impressed and very moved by what he heard.

He too became an integral part of my time and sojourner in America than any through contributions and loans he took from the Alpena bank in my behalf to support my studies throughout my stay in the USA and short stay in Liberia, West Africa.

It was through kindness of Mr. Ramsey and his sponsorship that enabled Michigan Technological University at Houghton to accept me do a Masters program in Biological Sciences from 1971 to 1973.

L – R: Dr. Alhasan Ceesay, Prof. Sulayman Nyang, Mr. Clloyd Ramsey and Prof. Francis Conti

It was Mr. Cloyd Ramsey who came to my rescuer when things went very bad and unbearable and practically unsafe for me after the military coup d'etat against William Tolbert' administration of Liberia in 1981. He provided a round trip Air ticket to the USA and supporting it with invitation for me as their guest at Sandusky, Michigan December 1981.

The invitation secured me a B-2 Visa to Detroit, Michigan. I arrived in New York 1:15 pm 20 December 1981. I prayed on disembarking and I was grateful and thankful to God and Cloyd Ramsey having set foot once more on US soil. I thank Cloyd ceaselessly in my heart for having helped me escape to America despite the ignominy of being in exile and to seek asylum soon.

I caught my flight to Detroit, Michigan around 3:45 pm same day. The Ramseys were at the Detroit Metropolitan International arrivals terminal waiting to receive me. They must have noted the fatigue in my face, if not the sorrow of leaving my beloved Gambia and people behind for an indefinite time. They welcomed me graciously and we headed for Sandusky, a small village in Michigan. I therein and then became part of the Ramsey family.

Life has it that when some of us were created the mould broke. Most give their time and money to their own families or to work that brings them some happiness and some money. Cloyd Ramsey is among a few who give themselves wholly and unselfishly to others.

I can never be able to repay or tell how devoted Ramsey is in sharing life with the needy unless you meet him. In brief, Mr. Ramsey and wife Narrate fed and sheltered me when I needed food and place to stay until I get my feet back on earth. He was my salvation voice in the wilderness of life's rugged road.

I stayed as their guest in Sandusky until it was time to seek asylum at the Immigration and Nationality Service (INS) in Detroit. There was no other situation less tense and so empty of hope than this next phase in my life. Life became an abyss of despair which only God and good friends, like the Ramseys, pulled me out from underneath. Shakespeare said, "Between the acting of a dreadful thing and the first motion; all the interim is like a phantasm, or a hideous dream.

The genius and mortals instruments like to a little kingdom, suffers then the nature of an insurrection." Indeed an insurrection has been going on in my head during those horrible days of the coup d'etat of April 15th 1980 I became aware of the need to muster courage, strength and endurance to prepare myself for the coming exile days and form it may take. Again, Mr. Ramsey contacted the Gambia several time to no avail to verify and correct a possible misunderstanding that may have occurred. Several friends and legislators Ramsey contacted advised that I seek asylum from the INS. Senator Carl Levin sent us a package of three copies of Form 1-589 for my use on 6th January 1982.

We took the bull by the horns, completed the forms and Ramsey and I proceeded to INS office at Mount Elliot Street, Detroit, Michigan on the 22nd February 1982, were I was subsequently interviewed separately and told action will be rendered in four months earliest.

If wishes were horses beggars would gallop to heaven for it took well more than eight months before any reply came and only after numerous INS court hearings did we get some semblance of partial positive direction. The final act was left with the State Department and vice president's office.

Things were so delayed and difficult that I asked Ramsey to take me to the Catholic Mission for me to seek Sanctuary or more public help and support. We landed at St. Paul's' Cathedral, Diocese of Michigan, where Hugh Davis led me to the refugee office of the Diocese.

On hearing my story the refugee co-coordinator, Mrs. Patricia Koblinsky called rev. Hugh C. White, advisor to then reigning Bishop of the Diocese, Bishop Coleman

Mcgehee Jr. The Diocese received and let me stay at 44 Ledyard Street in Detroit. In the mean time Ramsey sent the following appeal to the INS office at Mount Elliot in Detroit, Michigan:

TO WHOM IT MAY CONCERN

This letter is to acknowledge my association with Alhasan Ceesay, over a period of fifteen years. During that time I have found him to be a young man of very high ideals. His only interest in life has been to obtain an education and return to serve his home country and help his people.

I have personally invested thousands of dollars in Alhasan Ceesay because it seemed to me to be a very efficient way to help the impoverished people from his country that has had a great deal less than I have.

If anyone were to follow the course of his life, he would see that his motives most certainly were not to simply escape the futility of his home country and live that, good life here. There is no doubt in my mind that the dangers that he describes do exist for him. Even if these were less than perfect proof, would you like to take the chance of being wrong and find out that he had been imprison or worse killed for no reason at all?

Please save this man. If you cannot do it for his sake, then consider the investment made by concerned individuals, other organizations and myself. Thank you for your serious considerations of this matter. Signed: Cloyd Ramsey, Sandusky, Michigan, USA

My next Alpena Samaritan and brother in Chris as well as profession was Dr. Charles T. Egli, who I met almost about the same time I did with Ramsey. He was a Surgeon working for the Medical Arts Clinic at the time of our meeting.

He came into the radar after a speech I gave to the Alpena Medical Association. He too has contributed prominently and was instrumental in having the medical Association comes to my aid with a donation of $400 towards my second semester fees at Alpena Community College.

By this miracle I was able to complete payment for the second semester at college. Charles, as he prefers being called, is a surgeon and devoted Christian who also became very close friend and had done a lot to encourage my efforts.

His rallying for assistance continued throughout his days at the Medical Arts Clinic. For you to note Dr. Egli's closeness here is a letter he sent in my behalf during my petitioning for asylum in the USA. It read:

Medical Arts Clinic

Alpena, Michigan

November 14, 1986

RE: Deportation Notice on Alhasan Ceesay

Dear Senator Levin,

Alhasan Ceeesay was a college student in Alpena many years ago when I first met him and was very much impressed by his sincerity and enthusiasm.

He went onto graduate school at Michigan Technological University in Houghton, Michigan, in hopes of getting into medical school. He tried very hard to get into medical school in Africa.

He was receiving no support from his own country because it considered him a political agitator and tribalist.

Alhasan Ceesay on his own initiative was able to get into medical school in Monrovia Liberia and succeeded in taking two years medical education before he fled for safety to the USA. He later sought political asylum in the USA for fear of persecution due to the aftermath of an attempted coup in July 181.

It has always been his desire to complete his medical training and return to the Gambia when the climate warrants. For almost five years now, Alhasan has been trying to receive asylum, during which time his chances at medical school are affected. Most recently he received a letter from INS judge ordering his deportation. The deportation of Alhasan Ceesay back to the Gambia would result in his certain death or imprisonment and would constitute another tragedy in the way our government handles people like Alhasan.

In a country where there are so many illegal aliens it seems that there must be some place for one more refugee. I beg you to personally consider Alhasan's case.

Sincerely

Dr. Charles T. Egli, MD

Mr. Homer Shepard, resident of Flint Michigan, was also very kind to me while at Flint. He offered to lodge me during the summer of 1969 on securing a full time job at the St. Joseph Hospital on Flint, Michigan as nurse assistant.

Homer and wife offered to help defray rent expenses, which were taking a quarter of my earnings. With this help I was able to return to Alpena Community College at the end of the summer and pay my dorm and food bills and still had some pocket money to buy pens and other sundries during the semester.

God blesses his heart. We lost contact since my return to Africa. All letters to his address were redirected, as addressee no longer leaves here.

Bishop Coleman Mcgehee had already blessed efforts of the hastily formed CEESAY COMMITTEE. It became the Adhoc committee and my Pegasus wing.

Like any normal human gatherings we had our different ideas as to how to approach the asylum problem but all of it steered towards or sought better ways to meet the challenges and enigma about to end all that I stood for and worked hard for in life. The brain storming sessions were very pragmatic if not practical and well-intended discussions.

One of the exploratory searches for solutions led us to Mayor Harvey Sloan of Louisville, Kentucky. I met Mayor Sloan in 1976 when I was trying to get into medical school at the University of Louisville.

Also we used to write each other while I was in Monrovia, Liberia, West Africa. I was invited to his office early February 1983, and was given opportunity to talk with key aids at the Louisville City Hall while he attended other state affairs.

His executive aids, Sharon Wilbert and Mrs. Blanche reviewed my case along with information already in my file open in my name. They concluded that I did deserve help and I was asked to speak to Mrs. Joyce J. Rayzer, Director, and Health Affairs for the Mayor. Joyce contacted the Dean of the Medical School and gave him an in-depth briefing of my background and precarious situation I was faced with.

Two weeks later on February 28th 1983, I received the following letter from Joyce in behalf of Mayor Harvey Sloan. It read thus:

Office of the Director of Safety

City Hall

Louisville, Kentucky 40202

28 February 1983

Dear Mr. Ceesay,

It appears, as the old saying goes, that I have good news and bad news. I have been in contact with the University Of Louisville School Of Medicine with regards to your admission at the fall term. I have spoken to Dr. Donald Kemetz, Dean of the Medical School, and Mr. Harold Adams, Special Assistance to the president of the University of Louisville.

Both of these administrators upon reviewing the information you sent me feel that you are a very good candidate for the minority admission program.There is however, one issue, which must be resolved favorably before your admission to medical school, or the financing and packaging necessary to begging this endeavor can be given serious considerations.

The issue, which must be resolved, is the financial determination base on whether you would be granted asylum in the country. Without the asylum being granted and hence financial aid the university cannot proceed with your request for admission this fall because your legal status would be too tenuous for them to invest hard cash in your future medical development under such nebulous state.

It appears that you must begin medical school anew. The two years completed at Liberia, cannot be accepted for transfer. You will start as freshman upon being granted asylum in USA. Again, try and find resolution to granting you asylum.

I have been assured that everything that can be done for you will be done immediately upon a favourable notice of your asylum. Everybody in the Mayor's office says hello, and we are sending you our prayers.

Sincerely

Joyce J. Rayzer

Director, Health Affairs

This was the impact Mayor Harvey Sloan had. In addition Mayor Harvey Sloan sent the following directly from his desk to the INS pleasing for them to grant me asylum.

City Hall

Office of the Mayor

Louisville, KY 40202

November 7, 1983

Alhasan S. Ceesay of the Gambia has contacted this office in an effort to gain political asylum in other to complete his medical education at the University of Louisville. I know that he is dedicated individual and is more desirous of providing needed medical aid to his fellow man. Mr. Ceesay petitioned for political asylum in February 22, 1982 due to a purge, which followed a failed coup in the Gambia.

The Medical school at the university of Louisville is currently processing his application for the 1984/85 academic years. It would be most helpful if you could assist him in expediting his papers. He will not be admitted unless a written statement confirming his residency status is available.

Since he has already lost two years awaiting residency confirmation, it would be deeply appreciated if you could assist this young man in any way possible. If my staff or I can be any further assistance in the matter, please do not hesitate to contact this office.

Sincerely

Harvey L Sloan

Mayor Louisville

Let us for a moment revert to Bishop Coleman McGehee at the Episcopal Diocese of Michigan in Detroit Michigan. Below is letter sent to the INS director, Edwin Chauvin at Mount Elliot in Detroit, Michigan

Office of the Bishop

4800 Woodward Avenue

Detroit, Michigan 48201

24 October 1983

Dear Mr. Chauvin,

As Bishop for the Episcopal diocese of Michigan, located in Detroit, Michigan, I write you this letter on behalf of Alhasan S. Ceesay, a petitioner for political asylum in the United States. As you may note from the file Mr. Ceesay seeks political asylum base on his fear of political persecution and danger to his physical safety and well being by the government, were he to be returned by the INS to his country the Gambia. Mr. Ceesay's life will disclose to you, he was active opponent of the political regime in the Gambia.

After protesting incarceration of his friends, Mr. Ceesay was placed on a list of individuals who were allegedly involved in criminal activity and who were involved with the Movement for Justice in Africa (MOJA) and were sought for interrogation by the Gambia government.

The Gambia government has singled our Mr. Ceesay because of his political opposition and has prevented him from continuing his medical education in Liberia by cutting off his financial assistance and by asking the Liberian government to return Mr. Ceesay to the Gambia.

I am personally acquainted with Mr. Ceesay, and believe him to be an individual who is worthy of support of the Episcopal Dioceses of Michigan. I feel that it took great courage for Mr. Ceesay to stand up for human rights and to publicly oppose the political regime in the Gambia.

I am convinced that Mr. Ceesay is an altruistic individual who deserves to pursue his medical training to benefit, both in the United States and perhaps elsewhere, those individuals who might be helped by his medical ability.

Mr. Ceesay has already establish his medical science aptitude in his studies at Medical School in Liberia, and he has applied to and been accepted by the School of Medicine at the University of Louisville, Kentucky, with tuition to be paid by that institution, upon his authorization to remain in the United States.

Mr. Ceesay has also sought authorization to engage in employment pending the outcome of his asylum request, he proposes to assist in medical research at the university should his employment authorization be granted by your office.

Therefore, on behalf of Mr. Ceesay as well as the members of my Diocese, I would urge you to give favorable consideration to Mr. Ceesay's petition and expedite his request for employment and his political asylum petition in every possible way so that his efforts to enter the University of Louisville School of Medicine may not be delayed any longer than may be necessary by legal and administrative procedures which you office follows.

Please feel free to contact me if I can be of any assistance in helping you to reach your determination on this matter. I fervently believed that, upon your investigation of Mr. Ceesay's case, you would reach the conclusions that he would be an asset to the United States, and that his fears as to his persecution and personal safety should he return to the Gambia, have firm foundation in fact.

Very truly yours

(The Rt. Rev.) H. Coleman McGehee, Jr.

Bishop of Michigan

The Bishop of Michigan, H. Coleman McGehee followed the above with a letter to then vice president George Bush Sr. Who sent the following tars reply.

The Vice President

Washington, D. C

April 25, 1984

Dear Rev. McGehee,

Thank you for your recent letter concerning Alhasan S. Ceesay.

It was thoughtful of you to write and I appreciate your having taken the time to bring Mr. Ceesay's case to my attention. I have asked the State Department to review all asylum cases and human rights violations, which are brought to my attention.

I have, therefore shared your letter and the enclosures with officials at the Department of State and asked that they review Mr. Ceesay's request and write to you directly. I have also asked that a copy of their response be forwarded to my office. With best wishes

Sincerely

George Bush

Bishop McGehhee, Bishop Mason, Rev. Hugh C. white, Rev. David Brower, Rev. Bill Woods, Rev. Virgil Jones, and Rev. Mark D. Meyer all touched my heart in similar fashions Hence here is my collective feeling and experience in a nut shell about these devoted men of Christ.

All of the priests lived in Detroit, Michigan except Rev. Mark D. Meyer, who lived in Plain view, Texas, USA. I lived with Rev. Mark Meyer in 1989 after hurricane Hugo devastated our campus at Montserrat, West Indies. The rest of the above I met while trying to defray deportation notice from the INS. Those were challenging and nerving political moments for m family and I.

These men of God never docked when told about my nightmare. These true believers became unique brothers I would like to share few outstanding things they did in style engraved in simple devotion to Christ's dictum. I write because these men impressed me in their interpretations and devotion to the Gospel of Christ.

Hence forgive me if I became a bit sentimental in relaying help they gave to me at various challenging times of my life. They were personal pastors for me. These were the beacon of hope and faith that stood by me when it was all doom and gloomy for me. They were simple people, humble ones at that, I can confide with, debate with, and had shoulders on which to cry my heart out without being embarrassed and above all expect a little prayer at the end of it.

Then guess what? We would be on tract trying to get hold of friends of theirs and people that might lighten my burden. Their devotion to justice and fairness was magnanimous and are my brothers in Christ. Rev. Mark Meyer, on being told the hardship I endured in Montserrat from hurricane Hugo gave me a room and gifts more than ten thousand u.s. dollars to help me complete my pre-clinics at the American University School of Medicine.

I learnt from these men of God that there is a special strength that can sustain us through almost any difficulty. That strength comes from God and from kind hearts like these Samaritans of good will. The strength comes from partly within but even more, it comes from faith and love of those close to us.

These men gave themselves wholly and as unselfishly to others in need when I met them at the Episcopalian diocese of Michigan. They devoted time to my cause and dropped selfish interests aside to help me fight my case against the INS while I was up to my neck in legal and political mud. I found nothing in these men but admirable integrity, honesty and unswerving commitment to leading life devoted to God, the Bible and in helping the downtrodden. I always feel elated whenever I get chance to speak to these kind hearts from afar. Meeting them makes me feel reunited with my best friends.

I rather have a million more like then than multi millionaires that do not care about the plight of the common man. Again, I applaud contribution and friendship these men touched my heart and life with. God blesses them.

My family, villagers and I are extremely indebted to them. These men translated their concerns, and love of humanity and continued to be my good Samaritans and a bridge over trouble waters. These believe in the worthiness and sanctity of life.

And above all they ascribe to the power of knowledge and justice over ignorance. We look forward to the day we can serenade them amongst us in the smiling coast of the Gambia. We pray they keep fit to be able to join us in the opening ceremony of the Manding Medical Centre at Njawara village, the Gambia, West Africa.

These men translated their deep faith, concerns, and love of humanity. I opted to do my clinical rotations in Colchester, Essex, UK in 1990 and chanced to meet the

Robinson's. Keith Robinson vested my newly born baby girl, Famatanding Ceesay, at the Colchester County Hospital, which marked our first meeting. This slightly shy bloke impressed me a lot. He was all smiles and fund. He titled the little ears of my daughter and told her not to be as bad as her daddy.

We all laughed over it. We from that moment liked each other and he became one of my inseparable unique Brits. Keith and wife would visit the Gambia and my girls loved them to bits. t for the presents he takes to them each time but because of his amiable personality, altruistic, very caring human he is.

He had spent boxes of monetary aid towards my NGO, Manding Medical Centre at Njawara village, and the Gambia. On the forming of the Friends Manding Charitable Trust, he was unanimously voted chairman of the charity by the members.

He had since inspiration of the Friends of Manding Charitable Trust worn the cap admirably and did a job well done for the charity. Also he had been instrumental in the Gambibazaar held every fortnight in Colchester to help raise funs for Manding Medical Centre's goals back in the Gambia. He is committed to seeing the center come to fruition for the villagers of the Gambia and any that would need its service.

Personally, he and his wife had been my lifeline and support. They have always come to my aid the call of expectation and I remain profoundly grateful to him and his wife Lorna V. Robinson. Ten years ago I was on the verge of preparing becoming a consultant and return to serve the Gambia.

Today an untold anguish my life went through in these years was dampened by kindness of Lorna and Keith Robinson and many other kind and generous Brits. They are my Colchester Samaritans and Njawara villager's angels with golden hearts. We are working hard to seeing that Manding Medical center transcends the dream it was to reality for the Lower Badibou region.

Its service is much needed by the villagers. God blesses their hearts. In Manchester many helped but few match Elhaj Asfaque Ahammed, Neville Brown, Kofi Awudo and Ahmed Nizami.

Elh. Asfaque Ahammed is proprietor of Punjab Collection located at Wilmslow Road in Manchester. A lot has already been revealed about the kindness and generosity of this gentile heart and family in my first book, "The legend again all odds."

Asfaque Ahammed has since my early days in Manchester to today been benevolent towards me. He gives me food and money any time he thinks or feels that I am on the brink of collapsing because of joblessness, hunger, and worries about the state of my equally beleaguered family back home. Only God can reward such humble good people. I first met Neville in Montserrat, West Indies, while I was a medical student at the American University of the Caribbean.

We have ever since been cordial and upon finding me out in Manchester he had steadfastly kept that friendship ablaze. He in various ways would come to my aid with small but significant donations at the time. He even helped in securing a job at Belfry House Hotel at Hands Forth in 2006.

He is kindhearted fellow and my Montserrat. Kofi Awudo is Toggles gentleman I also met through his link with Neville Brown. He turned to be very kind and generous to me. He bought me shoes and shirts to allow me start work at the above hotel.

Years later on my return from Glasgow, Scotland he was the one that lodged me free of charge for three winter months. He is of exceptional quality and humane person. I remain grateful both fellows. I met Mr. Ahamed Nizami in 2008, an angel in human flesh, at Waseem's work place in Manchester.

This lawyer turned Editor and I gelled from that hour to today. He is currently the Chief Editor of the Khalish Magazine, an Urdu language magazine in UK and worldwide.

He also doubles as one of the Pakistani group leader in Manchester. On knowing my predicaments his benevolence surfaced.

There nod then he promised to help me with some the problems pulling me down and also indicated interest in helping my NGO Manding Medical Centre get financial aid to get a head start on the provision of its goals for the villagers.

In addition he proposed a fun raising idea using his medium and other avenues that may come to light. We tentatively initiated, depending on approval and provisos set by Keith Robinson, Chairman of Friends of Manding Charitable Trust in Colchester been met, formation of the Manchester manding Medical Center Annex to be office at 9 knowley Street in Manchester.

To further demonstrate his kindness and interest in my goal Ahmed Nizami donated fees for all three PLAB exams I took in 2009. Gentle hearts like Ganem Hadied and others felt sorry that my life became an unkind and rough ride for me.

He said, "Ceesay, I wish I can help more to get you out of the limbo you found yourself. Just believe in God and this pain will one day pass like history." Mahmud Adam also marched Ganem's effort by collecting money from the Liverpool mosque.

Both monies were used for my exam fees and for which kindness I remain eternally grateful to all donors. Mohamed Salam of Greenhey business in Manchester was another Good Samaritan that came to my aid when I was left to sleep in cold weather at Alexandra Park. Upon contacting him he kindly offered me room in one of his flats in Manchester.

He was very kind and generous towards me. We have many times prayed together for my eventual breaking out of nightmarish bad luck life had been to me in recent times.

Last but not the least is Sami Bati from Algeria who I stayed with at 245 Great Western Street and who relentlessly called and ask people and friends to come to aid. He raised a bundle to help me pay school fees for my daughters in the Gambia and feed my bones.

My brother Abdullah Hashim and wife Asiya Qadri were very kind Bangladesh cum Pakistani couple I met during the most challenging times of my life. Their kindness is yet to be matched by their peers. I met the couple while sleeping rough in the street of Manchester as Mohamed Salam' offer of a place came to an abrupt end.

The place was rented to a family leaving me homeless with no place to go except spend the nights at cold and treacherous Alexandra Park. It was very risky but being jobless it was the only option left to me.

Hence, it was a miracle when this God fearing Good Samaritan couple came to my rescue. They not only lodged me temporally at their other flat at 2 Sway field in Manchester but also continued to shower me with gifts and food. I certainly look forward to hosting and having my villagers and family serenade this unusually kind and generous couple from Bangladesh.

Yankuba Samateh and dear friend Abdal Nasser deserve a mention with gratitude and thanks for kindness and generosity they showered me with during these dark days and for constantly reminding me that I am more than capable of bringing my dream to fruition for the villagers.

Mrs. Roheyata Corr-Sey, a cousin, remained the most supportive and one that kept encouraging me more than any family member had done during this sojourn of mine. God blesses her and her family. I look forward to being able to thank her in person for insisting that blood is thicker than water and for being with me in thick and thin of this murderous trail.

I just have to have continued faith; confidence to do it and the universe will cooperate to justify these days difficulty. My life being as mythical as Pelebstine fever, it was full of ups and downs and again it was Ahamed Nizami who offered to lodge me when I was asked to leave my previous address where I was renting.

His kindness is phenomenal and transience's mortals. I look forward to him being my guest in the Gambia. Worth mentioning is Abdullah Shahim, a young Bangladeshi fellow who practiced his believe that we are all God's children and do need to help the "miskin" whenever we can.

He has graced my life with kindness and brotherhood that any human being yearns to get. He and his wife Asiya Padri have been one of the bright experiences of my UK sojourn. God bless their hearts. Asiya is a shining beauty and sunshine of Abdullah Shahim.

Each day became a specific thrill that lead to that exhilarating moment of victory for mankind. It was a hard challenge and a march placed before me. It is a march I will pursue towards the day I would once again be able to serve the Gambia as a physician.

Friends such as Lorna Robinson, Eliza Jones, Mahmud Adam, Ganem Hadied, Abdinnisir, Faisal, Yusuf Ali, Ishfaque Ahmed, Ahmed Nizami, Abdullah Shahim, and countless angels all suffered my pain and felt way into my heart through compassion as I plied through financial inadequacies.

Angels like Faisal, Abdul Rhaseed, Abdinnisir, Yusuf Ali, and Mahmud Adam deserved to be classed as paragons of kindness. These Somalis are among many who refused to let me bit the dust because of foot dragging visa problem. They encouraged by sharing food and they had with me and made certain that I persevere for a bright day for family and country. These are people who help lift my feet when my wings could not remember how to fly away from hardship.

Faisal would on weekends prepare hot and well spiced Spaghetti and meat, or buy food for me from the next door restraint. Abdinnisir Hassan in almost tearful manner would push me into going to get food.

On top of this generosity these folks let me stay in their flat at 284 Great Western Street, Manchester while my lawyer fight not only to untangle but to get the Home Office act on change of status request I made to that office back in 2004.

I feel favored, if not blessed having to face these inhuman challenges without losing my sanity. Being in the belly of a ferocious beast is more comfortable than life I am currently saddled. I feel like being at the interface between Purgatory and hell on earth.

Simply put, my experience was no domain for the weak. The dilemma in this life remains ceaselessly changing. These few, this band of altruistic brothers kept me going through many a dark hour of my life in America and Great Britain. They stood tall for me among many in caring for the plight of those who they never met in poverty stricken parts of the world.

Friends like these are angels who lift us to our feet when our wings have trouble remembering how to fly. In this almost inhospitable life friends like these are a great gift indeed. Tinged with trepidations for what the future can sing I picked up courage and inspiration knowing that good comes out of fighting for what one believes in. Life has taught me how to look after myself and that things do not just happen, people make it happen.

And so the villagers and I appeal for your help and participation with Manding Medical Centre. Together we can walk on water and make this dream of providing medical aid to villages become worthy cause for generations.

I have learnt not to rest on my oars else I fall into a deep and turbulent sea of troubles. I have to keep running in order to be with the best or where I am. I will continue to not only learn to improve my performance but to work hard to see that this dream of providing a much needed medical aid to villagers is brought to fruition.

Dalliance said, "Say of me what you will and the morrow will judge you, and your words shall be a witness before its judgment and a testimony before its justice. I came to say a word and I shall utter it. Should death take me ere I give voice the morrow shall utter it. That which alone I do today shall be proclaimed before the people in the days to come."

Late Auntie Meta Ndow & Alasan Mballow Jr. Gambia 2015

Have your manuscript become a book by submitting it for possible publication to acquisitions publishes Kunsa. Com

Please contact us to expose your work globally.

My Rohey Ceesay hard at studies, Manchester 2015

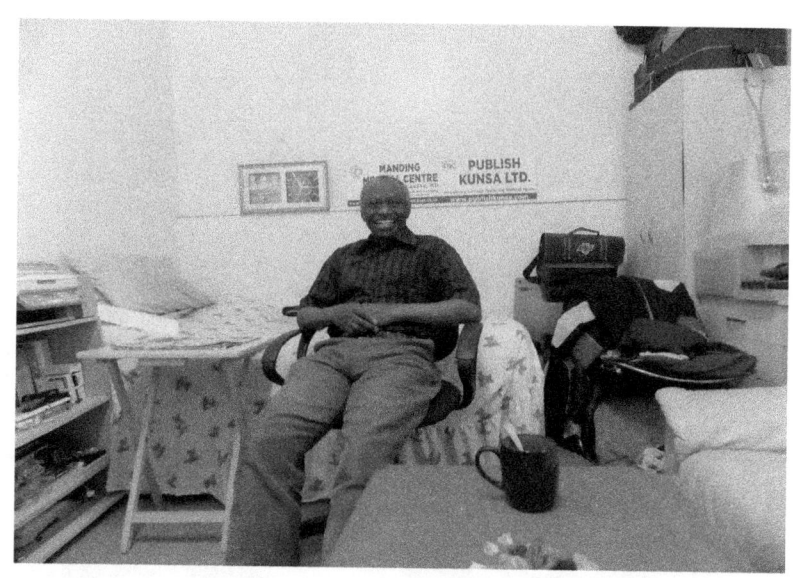

Dr. Alhasan Ceesay taking break from writing books

www.ingramcontent.com/pod-product-compliance
Lightning Source LLC
Chambersburg PA
CBHW051031160426
43193CB00010B/907